DATE DUE

NOV 1 4 2000	FEB 1 3 2007
FEB - 3 2001	
SEP 2 1 2001	
DEC 0 2 2001	
MAR 0 8 2002	
MAR 1 7 2002	
OCT - 3 2002	
NOV 1 3 2002	
JAN 2 7 2003	
AUG 2 1 2003	
NOV 1 1 2003	
APR 2 3 2004	
FEB 1 9 2005	
(APR - 2 2005	RENEWALS
	362-0438

The Library Store   #47-0106

CHOOSE
CALIFORNIA FOR
RETIREMENT

Choose Retirement Series

CHOOSE CALIFORNIA FOR RETIREMENT

Retirement

Discoveries

for Every

Budget

The Globe Pequot Press

Old Saybrook, CT

JOHN HOWELLS,
DON MERWIN, AND
JOSEPH LUBOW

Cover and text design: Laura Augustine
Cover photos: (upper left and lower right) ©Photo Disc; (upper right) 1997 Digital Vision Ltd.

Library of Congress Cataloging-in-Publication Data

Howells, John, 1928–
    Choose California for retirement : retirement discoveries for every budget / by John M. Howells, Don Merwin, and Joseph Lubow. —1st ed.
        p.   cm. — (Choose retirement series)
    Includes index.
    ISBN 0-7627-0255-9
    1. California—Guidebooks.   2. Retirement, Places of—California—Guidebooks.
3. Cost and standard of living—California.
I. Merwin, Don, 1928–   .   II. Lubow, Joseph.   III. Title.   IV. Series.
F859.3.H74   1998
979.4'053—dc21   98–19529
                                                                        CIP

Manufactured in the United States of America
First Edition/First Printing

CONTENTS

Help Us Keep This Guide Up to Date

Every effort has been made by the authors and editors to make this guide as accurate and useful as possible. However, many things can change after a guide is published—establishments close, phone numbers change, facilities come under new management, housing costs fluctuate, and so on.

We would love to hear from you concerning your experiences with this guide and how you feel it could be made better and be kept up to date. While we may not be able to respond to all comments and suggestions, we'll take them to heart and we'll make certain to share them with the author. Please send your comments and suggestions to the following address:

The Globe Pequot Press
Reader Response/Editorial Department
P.O. Box 833
Old Saybrook, CT 06475

Or you may e-mail us at:

editorial@globe-pequot.com

Thanks for your input and happy travels!

CALIFORNIA

Introduction

California, it is frequently said, is a "state of mind." That well may be true, but California is also 158,869 square miles of mountains, deserts, woods, meadows, and jam-packed cities, making it, geographically, the third largest state in the Union. With more than 32 million inhabitants, it is, by a wide margin, the nation's most populous. For these and many other reasons, it is almost certainly the nation's most diverse state.

If California were an independent nation, it would rank high among the world's countries in both size and population. Not only is the state large enough to contain several smaller nations, it contains a wider variety of climates than almost any nation in the world. Most people are familiar with the way Southern California's semitropical paradise contrasts with Sierra Nevada alpine meadows. And, of course, there's Mojave Desert's harsh, dry sagebrush landscape contrasting with the lush fields of flowers and and vegetables in the interior valleys, or with the pine and hardwood forests of the northern portions of the state.

What that means for retirees deciding to move there is that their lifestyle options are almost unlimited.

There is a definite difference between the folks who live in the extreme western part of the nation and those who live in the East, Midwest, and South. Personalities and worldviews vary with each section. Sometimes the differences are subtle. The reasons for the differences are partly historical and partly environmental.

Folks who live in the southern portions of the United States are, by tradition, rural and outdoor-oriented. Midwesterners share much of the Southern tradition, yet larger cities, larger farms, and industrial development, combined with a history of European immigration and influence, distinguish them from Southerners.

The Eastern mindset, on the other hand, is shaped by closely packed cities, little open space, and an orientation toward business and industry. In heavily populated areas the friendliness and hospitality of the South and Midwest simply are not possible.

The West Coast has a comparatively short history, and, with the exception of a few Native Americans, it is populated principally by newcomers from every part of the country and the world. As a result, Southern hospitality mixes with Northeastern reserve, and the love of open spaces mixes with a love of the city. The result is a multifaceted, laid-back lifestyle.

Yes, the West Coast has earned a reputation for being laid-back. So what's wrong with kicking back and enjoying life? We're convinced you'll live longer and enjoy life more. We have friends in Connecticut who think nothing of commuting an hour and a half each way to work. That's almost two extra working days a week—ninety working days a year—staring out a train window! In contrast, most Californians complain bitterly if their commutes are longer than twenty minutes (except for those around Los Angeles, where businesspeople spend their spare time parked on freeways).

Another East-West difference is the attitude toward education for older residents. Western community colleges and adult education programs are accessible and liberally patronized by senior citizens. Many universities waive fees for those over sixty-five, welcoming them and their potential contributions to the system.

A friend who moved West after spending most of his life in New York City made this observation: "A big difference I see between East Coast and West Coast living is a sense of space and belonging. In New York I always felt that I *belonged* to a certain neighborhood, and I felt perfectly comfortable there. When I went elsewhere, I felt almost as if I was intruding—that I didn't belong. But in the West, I don't feel this restricted sense of neighborhood. Everywhere belongs to me, and I don't feel out of place no matter where I am."

Two factors account for this. One is the historical fact that the West Coast is still in the process of being settled; people have no deeply ingrained sense of neighborhood. Western families tend to live in one house for short periods; when they can afford to upgrade their lifestyle, they trade for a more expensive home in another neighborhood. They seldom develop deep roots, binding friendships, or loyalty to one locale; the new one is always better than the last.

The second factor is the environmental circumstance of so much open land. Much of it actually belongs to everyone. A huge percentage of land in Western states is in nationally owned forests, deserts, and mountain slopes. Unlike on the East Coast—where just about every acre is fenced and posted as private property—most Western land is public and open for anyone to enjoy. Almost 50 percent of the land in California and Oregon belongs to the U.S. government. Nevada is 85 percent federally owned, and Arizona, 44 percent. Compare this with only 3.8 percent in New England, along the Eastern seaboard, and in the Midwestern states.

Openness means more than forests and deserts. The ocean also belongs to the people. Unlike the Atlantic and Gulf shores, where property owners own the beach in front of their homes and can post No Trespassing signs, Pacific beaches belong to everyone. By law, property owners must provide public access to their beachfront properties; their ownership extends only to a certain distance above the high tide line. You can stroll along any beach you please, secure in the knowledge that it is as much your property as anyone else's.

Because West Coast weather is mild and generally pleasant year-round, people tend toward outdoor activities. Most live within a few hours' drive of excellent ski country or uncrowded beaches. They can enjoy snow sports in the afternoon, then drive down the mountain to swim in a pool or relax in a hot tub the same evening. Outdoor living is the hallmark of Westerners.

The West Coast offers the most amazing smorgasbord of retirement choices imaginable. Choose from mountain communities with alpine winters, deserts that look more like the Sahara than the Sahara, farmlands reminiscent of Iowa, rugged coasts as pretty as the Spanish Mediterranean, and beaches as smooth as Hawaii's (albeit with colder waters). Within an hour or so of most retirement locations, you can be hunting deer, fishing for trout, or trolling for salmon. From a rustic cabin, deeply isolated within a redwood forest, you can drive for thirty minutes to an art museum, a theater, or an ocean beach. From a city home you can drive twenty minutes to a wild and scenic wilderness. Almost any ecological, environmental, or climatic feature can be found on the West Coast.

True, some California locations have smog and air pollution at least as bad as that in many Eastern cities. (Los Angeles has dramatically cleaned up its act over the last two decades, however.) But most of the state enjoys pristine, clear air.

California Tax Information

California Franchise Tax Board
P.O. Box 942840, Sacramento, CA 94240–0040
(800) 852–5711

Personal Income Tax
Ranges from 1 percent to 11 percent, depending on income, marital status, and other factors.

Property Taxes
All real and personal property is subject to local tax. Some intangibles are subject to state taxation. Maximum amount of tax cannot exceed 1 percent of the full cash value of the property. In relation to personal income, property tax collections are in the lowest third among the fifty states.

Estate Tax/Inheritance Tax
California does not impose an estate tax or an inheritance tax. It imposes only a pick-up tax, which is a portion of the federal estate tax and does not increase the total tax owed.

Sales Tax
Varies by county; up to a maximum of 8.5 percent.

What about water? Isn't the West always in a drought of some sort? Not really. Some mountain areas in California consistently get so much rain it's ridiculous—more than 60 inches a season (and that's nothing compared to parts of Oregon and Washington)—while places not far away in the desert are lucky to see a couple of inches all year. But one important similarity is that, as a general rule, not much rain ever falls in the summer. In the mountains you might catch some summer rain, and even thunder storms, but elsewhere you can pretty much count on leaving your waterproof hat at home when golfing, fishing, or hiking. This arrangement is perfect for tourists and retirees, but it is a little difficult for farmers—no rain during the growing season, and too much rain when they don't need it. Fortunately, a system of irrigation remedies this situation, permitting California to be one of the most productive of all the farming states. Another nice thing about the weather here is a low relative humidity. This means gentler hot days, more comfortable cool days, and far, far fewer bugs such as cockroaches and mosquitoes.

Along the ocean temperatures vary little from season to season. It is pleasant year-round from San Diego to Eureka. Granted, the farther north, the cooler the temperatures, but they remain remarkably stable regardless of the season. This temperature stability is due to the chain of low, coastal mountains that runs the length of the entire West Coast, from Washington's Puget Sound to San Diego. This ridge separates the coast from the inland valleys and prevents the cool Pacific air from sweeping eastward.

A natural air-conditioning system occurs when the sun heats up the inland valley air. This warm air rises, creating low pressure that then draws air from the ocean across the coast and over the mountains to cool things off. If it weren't for this occurrence, the coast would be as hot as the interior valleys. In the winter the air currents are stable and the cooler air stays offshore, allowing both beaches and inland to bask in the sunshine. Often the relative heat waves of the coastal lands occur in November, with eighty degrees common, as opposed to the seventy-degree days of August.

The coastal towns, therefore, are for those who don't like air-conditioning and hate freezing weather. Los Angeles is a bit different, since the mountains are farther from the coast and the sun heats the entire coastal plain. However, the ocean breeze performs somewhat the same natural air-conditioning function. That's why Los Angeles has such pleasant weather: warm in winter but rarely extremely hot in summer. This climate is exactly why so many people live there.

Through the coastal valleys north, across the San Joaquin and Sacramento Valleys, through Oregon and Washington, the climate patterns are similar—hot, sunny summers and mild winters. The farther north, the cooler the summer weather and the greater the likelihood of a touch of snow in winter. But all along the coast, rain comes in the winter. This causes a strange switch in seasons. Unlike the green, Eastern summers, things turn brown in the summer, sometimes by the first of June, and then brilliant green in November, when the rains begin to fall. This is agricultural land, lush when irrigated. The people living there enjoy a mild climate and snow-free winters.

On the other side of the valleys is yet another range of mountains, high and forbidding. These run in an almost unbroken chain from the Canadian Rockies to the Andes in South America. On the slopes and foothills of these mountains is a third climate system. It was along this uplift, in California's Sierra Nevada range, that the early-day miners found gold and settled during the West's infancy. After a brief flurry of mining activity, the area was almost deserted. Much of it is rolling country, forested with hardwood and pine. Cold-water rivers teeming with trout tumble from the mountains on their way to the ocean. Folks who live here like the mild four seasons and the rustic, forest atmosphere— plus the knowledge that big-city convenience is a short distance away.

High mountains, deep snow, ski lifts, and tall trees characterize the next level of Western living. The high Sierra, with crystal-clear air and brisk mornings, attracts a special breed of retirees. These folks either are not afraid of snow or they are not afraid to admit they hate it and leave every winter; in some places the snow level reaches 12 feet. But summer in the Sierra is beautiful.

Californians are not slaves to fad and fashion, as people tend to believe. We don't rush out and buy clothes simply because some magazine dictates that this year's fashions must be different. Few restaurants require ties, because California men seldom wear them. Women can wear slacks, blue jeans, or fancy dresses for any occasion.

Are there really affordable places in California, without smog and without horrendous traffic? By and large, the closer you get to the coast—at least south of Mendocino—the more you pay for housing. But there are exceptions even to that rule. Contrary to popular stereotype, California is not all palm trees, movie stars, and surfers. Much of the state, particularly the northern part, is rural in character. Small towns set in national forests or in the wine country are pretty much like small towns everywhere when it comes to cost of living and lifestyles. The Northern California coast is as different from Southern California resort and surfing areas as New England towns are from the Florida beaches. Are there places with hunting and fishing, for gardening and for sociability, with a four-season climate? The unqualified answer: Yes!

A few years ago, we might not have paid as much attention to California's urban areas, particularly San Francisco and Los Angeles, in our discussion of potential retirement sites. There is, however, strong evidence that a rapidly increasing number of retirees are having second thoughts about the joys of suburban living and opting for the stimulation of the metropolis. Safe, comfortable neighborhoods in big cities are likely to be expensive. Yet for those willing and able to pay the price, they may be well worth it.

THE SAN DIEGO AREA

Although most people think of the Los Angeles area and the San Francisco Bay area as the focus of life in California, San Diego has begun to capture the hearts of millions as a wonderful place to live. More than 2.7 million people live in the county, with 1.2 million of them in the balmy city of San Diego.

Stretching north from the U.S.–Mexico border to the Orange and Riverside county lines, and west from the coast over the coastal range into the desert, San Diego County offers a variety of climates, terrain, and lifestyles. With its industry focus on the Pacific Rim and Latin America, the area is filled with diverse cultures, adding depth to the American lifestyle.

With mild weather along the coast and warmer weather in the inland valley, outdoor recreation is often the priority in the leisure time of residents. There are, for instance, seventy-two golf courses in the county! Lakes and rivers are open to boaters, sport fishers, and water-skiers. The ocean seems to always beckon residents and tourists alike to its shores.

For most of the county, annual rainfall totals are less than 12 inches, a far cry from the weather patterns around San Francisco Bay. Average high temperatures run from the fifties and sixties in the winter to the seventies and eighties in the summer. Average lows rarely fall below forty degrees, and most nights are in the fifties.

The county splits generally into three regions: coast, inland valley, and mountains. Regardless of which region you choose to live in, you have easy access to the others.

The coast, the most heavily populated area (starting at the Mexican border and ending at Oceanside), is filled with beaches, estuaries, lagoons, river mouths, and lakes. The Pacific Ocean's moderate to high waves bring surfers from around the world. Yet the ocean has its periods of calm time, too. Its natural and human-made protections of coves and seawalls give swimmers opportunities to have great fun. Its breezes stimulate the sailors, and its wild shores delight the hikers.

The inland valleys, a little warmer than the coast, are heavily agriculturally based, with a few cities of moderate size. Here the land lover rules,

SAN DIEGO
AREA

with hiking, biking, and horseback trails over rolling hills. Lakes offer swimming, picnicking, and boating. The backdrop of mountains adds beauty, and this proximity offers quick access to mountain activities.

The mountains themselves harbor few communities, which helps to maintain the ecological balance. Temperatures here are cooler and the weather has more moisture, yet fishers and hunters enjoy the game, and mountain hikers and riders return again and again to experience the area's beauty.

There are a few desert spots to the east of the mountains, though most of the desert is in Riverside and Imperial Counties. See Chapter 3, *The Desert*.

History and culture, from indigenous to global, can be found throughout the county. The city of San Diego is famous for its various museums, but other towns and cities have their own unique histories available to all. The arts are also respected and promoted. Publicly-funded performing and visual arts complexes bring a diversity of cultures and styles to local communities.

Nearby is the border with Mexico, an easy place to cross to enjoy another country's culture. To the north are Orange and Riverside Counties, from Palm Springs west to Laguna Beach, offering everything but snow to residents and visitors.

San Diego

The city of San Diego, just a few miles north of the Mexican border, is the sixth largest city in the United States and the second largest in California. Yet with amazing earnestness it has brought together its varied communities and its business and tourist interests to form a cohesive city. It has, furthermore, influenced the whole of San Diego County: Its magnetism attracts thousands of new residents to the area each year.

San Diego was first noted in 1542 by Portuguese explorer Juan Rodriguez Cabrillo, sailing under a Spanish flag. It was again visited sixty years later by Sebastian Vizcaino. In 1769 an expedition brought Father Junipero Serra, who later founded Mission San Diego de Alcala. That year is considered the official birth date of the city.

When the United States defeated Mexico in the Mexican War (1846–48), California became a U.S. territory. And it was shortly after this time that San Diego started to develop. In 1901 the U.S. Navy chose San Diego as a major base, giving the city a solid economic foundation to attract and develop all types of industry. San Diego would eventually become the headquarters of the Pacific Fleet and many other administrative bodies of the entire navy. Today there are 1.2 million people living in the city, with another 1.5 million in the surrounding towns and cities.

San Diego boats some the best weather in the United States. Mild coastal temperatures with plenty of sun and pleasant breezes make the city a favorite place to live or visit. The area has average minimum winter temperatures in the high forties and average highs in the mid-sixties. Summer average temperatures range from the mid-sixties to the high seventies. Though days with temperatures over ninety degrees are infrequent, they do occur. Lows below freezing are quite rare, however. Rainfall averages about 10 inches per year.

The city is the hub to its suburban spokes. The city's draw for jobs and entertainment is nevertheless reciprocated when special events occur in these smaller cities and towns.

But San Diego has special events year-round. In January the Martin Luther King Day Parade runs through downtown; Ocean Beach Sandcastle Event is held in October. In April, Day of the Docks, a sportfishing festival, is celebrated at the San Diego Sportfishing Landing. San Diego celebrates Cinco de Mayo and other ethnic holidays as well. In addition, there are the rodeo, the San Diego American Indian Cultural Days in May, La Jolla Festival of the Arts and Food Faire in June, and the Naval Air Station Miramar Air Show in August.

Neighborhoods are the key to a city. San Diego's neighborhoods reflect the economic, social, and racial diversity of a metropolitan area. Old, original communities mix with planned ones. From La Jolla in the north, with average incomes of $50,000 and average housing costs of $460,000, to the Logan Heights area, with median income of $25,000 and the average value of homes around $90,000, the span is great. But as part of a larger city, each aids the others with its presence, its sights, and its peoples.

Recreation and Culture

A city of immense size that dates its present life at more than 200 years is bound to offer residents and visitors many historical sites. San Diego's Cabrillo National Monument honors the first European credited with visiting the bay. Walk to the Point Loma lighthouse from the visitors center.

Two parts of town—Old Town and Gaslamp Quarter—have been restored and cater to the tourist's needs. The history of the area is preserved and displayed at the Museum of San Diego History and at maritime, railroad, natural history, aerospace, and automotive museums, most of which are located in Balboa Park.

Balboa Park is a 1,200-acre expanse inside the city, originally designated by the city planners in 1868. Housed in the park are over a dozen museums, a botanical garden, the San Diego Zoo, the Starlight Bowl, and the Old Globe Theatre complex. The Fleet Space Theater and Science Center, the Japanese Friendship Gardens, a model railroad museum, the San Diego Museum of Art, Timken Museum of Art, Museum of Photographic Arts, and the main site of the Mingei International Museum of World Folk Art all have regular exhibitions. The park contains one of the densest concentrations of museums in the country.

For all that Balboa Park offers, there are many more museums around the city. Centro Cultural de la Raza focuses on the art of Native North and Central Americans. The Chinese Museum on Chinatown preserves Chinese immigrants' history. The Children's Museum of San Diego, the Museum of Contemporary Art, the San Diego Art Institute, the Firehouse Museum, and Heritage Park Village are also all in the city.

For theater, besides the Old Globe and Starlight Amphitheatre, San Diego's Lyceum Theatre is the home of the San Diego Repertory Theatre. The La Jolla Playhouse, started by Gregory Peck, Dorothy McGuire, and Mel Ferrer, continues to produce innovative drama. Smaller drama groups test the waters and push the envelope in their choices of materials.

Jazz clubs have made their way back into the city's social life. The area's large Hispanic community adds Latin flavors to the musical heritage of the city. Rock, alternative rock, blues, and folk all play their part in the nightlife of this metropolis.

Urban environments like San Diego offer splendid street walking and park strolling. The beaches offer the open-air feel of the Pacific, while walking the Gaslamp Quarter and Old Town makes one feel the heartbeat rhythms of San Diego. Parks around the city, from Balboa Park to the Cabrillo Monument and others, can be walked safely. On the edge of the city is Torrey Pines State Beach, where hiking is encouraged.

From La Jolla to Chula Vista, surfing and swimming are two of the most popular pastimes. Try Mission Bay Park for boating, fishing, and swimming, as well as waterskiing, Jet Skiing, bicycling, or kite flying. Tijuana, Mexico, is a bus ride away, offering inexpensive shopping and a taste of the local culture.

Real Estate

There is a limited inventory of downtown condos and townhouses priced from $100,000 to $250,000. There are, however, senior townhouse complexes that offer organized activities, such as communal dinners and daytrips for shopping and sightseeing. Older downtown homes range from $175,000 to $350,000. Three-bedroom, two-bath homes in surrounding neighborhoods such as Claremont, Del Cerro, and College Grove sell from $190,000 to $300,000.

The nearby island community of Coronado features executive living at its best. Condos sell from $210,000 to $300,000 for two bedrooms and two baths. Waterfront or water-view condos sell from $299,000 to $500,000. Single-family homes in established Coronado neighborhoods generally are priced over $500,000.

The average San Diego rental is about $650, with significant variations by geographic location.

Medical Care

Few places in the world offer better medical care than San Diego. More than two dozen hospitals and research centers are within the metropolitan area. There is a high number of doctors per capita as well.

When Grandkids Visit

With Balboa Park alone, the grandkids could be kept satisfied for many visits. The San Diego Zoo, one of the world's most famous, has giant pandas among the hundreds of animals cared for by the expert staff. The Reuben H. Fleet Center has an OmniMax film and museum. See Recreation and Culture above for a list of other Balboa Park attractions.

Other things to do with visiting grandchildren could include the following:

- Mission Bay Park and Torrey Pines State Reserve are great for swimming, surfing, walking, and picnicking. Sea World is near Mission Bay, and the Birch Aquarium is near Torrey Pines.
- Trips on Coaster, the commuter train that runs from San Diego north to Oceanside, or the Trolley, which runs to the eastern suburbs of San Diego, can be fun for young kids. A stop in Carlsbad (on the Coaster) could mean a visit to the Children's Museum there.

- Drive out to Escondido for the San Diego Wild Animal Park or to any of a number of lakes or state and regional parks and missions.
- For lots of other ideas, take a look at the sections on other San Diego County cities.

Addresses and Connections

Chamber of Commerce: 402 West Broadway, Suite 1000, San Diego, CA 92101–3585

Senior Center: Clairemont Friendship Senior Center, 4425 Bannock Avenue, San Diego, CA 92117; Mira Mesa Senior Center, 6460 Mira Mesa Boulevard, San Diego, CA 92126; Rancho Bernardo Joslyn Center, 18402 West Bernardo Drive, San Diego, CA 92127

Newspaper: San Diego Union-Tribune, P.O. Box 191, San Diego, CA 92108

Airport: San Diego International Airport (formerly Lindbergh Field); Montgomery Airport is considered the auxiliary city field.

Bus/Train: Amtrak has service from San Diego northward, and San Diego is the southern terminus for Coaster, the commuter rail line, which has its northern terminus in Oceanside. San Diego Metropolitan Transit District runs buses and trolleys within San Diego and among the cities to the east. The Downtown and Old Town Trolleys run in their respective areas. A ferry connects San Diego with Coronado.

Internet: http://usacitylink.com/sandiego/default.html
http://www.sannet.gov/
http://intergate.coronado.k12.ca.us/faculty/tlshook/sdarea.html
http://la.yahoo.com/Cities/San_Diego/

San Diego Weather

	JAN.	APR.	JUL.	OCT.	RAIN	SNOW
	\multicolumn{6}{In degrees Fahrenheit}					
DAILY HIGHS	66	68	76	75	10"	—
DAILY LOWS	49	56	66	61		

La Jolla

The meaning of La Jolla (pronounced *la HOya*) is unclear. It may mean "jewel" in Spanish, yet the word does not do justice to the beauty of this seaside community. Although La Jolla is the northern coastal section of the city of San Diego, its unique atmosphere has made it known around the world.

Torrey Pines State Reserve is to the north, and Mount Soledad in its southeast. On its western coastline, La Jolla offers beaches and coves.

La Jolla also may mean "cave," and its caves at La Jolla Cove are 350 feet high. Also at the cove are sharp cliffs and an underwater park. Other beach areas include Black's, La Jolla Shores, Shell, Boomer, and Wipeout.

Experienced surfers like Windandsea Beach. Pacific Beach has a 3-mile concrete boardwalk that is great for skateboarding and in-line skating, as well as for walking, bicycling, and running. Mission Beach is safe for children and includes a roller coaster (at Belmont Park) and 4600-acre Mission Bay Park.

The peninsula that creates the La Jolla area is 14 miles from downtown San Diego and 35 miles from the Mexican border. It has no heavy industry or railroads. The climate, with summer highs around seventy-eight degrees and winter lows between forty-five and fifty degrees, is mild and pleasant, with only about 10 inches of rainfall in an average year.

Originally settled by Native Americans more than 3,000 years ago, the town began developing after 400 acres of Pueblo lands were bought by Frank T. Botsford in 1886. About 350 people lived here at the turn of the century, but with the growth of tourism, the establishment of the Scripps Institute of Oceanography and later the University of California, San Diego campus, the population now nears 35,000.

Recreation and Culture

The appeal of La Jolla is its beauty, so outdoor activities are big. From the cliffs and caves at La Jolla Cove to the sandy calm beaches of La Jolla Shores Beach and Pacific Beach, there are activities for a variety of skill levels to please almost everyone.

Scuba diving, spelunking, and cliff climbing at advanced skill levels are needed at La Jolla Cove. Windandsea Beach is a well-known surfer's beach, but the waters are too rough for safe swimming. For that, try La Jolla Shores Beach, where the sand and surf create a family spot. The Shores also has picnic areas and sand-beach activities for kids. Scuba diving is easy here, allowing the diver opportunities for views of the undersea preserves.

Another beach of note is Pacific Beach. A 3-mile-long concrete boardwalk gives walkers and runners, skateboarders and in-line skaters plenty of room to roam. And the Crystal Pier is great for fishing. Mission Bay adjoins the 4600-acre Mission Bay Park with picnic and other park facilities. It is directly across from the Giant Dipper Roller Coaster at Belmont Park.

There are several parks to enjoy. La Jolla Strand, Nicholson's point, Coast Boulevard, Ellen Browning Scripps, and Kellogg are city parks along the coastline. Soledad City Park is on Mount Soledad. Kate O'Sessions Memorial City Park is to the south.

Torrey Pines State Reserve has bicycle paths and walking trails. La Jolla is an environmentally conscious area, so there is an emphasis on alternative travel in town, too. Enjoy a walk on the UC of San Diego campus as well.

Golf courses number more than seventy in the San Diego area; La Jolla has two. There are six tennis clubs and centers within a short driving distance. Professional sports teams have their bases in San Diego.

Cultural life in a university-campus area is a given. There are several art galleries and museums in La Jolla. Recently opened is the Mingei International Museum of Folk Art at University Town Centre, a satellite of the Balboa Park Museum in San Diego. The Stuart Collection of Sculpture Art is at UCSD, and the Museum of Contemporary Art opened its doors to rave critical reviews. The Atheneum Music and Arts Library also has art exhibits.

The La Jolla Chamber Society, one of five San Diego musical organizations, puts on Summerfest and also sponsors Concerts by the Sea at Scripps Park above La Jolla Cove. Local live theater is produced by the La Jolla Playhouse (founded in 1947 by Gregory Peck) and the La Jolla Stage Company, with a number of other theater groups throughout the city and county of San Diego.

The Scripps Institute of Oceanography and the Stephen Birch Aquarium-Museum offer classes and tours as well as exhibits.

Day trips to Tijuana and the northern area of Baja California, Mexico, can be of great interest. Trips to other state and national preserves in the area or into the desert of the Imperial Valley will give the day-tripper changing perspectives on life in southern California.

Real Estate

In La Jolla the most affordable home prices are for condominiums and townhouses. Two-bedroom condos are available from $160,000 to $300,000. Two-bedroom luxury condos and townhouses with ocean views and access sell for up to $1 million. Homes with three bedrooms and one bath start at $350,000. Most rentals are $700 and up.

Medical Care

There are three major hospital facilities in La Jolla: Scripps Memorial Hospital, Scripps Clinic and Research Foundation, and the Veterans Administration Medical Center. A full range of doctors practice medicine in town. Alternative medical care is also available in La Jolla.

When Grandkids Visit

La Jolla's beaches and parks can fill any child's day (see Recreation and Culture, above). A special children's pool is located south of Boomer Beach on Coast Boulevard. A concrete breakwater keeps the area safe from strong waves.

San Diego offers a multitude of activities, centered mostly on Balboa Park. (See the section on San Diego for more information.)

Addresses and Connections

Chamber of Commerce: La Jolla Town Council, 7734 Herschel, La Jolla, CA 92038

Senior Center: Senior Center at Sunset Cliffs Boulevard, 1371 Sunset Cliffs Boulevard, San Diego, CA 92107; West City Center, 3249 Fordham Street, San Diego, CA 92110

Senior Services: San Diego Senior Citizen Services, 202 C Street, San Diego, CA 92101

Newspaper: San Diego Union-Tribune, 350 Camino de la Reina, San Diego, CA 92108

La Jolla Light (weekly), 450 Pearl Street, La Jolla, CA 92038

La Jolla Village News, P.O. Box 9550, San Diego, CA 92169

Airport: San Diego International Airport (also known as Lindbergh Field)

Bus/Train: Amtrak can be reached in downtown San Diego. Greyhound stops here. Coaster (Coast Express Rail) provides commuter train service from as far away as Oceanside. North County Transit buses connect with towns and cities throughout the northern area of San Diego County. San Diego Transit provides local service and connections to downtown as well.

Internet: http://www.iaco.com/features/lajolla/homepage.htm
http://la.yahoo.com/Cities/La_Jolla/

La Jolla Weather

	JAN.	APR.	JUL.	OCT.	RAIN	SNOW
		In degrees Fahrenheit				
DAILY HIGHS	66	68	76	75	10"	—
DAILY LOWS	49	56	66	61		

East San Diego: La Mesa and El Cajon

East County, once a home to Native American settlers, later became part of the lands of the Mission San Diego de Alcala. Here cattle and sheep grazed until the land grants gave way to subdivision in the 1890s. Even then, lemon groves and other fruits were grown in this rural community.

The times changed as the railroad, and later the flume that carried water from the surrounding mountains, were built. As more industry and military personnel settled in the area, San Diego needed to grow. Small communities, once the site of ranches, farms, and vineyards, began to develop into residential and light industrial cities. The quiet towns of El Cajon and La Mesa slowly evolved into modern suburban communities.

El Cajon ("the box" in Spanish) is, in fact, boxed in by the mountains to the west and east, by the hills of La Mesa to the south, and by the upper valley to the north. Its population of 100,000 surrounds Interstate 8 about 18 miles east of San Diego Bay. Thirty miles from Baja California in Mexico and 130 miles south of Los Angeles, this inland city claims 5,000 businesses and more than thirty large employers.

La Mesa ("the table" in Spanish) abuts El Cajon and runs to the San Diego city line. Called "The Jewel of the Hills," La Mesa casts its view from 540 feet above sea level into the inland valley and mountains that surround El Cajon. Home to more than 50,000 people, the city begins as a continuation of east San Diego but ends as a residential suburb.

The climates of El Cajon and La Mesa are slightly different. La Mesa experiences warmer temperatures in winter and in summer than El Cajon. La Mesa also averages two more inches of rainfall annually. In winter, La Mesa has lows about forty-five degrees on average, with highs in the sixties. Summer there sees lows of sixty and highs in the low to mid-eighties. In contrast, El Cajon's winters average lows in the mid-thirties with highs in the mid-sixties. Summers there are cooler in the morning (upper fifties) and hotter during the day (high eighties).

Each city boasts of its festivals. La Mesa holds Oktoberfest every year as well as the Back to the '50s Car Show and Street Festival. El Cajon holds the International Friendship Festival, and the Magnolia Festival of Arts Plus Jazz brings nationally known jazz musicians to the juried arts show. The Mother Goose Parade turns the streets of El Cajon into a sea of youngsters and parents who strain to see the fairy-tale characters, musicians, and floats. La Mesa's Old Fashioned Christmas Village is held over two weekends in December. Both cities have farmers' markets.

Recreation and Culture

These communities offer a range of outdoor activities for everyone. From the small parks to the regional and county open spaces, the area offers horseback riding, walking, jogging, bicycling, camping, golf courses, tennis courts, and public pools. There are fourteen parks in La Mesa alone! Boating and fishing are permitted at Lake Murray Park.

El Cajon is the site of the Cajon Speedway, a ⅜-mile oval track for motor sports. Proximity to San Diego opens the door to many easy trips to attractions and events in the city. The convenience of the freeway system also makes north county day trips agreeable. Baja California, Mexico, is a quick 30-mile trip away. And north on I–15 will bring you first to Escondido, home of the San Diego Zoo Wild Animal Park, and eventually into Orange and Riverside Counties.

The arts are well represented in these cities. The Wieghorst Museum in El Cajon exhibits works of Olaf Wieghorst, "Dean of Western Art." Wieghorst is known internationally for his depictions of the West. Heritage of the Americas Museum, located on the campus of Cuyamaca College (one of two community colleges serving the cities), focuses on the history, culture, and natural history of the Americas, through art and archaeology.

Theater comes in the form of musicals and drama. The Christian Community Theatre performs musicals in Mount Helix Amphitheatre, while the Lamplighters Community Theatre is at the La Mesa Community Center. In El Cajon, try the East County Performing Arts Center–Theatre East.

Real Estate

There is a constant supply of smaller two- and three-bedroom, one-bath homes priced in the $115,000 to $250,000 range. Four-bedroom, three-bath homes range in price from $300,000 to $380,000. Nice condominiums are priced from $75,000 to $150,000. The average rent for a two-bedroom apartment is $585.

Medical Care

There are two hospitals in El Cajon and La Mesa: Scripps Hospital East County and Grossmont Hospital. There are several additional hospitals in the San Diego area, including Kaiser Permanente and UCSD Medical Center and Thorton Hospital–La Jolla.

When Grandkids Visit

Keeping the grandkids entertained in East County is easy to do. Walking, hiking, bicycling, and swimming in the public pools or nearby lakes can produce days of fun. La Mesa has fourteen parks and El Cajon nine. Outside their borders are more regional and state parks within easy driving distance. Try Lake Poway and its surrounding areas, for example.

A short drive to Balboa Park in San Diego adds the world-famous San Diego Zoo, botanical gardens, and lots of museums. Sea World in Mission Bay and San Diego Wild Animal Park in Escondido each can be all-day trips. And beach activities beside the Pacific Ocean are available from Chula Vista, south of San Diego, to Oceanside, near the border with Orange County. See the sections devoted to the San Diego County cities for more ideas.

Addresses and Connections

Chamber of Commerce: East County Chamber of Commerce, 201 South Magnolia, El Cajon, CA 91946

Senior Center: La Mesa Senior Adult Center, 8450 La Mesa Boulevard, La Mesa, CA 91941–5306

Newspaper: San Diego Union-Tribune, 350 Camino de la Reina, San Diego, CA 92108; *Daily Californian*, 1000 Pioneer Way, El Cajon, CA 91946; The *El Cajon Eagle*, P.O. Box 127, Lemon Grove, CA 91946; La Mesa Forum, 4341 Spring Street, La Mesa, CA 91941

Airport: San Diego International Airport is the major airport for the county as a whole. In addition, East County has general aviation services at Gillespie Field.

Bus/Train: Greyhound and Amtrak are available in San Diego. Other options include the San Diego Trolley and Transit, which offers senior and disabled transportation; El Cajon Dial-A-Ride; El Cajon shuttle; and

East County Wheels. Also there are four East County Light Rail stops in La Mesa, as well as Dial-A-Ride and the San Diego Trolley and Transit.

Internet: (La Mesa): http://la.yahoo.com/Cities/La_Mesa
http://www.grossmont.k12.ca.us/docs/La_Mesa/gronet.html
(El Cajon): http://la.yahoo.com/Cities/El_Cajon

La Mesa Weather

	JAN.	APR.	JUL.	OCT.	RAIN	SNOW
		In degrees Fahrenheit				
DAILY HIGHS	58	73	83	73	13"	—
DAILY LOWS	45	53	61	50		

El Cajon Weather

	JAN.	APR.	JUL.	OCT.	RAIN	SNOW
		In degrees Fahrenheit				
DAILY HIGHS	67	74	88	81	10"	—
DAILY LOWS	37	46	58	49		

Escondido

Escondido, in the northern part of inland San Diego County, was incorporated in 1888, but its history predates that considerably. The Kumeyaay Indians lived in the area for centuries. The oak forests supplied them with acorns which, when ground, became the people's staple food.

In the late 1700s the Spanish settled the area and subjugated the Native population. Several decades later, in 1848, the United States won the Mexican War and the annexation of the state followed, but its army first suffered a terrible loss in battle in nearby San Pasqual in 1846.

Today, Escondido has 125,000 residents and continues to maintain an agricultural base while becoming the economic hub for the area. The city is 18 miles from the coast, 30 miles northeast of San Diego, and 100 miles south of Los Angeles. It is at an elevation of 684 feet above sea level amid rolling hills. Three lakes are in the area, and the mountains sit to the east.

Climate is mild, with a January average of sixty-seven degrees and a July average of eighty-one degrees. Annual rainfall averages about 13 inches.

The newest campus in the California State University system is CSU, San Marcos, 10 miles away. Palomar Community College has a branch in Escondido.

The Weekly Farmers Market is a regular social event. Festivals such as Cinco de Mayo and the Escondido street fairs bring the community together in celebration.

Recreation and Culture

Escondido and its surrounding areas lend themselves to the outdoor activities expected of a warm and sunny climate. Lakes Wohlford, Dixon, and Hodges offer the public fishing, boating, sailing, and windsurfing. Dixon Lake and Lake Wohlford have camping areas.

Hiking trails at various parks and walking, jogging, and bicycling around town are popular. There are more than a dozen golf courses in the area, including private clubs with championship courses. Public swimming is available at Grape Day and Washington Parks.

Four wineries are in the area and open for tasting. Several shopping malls in Escondido offer most of the major department stores.

History is also a part of the park system. Heritage Walk Museum in Grape Day Park in the heart of Escondido has maintained a train depot, blacksmith shop, and Victorian house. Furniture and tools from the period more than one hundred years ago fill the structures. Classes on blacksmithing are held.

San Pasqual Battlefield commemorates the fierce battle between the U.S. Army and the *Californios* aligned with Mexico in the Mexican War. The scout for the United States in that ill-fated battle was Kit Carson, and a regional park is named for him. Felicita Park protects the areas in which the Kumeyaay Indians lived. A small museum exhibits artifacts from the area.

Daley Ranch, 3,000 acres in the northeastern Escondido hills, is one-seventh the size of the city. The property, once a successful horse and cattle ranch, has been bought and will be preserved as recreational open space in the city. Horseback, biking, and hiking trails total 20 miles. Plans for further recreational options are still being discussed. In Poway, a similar passive recreation park, Blue Sky Ecological Reserve, is open to the public.

Further away from Escondido is the Palomar Observatory with its 200-inch telescope and a museum on Palomar Mountain, an hour northeast of the city. Mission San Luis Rey, the largest of the twenty-one missions in California, is open to the public. Follow SR 78 past Julian (a forty-five-minute drive) and visit Anza-Borrego Desert State Park to see desert flora and fauna.

A major attraction just east of Escondido is the San Diego Wild Animal Park. The park is split into areas for animals to live in the wild without danger from predators. Visitors travel on a monorail or walk along to view the animals.

The arts are an important factor in the lives of Escondido's residents. The California Center for the Arts has art galleries, a 400-seat theater, and a 1,600-seat concert hall. National groups, famed performers, and local talent grace the halls and walls. Vista, halfway to the coast, has the Avo Playhouse and the Moonlight Amphitheatre.

Real Estate

Median home price is $169,534, with most homes between $125,000 and $250,000. Half of all rentals fall between $450 and $650.

Medical Care

The Palomar-Pomerado Health System, serving 500,000 people, is made up of two hospitals, Palomar Medical Center in Escondido and Pomerado Hospital in Poway. Tri-Cities Hospital in Carlsbad is within twenty minutes of Escondido.

When Grandkids Visit

Hiking, biking, fishing, and swimming—both in and out of town—keep children enjoyably busy. Three lakes and many parks offer places for outdoor activities that few other areas rival. Head to other sites in San Diego, Orange, or Riverside Counties (see their sections in this book).

The Iceoplex Ice Center and the Ups 'n Downs Roller Rink give your grandchild a chance to skate. The San Diego Wild Animal Park will also thrill them. The Wave Waterpark in Vista can be another stop, with four slides and other water attractions. Head to the Pacific Ocean for the beach experience in Carlsbad or Oceanside.

Day trips to Sea World, Birch Aquarium, and other San Diego County sites will round out any child's vacation. See the sections on San Diego County cities for more ideas.

Addresses and Connections

Chamber of Commerce: 720 North Broadway, Escondido, CA 92025–1893

Senior Center: Joslyn Senior Center, 724 North Broadway, Escondido, CA 92025

Newspaper: North County Times, 207 East Pennsylvania Avenue, Escondido, CA 92025; *San Diego Union-Tribune,* 350 Camino de la Reina, San Diego, CA 92108; *Escondido News Reporter* (weekly), 210 South Juniper, Suite 205, Escondido, CA 92025; *Nueves Horizontes,* 419 North Ninth Avenue, Escondido, CA 92025–5034

Airport: San Diego International Airport and John Wayne Airport in Irvine are the closest major airports. McClellan-Palomar Airport in Carlsbad (10 miles away) has direct passenger service to Los Angeles. There are also small-plane airports in the area.

Bus/Train: Greyhound and Amtrack service, Escondido; North County Transit District (NCTD) provides local service and transfer service to San Diego and Oceanside. There is a regional transit center in Escondido.

Internet: http://la.yahoo.com/Cities/Escondido/

Escondido Weather

	JAN.	APR.	JUL.	OCT.	RAIN	SNOW
		In degrees Fahrenheit				
DAILY HIGHS	67	71	81	66	13"	—
DAILY LOWS	43	48	60	54		

Poway

Poway (PAU-wi), in the inland valley north of La Mesa, is a city of 50,000 people, but less than two centuries ago the area was basically uninhabited. During the years of control by the Mission San Diego de Alcala, the land was used for grazing, tended by the Native American labor force made up of members of the Dieguito and Luiseno peoples. The name Poway comes from these Native Americans and, though there is still disagreement, means either "the meeting of little valleys" or "end of the valley."

The first permanent settlement came in 1859, when Philip

Crosthwaite built an adobe house and began what later became a successful ranching endeavor by the property's subsequent buyers. Ranching was forced out of the valley as farmers succeeded in getting changes in laws that made ranching too difficult to continue. The valley went to crop agriculture exclusively. The valley's farmers grew grains and fruits in orchards and in vineyards. The area became well known for its raisins and peaches.

Cycles of real estate booms and busts ended in 1972 when the construction of Poway Dam ensured a dependable supply of water to the valley. Poway was incorporated in 1980.

The city is east of I–15, south of Escondido, 20 miles northeast of San Diego. Its base is at 480 feet above sea level but rises to 2,250 feet within the city limits.

A mild climate with low humidity and marine breezes keeps Poway a pleasant place. Winter highs average sixty-five degrees, with summer highs averaging seventy.

Since its roots are in agriculture, Poway attempts to maintain the rural sense while planning an urban environment. The city maintains 70 percent of its land as open space, providing a natural buffer to the urban sprawl to the south and west.

There are seventeen parks in and around Poway. Community Park contains a special dog park used by as many as 150 dogs each day. Old Poway Park holds the memories of the history of the valley with restored buildings and a locomotive. A farmers market is held here every Saturday.

Lake Poway, Poway Park, and Rexrode Wilderness Area are outside the city. Blue Sky Ecological Reserve is designed to protect several threatened animals and plants. The reserve is split into specialized areas for selected wildlife to live, but the proximity of the zones to each other creates a harmonic ecological habitat for all.

City events include the Old-Fashioned Fourth of July, Christmas in the Park, and Boardwalk Craft Market, a juried event. Poway also celebrates the Old West for two weeks each July. Included in the celebration is a rodeo sanctioned by the Professional Rodeo Cowboys Association.

Recreation and Culture

Poway maintains a family atmosphere in its 3,000 acres of open space. The city has about 50 miles of networked trails for hiking, horseback riding, walking, jogging, and running. There are plans for 25 more miles. Parks have picnic areas, and many have special sport and game facilities.

Community Park is a good example of a multi-use park. The park is the home of the community swim center, the Weingart Senior Center, baseball and soccer fields, and tennis and bocce courts. There is also an auditorium with a stage and, as mentioned before, a dog park. Two playground areas and a fitness center complete the package.

Old Poway Park's mission is "to preserve a living historic village." To that effect, the Heritage Museum, the transplanted International Order of Good Templars Hall (Poway's first public assembly), and the Nelson House are open on weekends. A blacksmith's shop and a gazebo were built, and a locomotive, trolley, and old cars are on display in a train barn. Two acres of greenery are for picnicking and strolling.

Lake Poway and the neighboring Rexrode Wilderness are important parts of outdoor life here. The lake is open for fishing, boating, sailing, and camping, and the wilderness area has trails. Boats are available for rent.

The Blue Sky Ecological Reserve remains basically undisturbed. Trails for horses and walkers bring visitors closer to the habitats of many local animal and plant species. Head east over the hills to the Anza-Borrego Desert Park for a different ecological experience.

Equestrian centers and ranches dot the area. Horses can be rented, and there are pony and hayrides, riding lessons, and boarding facilities.

Poway's cultural focus is the Poway Center for the Performing Arts. The 815-seat theater/concert hall provides a venue for professional performers, theater companies, and local school and community arts groups. In Escondido is a larger venue, the California Center for the Performing Arts. And since Poway is only 20 miles from San Diego, the arts in all forms are easily accessed.

Real Estate

The median sale price for a two-bedroom house is $250,000.

Medical Care

Pomerado Hospital serves the area. Palomar Medical Center is in Escondido. Both are part of the Palomar-Pomerado Health System, serving a population of 500,000. Poway and Escondido have a full array of private services and facilities as well.

When Grandkids Visit

As seen in the Recreation and Culture section, there are outdoor activities available in the parks of Poway. Swimming and hiking and playing are all available in town and throughout the county.

The beaches of Oceanside to the northwest or in San Diego to the southwest are great for daylong excursions. Other adventures in San Diego County appropriate for kids can be found at the Birch Aquarium in La Jolla, Balboa Park in San Diego, Sea World on Mission Bay, and the San Diego Wild Animal Park in Escondido.

Addresses and Connections

Chamber of Commerce: 12709 Poway Road, Poway, CA 92064

Senior Center: Weingart Center, 13094 Bowron Road, Poway, CA 92064

Newspaper: San Diego Union-Tribune, 350 Camino de la Reina, San Diego, CA 92108

Airport: San Diego International Airport is the major airport for the San Diego area; McClellan-Palomar has passenger service to Los Angeles International Airport, and Montgomery and Gillespie also have commercial air service.

Bus/Train: Amtrak is in San Diego. Greyhound stops in Poway. There is door-to-door intercity service for the elderly and handicapped. Commuter bus service to downtown San Diego and San Diego International Airport is also available.

Internet: http://la.yahoo.com/Cities/Poway/

Poway Weather

	JAN.	APR.	JUL.	OCT.	RAIN	SNOW
		In degrees Fahrenheit				
DAILY HIGHS	66	69	80	77	11"	—
DAILY LOWS	45	51	62	56		

Del Mar

As with most of the San Diego county coastal communities, Del Mar rises from the beach and continues up into the hills behind the city. It sits along the northern border of San Diego; in fact, the area known as

Del Mar Heights is actually within San Diego's city limits. With a population of 5,200 and a high median income ($54,250), Del Mar remains an exclusive, wealthy community.

A popular vacation spot for celebrities from Hollywood, Del Mar built its reputation on its premier racetrack (founded by Bing Crosby and Pat O'Brien), where thoroughbred horses race from late July to September. The track is at the Del Mar Fairgrounds, which offers year-round events including the Del Mar Fair, from mid-June to mid-July, and the Holiday of Lights, from late November to the end of the year.

The area offers much more than horse racing. From beaches and parks to restaurants and the nightlife of a major city, there is plenty to do.

Though its history goes back to the San Dieguito hunters around 9000 B.C., its modern residents first arrived in the late 1800s, after the California Southern Railroad laid tracks for a line between San Diego and San Bernardino. Theodore M. Loop, who owned property along the creek and oceanfront, built a weekend excursion site, a tent city. Later he laid out a half-mile-wide town along 2 miles of the railroad tracks.

Del Martians, as they are called, enjoy a beautiful climate and setting. Highs range from sixty-five to seventy-eight degrees, while the lows usually stay between forty-nine and sixty-seven degrees, depending upon the time of the year.

Del Mar has retained its historical residences and buildings. Strict enforcement of building codes maintains control over the environmental ambience of a village setting. For all this beauty, residents pay a high price for housing, with nearly two-thirds of all housing stock priced over $500,000 and 30 percent of available rentals at more than $1,000.

Del Mar means "of the sea." Though the city has been through booms and busts over the years, this seaside residential community coexists with its resort and racetrack visitors to keep Del Mar a great place to live.

Recreation and Culture

Though the beaches of Del Mar were the original draw for many people, Del Mar and the surrounding area offer a great variety of interests. For instance, the Torrey Pines State Reserve, to the south of Del Mar, is a 1,700-acre area of beach, marsh, and coastal bluffs. The last remaining Torrey pines are protected by this reserve. It is a great place to walk, collect shells, swim, and surf.

Another area of interest to the outdoors enthusiast is the San Dieguito River Valley Regional Park. This long-term project of planning, acquisition, and preservation follows the San Dieguito River from its mouth in Del Mar to its source inland on Volcano Mountain near the town of Julian, about 55 miles away. At present, hiking, equestrian, and biking trails are open in the area around Lake Hodges and San Pasqual Valley. Both Lake Hodges and Lake Sutherland are open for boating.

In the city limits, two parks are popular. Seagrove Park overlooks the Pacific and offers places to picnic and play. Quite a number of marriages have been held here. Powerhouse Park, where a summer concert series is held, has a children's park and picnic facilities. In addition, Seacliff Park at the south end of Powerhouse Park has dry garden plantings and walking paths. At the Fairgrounds, there are events throughout the year.

Golf courses of varying difficulties, including professional level, are available. Bicycle paths and hiking trails go into the valleys east of Del Mar. Hot-air ballooning is another popular local activity.

Theater in repertory is presented in Solana Beach, just north of Del Mar. Music venues include the major resorts and restaurants in town. Dining out in Del Mar can be a culinary treat.

Real Estate

In Del Mar, prices for smaller, three-bedroom homes start at $320,000. A variety of contemporary and Mediterranean-style homes and estates range in price from $520,000 to more than $1 million. Condos start in price at $300,000 and range up to $700,000 for townhouses with panoramic views and full amenities. The average rental is $926 per month.

Medical Care

Scripps Memorial Hospital La Jolla is a full-service hospital, and the Scripps Clinic is just south of Del Mar. There are several private medical practices in Del Mar and the surrounding communities.

When Grandkids Visit

Besides the hiking, bicycling, horseback riding, swimming, and surfing in and around Del Mar, the grandchildren (and their parents) will enjoy the attractions throughout San Diego and North County. For example, trips to the San Diego Zoo, other museum sites in Balboa Park, and Sea World (see "San Diego") and Wild Animal Park (see "Escondido") will fill their days with wonder and excitement. Basketball and tennis courts are at Court Road, and a children's park in Powerhouse Park will also help to keep the children occupied.

Addresses and Connections

Chamber of Commerce: 1104 Camino del Mar, Suite 214, Del Mar, CA 92014

Senior Center: There is no senior center in Del Mar.

Newspaper: San Diego Union-Tribune, 350 Camino de la Reina, San Diego, CA 92108; *North County Times,* 207 East Pennsylvania Avenue, Escondido, CA 92025; *Del Mar Sun,* P.O. Box 348, Del Mar, CA 92014; *North Coast Weekly Reader,* P.O. Box 85803, San Diego, CA 92186–5803

Airport: San Diego International Airport (Lindbergh Field); McClellan-Palomar Airport in Carlsbad has flights to Los Angeles and serves small planes.

Bus/Train: Amtrak and Coaster can be boarded at the Solano Beach and Sorrento Valley stations. North County Transit District serves communities along the coast from UC San Diego at La Jolla to Oceanside and from Encinitas to Camp Pendelton via La Costa and San Luis Rey.

Internet: http://www.cerf.net/softres/delmar/
http://la.yahoo.com/Cities/Del_Mar/

Del Mar Weather

	JAN.	APR.	JUL.	OCT.	RAIN	SNOW
		In degrees Fahrenheit				
DAILY HIGHS	61	70	75	75	10"	—
DAILY LOWS	50	54	65	58		

Carlsbad

Carlsbad is known as the "village by the sea." It was named after Karlsbad Spa in what is now the Czech Republic, because the mineral springs in Carlsbad produced water that was similar to that at the Czech spa. The mineral springs are still there, but the public has limited access to them.

Directly south of Oceanside along the coast, Carlsbad has protected and revitalized its core and expanded into the adjacent city areas. The 68,000 residents enjoy a mild coastal climate, with lows in the mid-forties to mid-fifties in winter and highs in the mid- to upper seventies in the summer. Average rainfall is about 7 inches.

The first residents of this area were the Luiseno Indians, dating back at least 8,000 years, who inhabited the areas around the three lagoons and along the coast. Later, in the 1700s, the Spanish began to establish pueblos. In San Luis Rey, the "King of the Missions" was built to control the lands and Native people in the area.

Eventually, the mission lands were subdivided and sold. In turn, these huge parcels were also subdivided and sold. But it was John Frazier in the 1880s who first struck a natural spring. He sold his property to Gerhard Shutte, who built a one-hundred-room hotel. This town, which had only a few hundred residents at that time, became known as "the greatest seaside sanitarium on the Pacific Coast." The building of the rail line from San Diego to San Bernardino made Carlsbad more accessible.

For a small city with a sizable population, Carlsbad maintains its original charm while occasionally accommodating enormous crowds for special events. The downtown is clean and open, and the areas of green around town are inviting places in which to walk. A large and active senior center is nearby.

Yet the village turns into a sea of people at its big events. The San Diego Marathon and the Carlsbad Triathalon events are run here, and the Carlsbad Village Faires, held on the first Sunday of May and November, are California's largest single-day street festivals.

Carlsbad is also known for its commercial flower growers. The city flower is the bird of paradise, which was developed here. In the early spring, the farms and hills are covered with wildflowers in a dramatic display of color.

Recreation and Culture

The location of the city 30 miles north of San Diego gives proximity to Los Angeles, Orange County, San Diego, and Baja California, Mexico. But the Carlsbad area itself offers much to see and do.

Agua Hedionda Lagoon (meaning "stinking water" in Spanish, a reference to the garbage the Native people had piled nearby when the Spanish first encamped there) is the place for Jet Skiing, sailboarding, and waterskiing. Rentals are available at Snug Harbor. Along with the Buena Vista and Batiquitos Lagoons, Agua Hedionda is great for fishing, bird-watching, and nature walks. Walking and jogging are also big on the seawall walkway along the bluffs at the beach. On a clear day, the view extends from Camp Pendleton in the north to La Jolla in the south. Carlsbad State Beach has more than 200 campsites with ocean views.

Windsurfing is done on the Pacific Ocean, along with swimming and surfing. A public swimming facility and golf and tennis courses are in town. At the airport you can have a barnstorming-plane ride. Moor your boat at the Oceanside Small Craft Harbor, just north of the Carlsbad city limits.

Carlsbad Arts Office has a guide to finding and understanding the public art around the city. The Antique Gas and Steam Engine Museum in Guajome Park in Vista, 5 miles east of Carlsbad, chronicles the history of this area and of California.

The Quail Botanical Gardens in nearby Encinitas, just south of the city, has a wide variety of local, regional, and other plants, trees, and shrubbery. The mission in San Luis Rey has been restored and is open to visitors. Del Mar Fairgrounds holds events all year-round. It is home to the Del Mar Race Track, which runs thoroughbreds from late July to the beginning of September.

The Mexican border is about forty-five minutes away. Leave the car home and take the Coaster to San Diego and the bus to Tijuana.

Real Estate

Carlsbad has an abundance of smaller, older homes within walking distance of downtown shops. The smaller downtown homes are priced from $200,000. A short distance away, newer homes dot the hillside and range in price from $300,000 to $500,000 and higher for homes with panoramic ocean views. Condominiums are rarely available.

Rentals of a one- or two-bedroom apartment start as low as $500 and can go to $1,250. Houses rent starting at about $700 and can be as high as $2,500 per month.

Medical Care

Tri-City Medical Center is a full-service hospital serving the north coast cities. Throughout Carlsbad and the region, hundreds of doctors practice. Alternative care is also available in the area.

When Grandkids Visit

About seventy-five minutes away from Carlsbad are Disneyland and Knott's Berry Farm. In Escondido is the San Diego Zoo Wild Animal Park; San Diego itself has the zoo in Balboa Park and Sea World (see "San

Diego" for more ideas). The Stephen Birch Aquarium is in La Jolla.

The beach and lagoon are still the main attractions for kids in Carlsbad (see Recreation and Culture, above). There is also the Carlsbad Children's Museum. Bicycling is in bicycle lanes within Carlsbad, but many of the surrounding parks along the coast have bicycle paths or trails.

Addresses and Connections

Chamber of Commerce: Carlsbad Convention and Visitors Bureau, P.O. Box 1246, Carlsbad, CA 92018

Senior Center: 799 Pine Avenue, Carlsbad, CA 92008–2428

Newspaper: North County Times, 207 East Pennsylvania Avenue, Escondido, CA 92025; *San Diego Union-Tribune,* 350 Camino de la Reina, San Diego, CA 92108; *Coast News* (weekly), P.O. Box 232–550, Encinitas, CA 92023; *Carlsbad Sun,* 2841 Loker Avenue East, Carlsbad CA 92008

Airport: McClellan-Palomar Airport has daily passenger service to Los Angeles International, plus accommodations for small aircraft. Oceanside Municipal Airport is a general aviation airport. San Diego International and John Wayne Airport in Irvine are the closest major airports.

Bus/Train: Amtrak stops in Oceanside; Coaster commuter rail stops in Carlsbad; Greyhound and Pacific Trailways are in Oceanside; and North County Transit District runs bus routes around the region.

Internet: http://ci.carlsbad.ca.us
http://la.yahoo.com/Cities/Carlsbad/

Carlsbad Weather

	JAN.	APR.	JUL.	OCT.	RAIN	SNOW
		In degrees Fahrenheit				
DAILY HIGHS	69	65	78	77	7"	—
DAILY LOWS	47	52	68	61		

Oceanside

Oceanside is the northernmost city in San Diego County, running from the border with Orange County down to the border with Carlsbad. From the 3.5 miles of sandy beaches to Mission San Luis Rey, Oceanside is a bundle of activity for residents and visitors alike.

More than 165,000 people live in Oceanside, making it one of the three most populated cities in San Diego. A major influence on the size and makeup of the population is the existence of the U.S. Marine Corps base at Camp Pendleton and its 45,000 military and civilian personnel.

The climate mirrors that of other nearby coastal communities: sunny and mild with ocean breezes. Average winter temperatures are in the mid-fifties and average summer temperatures are in the mid-seventies. Average rainfall is less than 11 inches a year.

Oceanside was originally the home of the Luiseno Indians, a hunting-and-gathering people, until the friars of Mission San Luis Rey became their masters. The mission itself, the largest and most profitable of all California missions, was built mostly by these Native Americans.

With the decision by the Santa Fe Railroad in the 1870s to build a rail line between San Diego and San Bernadino, Oceanside was born. In 1888, the year of incorporation, a wharf was built, but it was destroyed by a storm. It was later rebuilt at its present location.

During the twenties, Oceanside developed a reputation as a weekend playland for Hollywood. Several films were shot here. In 1934 the U.S. government bought the land now known as Camp Pendleton, and the city became a residential community for the base workers and visitors of the marine trainees, trainers, and administrators.

These two influences—the military and tourism—continue to be the driving economic and social forces in Oceanside today. Controversy exists over past and future growth and the demands it makes on city facilities and services. Yet, through it all, the residents work to keep Oceanside a wonderful and affordable place to live.

Oceanside has rebuilt its old fishing pier to an unbelievable 1,942 feet of wooden overwater length, making it a great place to walk as well as fish. The city also has a small-craft harbor with over 850 slips.

MiraCosta Community College serves the city's higher educational needs. University of California, San Diego is in La Jolla, and San Diego State University is in eastern San Diego. Palomar College and California State University, San Marcos are inland.

Camp Pendleton, the largest U.S. Marine base, has been called an "ecological oasis of coastal California." The area has been left alone as much as possible, allowing the habitats to survive and thrive. Portions of the base are open to the public with hiking and horseback-riding trails.

Annual events include Rough Water Swim and Harbor Days in September, a number of surfing competitions throughout the year, Freedom Days on the Fourth of July (with a parade and fireworks), the Holiday Parade of Lights, a boat parade in the harbor held in December, and the Juneteenth Cultural Celebration in June.

Recreation and Culture

No one need be bored in Oceanside. The beaches beckon for sun-bathing, swimming, surfing, and walking. Camp Pendleton has bicycle, walking, and horseback-riding trails. The pier awaits those who fish. How about boating or kayaking at the Snug Harbor Small Craft Harbor? Sportfishing and whale-watching will take you out into the ocean.

Four golf courses and dozens more to the south and east make this area a contender for golf paradise. Two community swimming pools are open.

Mission San Luis Rey, "The King of Missions," can be toured. The Antique Gas and Steam Museum is in nearby Vista.

Surfing is a way of life for many in Oceanside, and the California Surf Museum celebrates that life with surfing memorabilia. Don't forget to visit the International Gymnasts Hall of Fame.

The flower farms of Carlsbad and Encinitas are alive each spring with brilliant colors and flowing movement from Pacific breezes. The Audubon Nature Center is in Oceanside, and the Quail Botanical Gardens are in Encinitas.

Oceanside's past is recollected at the Oceanside Heritage Park and Museum, and there are historical tours of downtown. The Oceanside Museum of Art presents work of artists throughout the area as well as that of regional and nationally known artists.

The Seagaze Summer Concert Series is held each summer at the Amphitheatre at the pier. There are Sunday afternoon concerts at the Civic Center Pond. Sunshine Brooks Theater offers performances regularly. In nearby Vista, there are two theatrical groups.

Real Estate

Real estate prices tend to be lower than those in nearby Carlsbad. In 1994 the median cost of a home was $144,000.

Medical Care

Tri-Cities Hospital in neighboring Carlsbad provides full hospital services. Hundreds of physicians practice in the area.

When Grandkids Visit

What more could a kid want besides beaches, bicycling, a wild animal park (in Escondido), a zoo (in Balboa Park in San Diego), and an aquarium (in La Jolla)? How about ice and roller rinks, or kayaks for rent at the small-craft harbor?

Try the Audubon Nature Center or the Buena Vista Lagoon. Take a trip to Lake Hodges to see the Native American paintings on the rocks there.

Open the visiting circle wider, and there are mountain biking and horseback riding along the coast and inland. Head north to Disneyland or on to Los Angeles for Universal City, La Brea Tar Pits, and other attractions. Eastward will take you to the desert past Julian.

Addresses and Connections

Chamber of Commerce: 928 North Coast Highway, P.O. Box 1578, Oceanside, CA 92051–1578

Senior Center: 455 Country Club Lane, Oceanside, CA 92054–3439

Newspaper: North County Times, 207 East Pennsylvania Avenue, Escondido, CA 92025; *San Diego Union-Tribune,* 350 Camino de la Reina, San Diego, CA 92108; *Coast News* (weekly), P.O. Box 232–550, Encinitas, CA 92023; *Oceanside Sun* (bimonthly), 2841 Loker Avenue East, Carlsbad, CA 92008

Airport: McClellan-Palomar Airport in Carlsbad has passenger service. Oceanside Municipal Airport is for general aviation. San Diego International and John Wayne outside Anaheim are the nearest major airports.

Bus/Train: Amtrak; Coaster (northern terminus); Metrolink is the southern end to the Orange County Line (to Anaheim and Los Angeles with stops along the way); North County Transit District runs bus lines within the city and to adjoining cities.

Internet: http://ci.oceanside.ca.us
http://la.yahoo.com/Cities/Oceanside/

Oceanside Weather

	JAN.	APR.	JUL.	OCT.	RAIN	SNOW
		In degrees Fahrenheit				
DAILY HIGHS	69	65	78	77	7"	—
DAILY LOWS	47	52	68	61		

THE DESERT

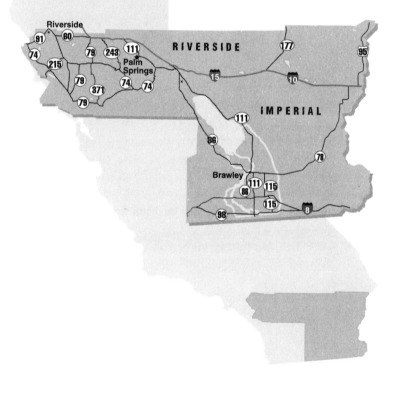

THE DESERT

None of California's diverse environments is more intriguing than the desert. It makes great demands of its inhabitants, but offers commensurate rewards. People can now live comfortably in places that were all but uninhabitable before air-conditioning became ubiquitous.

Not everybody responds favorably to the barren landscape the desert presents during the greater part of the year. For some even the drama of snowcapped mountains rising on the horizon fails to compensate for the lack of greenery. But for the desert rat (and there must be a lot of us, judging from the popularity of places like Phoenix and Scottsdale in Arizona), such a landscape provides a restful background for a life in the sun where gray, damp, chilly days are all but unknown.

And who can resist the explosion of color when the early spring rains bring the desert to life, with red, orange, yellow, and green replacing the usual shades of buff and brown?

In California's Mojave Desert communities there are few days when the temperature does not make it into the seventies. Prices are (except in the more luxurious neighborhoods of Palm Springs) more affordable than in most other California locales, and the pace of life is more leisurely. Small wonder that these are some of the fastest growing communities in the nation.

Riverside

Warm weather, lower housing costs, good public transportation, and tree-lined streets are some of the reasons why Riverside is experiencing rapid population growth. True, it is 53 miles from Los Angeles, but local services and attractions mean that it is not necessary to make that trip frequently.

Recreation and Culture

Water sports are popular in this area, where temperatures are moderate year-round and the annual rainfall total is only 10 inches. Skiing enthusiasts can find snow a short distance away from November through May. There are four golf courses, with weekday greens fees ranging from

$8.00 to $20.00. Tennis is available at nine parks, as well as at clubs and sports complexes.

No fewer than fourteen venues feature live performances, including opera, symphony, ballet, and theater. Four institutions of higher education contribute additional resources. There are six libraries and four museums.

Real Estate

The cost of living in Riverside is reported to be about 110 percent of the national average—lower than in most other California locations, particularly those fairly near a big city. A three-bedroom, two-bath house sells for from $135,000 to $149,500. Rentals of two-bedroom houses average $600 a month.

Medical Care

Riverside residents are served by four hospitals: Parkview Community Hospital, Riverside Community Hospital, Riverside General Hospital University Medical Center, and Kaiser Permanente Medical Care. The community has almost 2,000 physicians.

When Grandkids Visit

Take them horseback riding in any of the three county parks or the Lake Perris State Park, all of which feature equestrian trails. So what if you look funny on a horse. This is great riding country, and your grandchildren will respect you for trying.

Addresses and Connections

Chamber of Commerce: Greater Riverside Chambers of Commerce, 3685 Main Street, Suite 350, Riverside, CA 92501

Senior Services: Four senior centers serve older residents.

Newspaper: Press Enterprise, 3512 Fourteenth Street, Riverside, CA 92501–3878

Airport: Ontario International Airport is a short distance away.

Bus/Train: Greyhound Bus Lines provides interstate service. The Riverside Transit Agency (RTA) offers regional service as well as lines to Los Angeles and other more distant locations. The Metrolink commuter rail system ties Riverside to Los Angeles and other southern California cities.

Internet: http://www.riverside-chamber.com
http:// www.ci.riverside.ca.us

Riverside Weather

	JAN.	APR.	JUL.	OCT.	RAIN	SNOW
		In degrees Fahrenheit				
DAILY HIGHS	67	76	94	82	10"	—
DAILY LOWS	41	47	61	52		

Palm Springs/Desert Hot Springs/Palm Desert

Palm Springs (population 40,000) and its neighboring towns in the Coachella Valley (the population of 180,000 rises in winter to 240,000) are too far from Los Angeles to be geographically part of the LA area, but culturally and economically they are within its sphere of influence.

Palm Springs came into being in 1863 as a stop on the stagecoach line between Los Angeles and the New Mexico Territory and was developed as a residential community in the 1880s. It reached its peak as a playground for the rich and famous in the 1950s and '60s, losing favor during the '70s and '80s. It has again become very much the place to be during the '90s.

Throughout all these ups and downs, new towns sprang up throughout the valley, some of them with housing affordable for the rest of us who are neither rich nor famous. All of them offer the warm, dry desert climate, the freedom from urban crime and crowding, and the year-round outdoor living that movie stars and other millionaires flock there to enjoy. And all of them offer golf, golf, and more golf.

Today the Coachella Valley boasts sixty-nine golf courses, making it as close to paradise on earth as most golfers are likely to attain.

For those of us not addicted to banging little white balls across manicured meadows, there are countless other attractions in and around Palm Springs, including a wide choice of gourmet restaurants. Shopping is another favorite pastime, with countless shops and boutiques stocking everything you might ever need and many things you probably would not. We'll provide some of the details further along.

Recreation and Culture

Not into golf and glitz? How about rock climbing, bicycling, skiing, swimming, tennis, and croquet? All are offered within the area. The California Angels play exhibition baseball in season.

For the less athletically inclined there are more than a dozen museums in the valley, featuring everything from painting to military aircraft. Golf, Indian artifacts, local history, the human heart, and the Holocaust are among the other topics represented.

The performing arts are housed in the Annenberg Theater and the McCallum Theater for the Performing Arts, both of which feature internationally acclaimed artists in classical music, ballet, opera, and other genres. Theater finds a home in the High-Desert Playhouse Guild, the Palm Springs Playhouse, and the Plaza Theater.

The world of horticulture—especially desert horticulture—and the area's spectacular landscapes are the subjects of a number of gardens and nature preserves.

Real Estate

Palm Springs: Local realtors list one-family homes with two bedrooms and two baths for $140,000 and up. Some even include a swimming pool.

Desert Hot Springs: One-, two-, and three-bedroom homes are available from $115,000 to $400,000. Condos are priced at $55,000 for two-bedroom units. Almost all homes feature air-conditioning as an amenity.

Palm Desert: The beginning price here is about $125,000. As in other Cochella Valley communities, many homes include air-conditioning. If the house you buy does not, you will probably have to have it installed.

Medical Care

The Eisenhower Medical Center, the Betty Ford Center, and the Annenberg Center for Health Sciences are among the area's well-known medical facilities.

When Grandkids Visit

Show them the valley's scenic beauty from the air with a hot-air balloon ride. Dream Flights (800–933–5628) and A Natural High (888–32 FLY US) are two of the companies offering this experience.

Addresses and Connections

Chamber of Commerce: Desert Hot Springs Chamber of Commerce, 11711 West Drive, Desert Hot Springs, CA 92240; Palm Desert Chamber of Commerce, 72–940 Highway 111, Palm Desert, CA 92260

Senior Services: Palm Springs: Mizell Senior Center, 480 West

Amado, Palm Springs, CA 92262; City of Desert Hot Springs Senior Services, 11711 West Drive, Desert Hot Springs, CA 92240; Palm Desert: Senior and Volunteer Program, 73–750 Catalina Way, Palm Desert, CA 92260

Newspaper: Desert Sun, P.O. Box 190, Palm Springs, CA 92262

Airport: Palm Springs Regional Airport is the major passenger air site. Bermuda Dunes Airport supports commuter flights serving Los Angeles, Ontario, San Diego, and Phoenix. Thermal Airport provides for privately owned noncommercial aircraft, including fully loaded 727 jets.

Bus/Train: The SunLine Transit Agency provides frequent bus service within and between Palm Springs and its neighboring communities. Greyhound Lines and Thruway Motor Coach link the Palm Springs area with more distant locations.

Internet: (Palm Springs) http://www.ci.palm-springs.ca.us
(Desert Hot Springs) http://www.deserthotsprings.com
(Palm Desert) http://www.palm-desert.org

Palm Springs Weather

	JAN.	APR.	JUL.	OCT.	RAIN	SNOW
		In degrees Fahrenheit				
DAILY HIGHS	70	87	109	92	5"	—
DAILY LOWS	43	54	75	60		

Brawley

The Imperial Valley, known internationally for its fertile soil and its produce, is in the southeast corner of California, 125 miles from the nearest major California city (San Diego) and 60 miles from Yuma, Arizona. Here, the desert has been painted green with the aid of waters from the Colorado River, which runs along the border with Arizona.

The valley is hot, with average highs in summer ranging around 115 degrees. The valley is also dry and sunny, with about 2 inches of rainfall annually. There are a number of small towns with miles between them. To the north is the high desert. To the east and west are mountains. To the south is Baja California, Mexico. This is a quiet valley; the air is clean.

Within this desert land, the city of Brawley has grown to be its hub. Its 21,000 residents live their days at 113 feet below sea level, accepting, even embracing, the hot, dry days and cold nights. The climate extremes help make life a challenge. Yet many come, and few leave. Here lives a special breed.

Out here in the rural desert, 125 miles from San Diego, 210 miles from Los Angeles, and 230 miles from Phoenix, Arizona, there is room to expand. Brawley's population growth is astounding. Nearly 4,000 people arrived between 1990 and 1995. Predictions are for 40,000 to reside here by 2010. Since agriculture is the main industry, there is a seasonally fluctuating unemployment that averaged 22 percent in 1996.

Eighty percent of graduates of Imperial Valley high schools go on to college. Specialized job training is available to all. San Diego State University has a satellite campus in Calexico, less than 30 miles south. Imperial Valley College is in Imperial, a nearby community.

With twenty apartment complexes and eight mobile home parks, the Brawley area augments the older homes in the city's center and the new developments on the outskirts of town. There are also seniors' communities offering assisted living arrangements.

A car is required to move from one end of this swath of populated area, though Imperial Transit runs weekday buses among the cities and towns. Off-road vehicles function well on the dunes to the east and in the mountains to the west.

The Algodones Dunes (the Imperial Sand Dunes) are to the southeast; sand dunes run southwest-northwest below the Chocolate Mountains northeast of Brawley. (The Chocolate Mountains are inaccessible to the public; the U.S. Navy uses the area for gunnery testing.) The Salton Sea, an alkaline lake created when an accident during a Colorado River diversion program spilled water into an ancient dry seabed for two years, runs to the northwest of the city. The Sea is another 200 feet lower than Brawley.

The Superstition Mountains are to the west along with the Yuma Desert. From Niland in the north, 40 miles or so south to Calexico at the Mexican border, human beings control the sand, the water, and the way of life as best they can. But these surrounding areas, some protected by one or another government agency, control their own existence, regardless of who might think they are in charge.

Recreation and Culture

The desert and the mountains combine to offer rugged outdoor activities for the residents of the Brawley area. Camping, hunting, and fishing are available in all directions. The wilderness has become more accessible with the advent of off-road vehicles such as dune buggies. Be careful, though; the navy has taken over large stretches of desert and just about all of the mountains for bombing practice and for gunnery and parachute testing centers. Stay out!

The Bureau of Land Management manages several wilderness areas, such as the Coyote Mountains and the Jacumba Wilderness areas to the west and North Algodones Dunes and Indian Pass Wilderness areas to the east.

The inland Salton Sea, the accidental body of water in Imperial County, is popular for boating, boat fishing, and waterskiing. It is now a national wildlife refuge, so hunting is permitted only in designated areas at designated times of the year, and the public is limited to marked trails.

There are festivals aplenty in the region. The California Midwinter Fair in March, the Carrot Carnival, the Lettuce Ball, the Sweet Onion Festival, and the Sportsman and Agricultural Festival all celebrate the local agricultural industries. The Mariachi Festival, 16th of September and Cinqo de Mayo celebrations, Oktoberfest, and the Fourth of July Freedom Fest celebrate the cultural heritages of the area.

Imperial County arts organizations include Children's Theatre of the Desert; Desert Sundancers; Gospel Music of America; Hildago Society Ballet Folklorico; Imperial Valley Community Concert Association; Imperial Valley Master Chorale; Imperial Valley Symphony Association; Mostly Theatre Company; Street Level Theatre; Valley Jazz Big Band; and the Whimsical Theatre for the Performing Arts. The museums, such as Pioneer Park Museum and Quechan Tribal Museum, and art galleries such as the Imperial Valley Art Association Gallery and the San Diego State University Art Gallery, bring the history and art of the desert alive.

Real Estate

The average price of a home is $105,000.

Medical Care

Pioneers Memorial Hospital is an all-purpose, acute-care facility affiliated with Scripps Health in San Diego and Desert Hospital in Palm Springs. Clinicas de Salud del Pueblo is a community-based health-care facility.

When Grandkids Visit

Though the hot, dry climate may be a shock to children who visit from coastal or mountain areas, it is still possible for them to enjoy the sights and activities of the Imperial Valley. Use sunblock with a high SPF number, limit the amount of exposure to the sun, and drink fluids.

Most of the activities for children and families mirror those listed in Recreation and Culture, above.

Addresses and Connections

Chamber of Commerce: South Imperial Avenue, Brawley, CA 92227

Senior Center: There is no senior center in Brawley.

Newspaper: Imperial Valley Press, 135 South Plaza Avenue, Brawley, CA 92227

Airport: Imperial County Airport (10 miles south) has scheduled passenger service to LA International, San Diego, Ontario, and Yuma, Arizona. Brawley Municipal Airport is for general aviation.

Bus/Train: There are no train services; Greyhound stops here. Imperial Transit provides weekday service, connecting many Imperial Valley towns.

Internet: http://www.imperialcounty.com/brawley/index.html

http://bs.yahoo.com/Regional/U_S_States/California/Cities/Brawley/

Brawley Weather

	JAN.	APR.	JUL.	OCT.	RAIN	SNOW
		In degrees Fahrenheit				
DAILY HIGHS	69	85	107	91	3"	—
DAILY LOWS	39	52	74	57		

THE LOS ANGELES AREA

"Tinsel Town," "La La Land," even "Sin City"—you've heard them all. It is all too easy to dismiss the Los Angeles area as smoggy, crime-ridden, and artificial. But behind this superficial characterization lies America's second largest city and the host of wildly diverse suburbs, municipalities, and towns in its vicinity, all basking in beautiful weather year-round and enjoying an unequaled wealth of recreational and cultural resources. If there were any doubt about Los Angeles' standing as one of the world's great centers of culture, it was removed by the opening of the Getty Center. The Getty Center is not only a superb museum, but also a clear indication that Los Angeles must be taken seriously in this, as in so many areas of achievement.

Most people think of Los Angeles as the movie and television capital of the world, as indeed it is. But it is also a great financial, commercial, and manufacturing center. The most recent census figures place the population of Los Angeles County alone at more than nine million and of the metropolitan area (including two other counties) at fifteen million. If present trends continue, before very long this area will be the nation's largest urban center. Already, it is the Southern California lifestyle that people abroad, and increasingly at home, associate with life in the United States.

One reason for this is climate. When work occupied almost every waking hour for most people and leisure was rare, it didn't matter very much whether it was cold or hot, rainy or sunny. However, as more and more of our lives have shifted to the outdoors, the number of days when we can expect to enjoy sunshine and a comfortable temperature has become more important. This is true for people during their working years and doubly true for retirees.

It is hard for those of us who grew up in the East or Midwest to take in the fact that you can be swimming in the Pacific one day and skiing in towering mountains the next, with less than a three-hour trip from one to the other. But this is just another manifestation of the tremendous breadth of possibility that makes this area unique. If you are excited by the idea of living where almost anything is possible, the Los Angeles area deserves your serious consideration.

LOS ANGELES
AREA

Los Angeles

The City of Los Angeles (population 3.5 million) sprawls over a huge area within the even more gigantic Los Angeles County. It includes within its borders an urban downtown with a skyline to rival almost any city in the world, a second high-rise concentration in Century City, numerous other commercial centers, and an even greater number of residential neighborhoods, many of them so suburban in character that it is hard to believe they are part of a city.

Recreation and Culture

The city's great parks are filled with recreational facilities ranging from golf courses and tennis courts to hiking, rock climbing, horseback riding, and boating. Outstanding among them is Griffith Park, which in 1996 celebrated its hundredth anniversary. It is the largest municipal park and urban wilderness area in the United States, occupying more than 4,000 acres of natural terrain. Although there are ample recreational attractions in the park, much of it remains covered with California oak trees, wild sage, and manzanita at altitudes ranging from 384 to 1625 feet above sea level, with climates varying from semiarid chaparral foothills to forested valleys, and looking very much the way it did when it was the site of several Native American villages.

At the heart of the city's cultural life is the Music Center for the Performing Arts Complex, which contains the Dorothy Chandler Pavilion concert hall, the Ahmanson Theater, and the Mark Taper Forum. There is also the new Getty Center (ten years in the making), with its world-class art museums; the Hollywood Bowl (site of outdoor concerts with world-famous musicians and performers); the Los Angeles County Museum of Art; the Armand Hammer Museum of Art and Cultural Center; the History Center of the California Historical Society; the Southwest Museum; the Museum of Contemporary Art; and the city's other museums and galleries, far too numerous to list here. Clearly Los Angeles enjoys a wealth of cultural resources that few cities anywhere in the world can begin to rival.

Then there is the collection of colleges and universities that make Los Angeles one of the nation's educational centers. These include the University of California at Los Angeles (UCLA), the University of Southern California, California State University at Los Angeles, Loyola

Marymount University, Mount Saint Mary's College, Occidental College, Woodbury University, Yeshiva University of Los Angeles, and a number of junior colleges.

Altogether, there is no danger that either your body or your brain will suffer any lack of exercise and stimulation if you choose Los Angeles as your retirement home.

Real Estate

Is some of the world's most expensive real estate in Los Angeles? You bet it is! In Bel Air, homes range in price from $350,000 for two bedrooms and up to $600,000 for three bedrooms. Condos range in price from $229,000 to $599,000. In Hollywood condos range in price from $155,000 to $220,000.

That does not mean, however, that within or near to Los Angeles' 1,204-square-mile area there are no safe, comfortable, affordable neighborhoods. Thousand Oaks, for instance, is quite affordable and is within relatively close proximity to Los Angeles. There are few condominiums. There is a good supply of single-family homes. Three-bedroom, two-bath homes start at $250,000. Four-bedroom homes start as low as $275,000.

Medical Care

Los Angeles, the home of several of the world's most famous hospitals, is an international mecca for cutting-edge medical care. The University of California at Los Angeles (UCLA) Medical Center and the University of Southern California (USC) Medical Center are only two of the numerous major hospitals in the city.

When Grandkids Visit

The Laserium is a dazzling display of krypton and argon laser visuals performed under the stars inside the Griffith Park Planetarium.

Addresses and Connections

Chamber of Commerce: 350 South Bixel Street, Los Angeles, CA 90051

Senior Services: Los Angeles County Area Agency on Aging, 3175 West Sixth Street, Suite 414, Los Angeles, CA 90020

Newspaper: *Los Angeles Times*, Times Mirror Square, Los Angeles, CA 90053

Airport: The Los Angeles International Airport is accessible by public transportation.

Bus/Train: The Los Angeles County Metropolitan Transportation Authority (MTA) is the major transit provider in Los Angeles County. MTA is also responsible for funding the other transit providers in Los Angeles County. Metrolink is a regional commuter rail system serving Los Angeles, Orange, Ventura, San Bernardino, and Riverside Counties, as well as northern San Diego County. Amtrak has a major terminal at Union Station, and there is Metro Rail, a three-line rail system. Metro Rail is part of a regional train system that can take you as far as Ventura and into San Diego, Orange, Riverside, and San Bernardino Counties.

Internet: http://la.yahoo.com
http://www.lachamber.org
http://www.ci.la.ca.us

Los Angeles Weather

	JAN.	APR.	JUL.	OCT.	RAIN	SNOW
		In degrees Fahrenheit				
DAILY HIGHS	68	72	84	79	15"	—
DAILY LOWS	49	54	65	60		

Burbank

This Los Angeles suburb (population 100,000) styles itself "The Media Capital of the World." It has come a long way since its founding in 1887 when it consisted of approximately thirty residences, a furniture factory, and a few other businesses. The town was named after a dentist from Los Angeles, Dr. David Burbank, who had purchased more than 4,000 acres there in 1867. For several years Dr. Burbank operated an extremely successful sheep ranch. Surrounding Burbank were farms, vineyards, and orchards. The small community vigorously boomed until April 1888, when it became a victim of the land speculation bubble. Many people lost their property due to delinquent taxes, and development halted for two decades.

Burbank has come in for at least its share of spoofing. (Remember "beautiful downtown Burbank"?) Perhaps the reason for this is that by the middle of the current century it had become primarily an industrial town and lacked a downtown altogether. All that has changed, however, and there is something to Burbank's claim to be "the real Hollywood." Warner Brothers and the Walt Disney Company have their headquarters there, and *The Tonight Show* originates in NBC's Burbank studio. Countless other film- and broadcast-related companies also make their homes there.

Perhaps this media concentration is one reason for the wide choice of restaurants, theaters, and nightclubs, as well as the wonderful range of shops Burbank enjoys (in what really has become a beautiful and thriving downtown).

What makes this town particularly attractive is that it offers all this within the context of a strong family orientation and affordable housing.

Recreation and Culture

Three golf courses with greens fees as low as $12, numerous public tennis courts, a famous equestrian center, neighborhood parks scattered throughout the city—all combine to make Burbank a first-rate location for the physically active resident.

Six live theaters and two museum complexes support Burbank's claim to be an active center of the arts. As the home to the NBC television studios, Burbank offers residents and visitors free entertainment as members of the audiences of the numerous programs filmed there.

Real Estate

Burbank offers a wide variety of home prices. Single-family homes are available for anywhere between $205,000 and $495,000. Even those at the low end are in pleasant, safe, attractive neighborhoods. Condos sell for between $155,000 and $300,000.

Medical Care

Burbank is served by one of the Los Angeles area's outstanding hospitals, Providence Saint Joseph Medical Center, a 658-bed facility with a full range of services. Other resources include the Thompson Memorial Medical Center, Mullikin Medical Center–Burbank, and Burbank Urgent Care.

When Grandkids Visit

A tour of the nearby Universal Studios Hollywood will delight any youngster with the opportunity to see how films are made, visit historic sets, and view many decades of movie memorabilia.

Addresses and Connections

Chamber of Commerce: 200 West Magnolia Boulevard, Burbank, CA 91502

Senior Services: Joslyn Adult Center, 1301 West Olive Ave., Burbank, CA 91506

Newspaper: Burbank Leader, 220 North Glenoaks Boulevard, Burbank, CA 91502

Airport: The Burbank-Glendale-Pasadena Airport is conveniently located in Burbank. Los Angeles International Airport is about forty-five minutes away.

Bus/Train: The Metropolitan Transportation Authority (MTA) provides bus service both within Burbank and to Los Angeles and other locations. Commuter rail service to downtown Los Angeles and to numerous neighboring communities is provided by Metrolink from two Burbank stations. Amtrak offers train transportation to more distant locations.

Internet: http://burbank.acityline.com

Burbank Weather

	JAN.	APR.	JUL.	OCT.	RAIN	SNOW
		In degrees Fahrenheit				
DAILY HIGHS	68	75	90	82	16"	—
DAILY LOWS	41	48	61	54		

Pasadena

There are probably few Americans who do not visit this scenic city at the base of the San Gabriel Mountains once a year via television on New Year's Day. Then the Tournament of Roses holds sway, monopolizing the attention of football fans with the Rose Bowl game and the rest of the populace with the flower-filled parade.

In many parts of the country, viewers shivering in midwinter cold marvel at the Southern California sunshine that pours down on the shirt-sleeved spectators.

The weather in Pasadena really is that warm, the flowers are that plentiful and that beautiful, and the residents do feel that fortunate to be there—not just on New Year's Day, but year-round.

Pasadena is a suburb of Los Angeles, attached to it by freeways and bus and rail lines, but it is large enough (population 132,000), old enough (settled in the nineteenth century), and rich enough in commercial and cultural resources to be a very distinct city on its own.

Pasadena calls itself "Southern California's Crown Jewel"—its Indian-derived name has been taken to mean crown of the valley. Supporting that claim is its environmental and architectural beauty, its educational distinction (as the home of the California Institute of Technology), its outstanding cultural facilities (detailed below), and, of course, the Tournament of Roses, which helps to keep it in the world's eye.

The population is highly educated, with more than half having completed some postsecondary education, and well over a third holding college degrees. It is also highly diverse—approximately 47 percent white, 27 percent Latino, 18 percent African-American, and 8 percent Asian.

The trip to Los Angeles can take as little as fifteen minutes by the 110 Freeway (built largely along the route of California's first superhighway). Yet, in many ways, Pasadena remains part of an older, many would say better, California tradition.

Recreation and Culture

Horse-racing fans will enjoy the world-renowned Santa Anita Park, often described as America's most beautiful racetrack.

Golf courses in the Pasadena area include three operated by various governmental jurisdictions and several private country clubs. Weekday greens fees at the public courses are around $20. Facilities for swimming, tennis, hiking, and even ice-skating are also readily available.

Cultural offerings include a major symphony orchestra, at least four theaters featuring both major professional productions and local amateur companies, two choral groups, and a full calendar of events and activities in the visual arts.

Real Estate

Condominiums in this charming city are available starting at $100,000 for two bedrooms and starting at $160,000 for three bedrooms. Smaller two- and three-bedroom homes are readily available and range in price from $150,000 to $250,000. Older, more unique and charming homes sell from between $250,000 and $300,000, making Pasadena an affordable community.

Medical Care

Pasadena is home to a teaching hospital, a highly regarded acute-care hospital, and an abundance of other providers. Huntington Memorial Hospital, with 589 beds, is a nonprofit medical center serving the region. St. Luke Medical Center, with 162 beds, has served the community for fifty-five years.

When Grandkids Visit

Show the kids what a great skater you are at the Pasadena Ice Skating Center, a year-round facility. There is something unreal about zipping around on ice while outside the temperature is in the eighties and palm trees are blowing in tropical breezes.

Addresses and Connections

Chamber of Commerce: 117 East Colorado Boulevard, Suite 100, Pasadena, CA 91105

Senior Services: Center for Aging Resources, 447 North El Molino Avenue, Pasadena, CA 91101–1403

Newspaper: Pasadena Star-News, 525 East Colorado Boulevard, Pasadena, CA 91109; *Los Angeles Times,* One Market Square, Los Angeles, CA 90053

Airport: The Burbank-Glendale-Pasadena Airport (in Burbank, twenty minutes); Los Angeles International Airport (forty-five minutes)

Bus/Train: The Los Angeles County Metropolitan Transportation Authority (MTA) provides public bus service in Pasadena, connecting with all parts of the county. Foothill Transit provides regular and express bus service in the San Gabriel and Pomona Valleys. Los Angeles City Department of Transportation operates commuter express lines from Encino to Pasadena that stop in Burbank and Glendale. The Pasadena Blue Line, scheduled to open in 2002, is an extension of the light rail transit system that will link Pasadena with downtown Los Angeles and on to Long Beach. There is also a Dial-A-Ride for seniors and the disabled.

Internet: http://www.pasadena-chamber.org
http://www.citycent.com/CCC/Pasadena/index.html

Pasadena Weather

	JAN.	APR.	JUL.	OCT.	RAIN	SNOW
		In degrees Fahrenheit				
DAILY HIGHS	68	75	89	82	19"	—
DAILY LOWS	44	49	61	55		

Santa Monica

Three miles of sun-drenched coastline, with some of the most famous (and frequently filmed) beaches in the world, give Santa Monica (population 87,000) its unique character. It is, however, much more than a coastal resort community—it offers a wide range of residential areas and recreational and cultural attractions, not to mention fast and easy access to Los Angeles, with all its rich and varied resources. It is not hard, when you are walking its palm tree–lined boulevards or browsing in its upscale shopping malls, to imagine you are in the south of France.

Together with its neighboring communities of Pacific Palisades and Marina del Rey, it numbers among its residents dignified older couples seeking a quiet retirement in an almost perfect climate; wealthy entrepreneurs luxuriating in mountaintop villas with sweeping ocean views; sun-worshiping bodybuilders still posturing on the sand in an evocation of the famous Muscle Beach that launched a fitness craze sixty-five years ago; and hippie survivors attempting to re-create the world of the 1960s in the beachfront coffee houses and cafes.

Recreation and Culture

Swimming, surfing, and bicycle riding on a 26-mile beachfront trail are popular features of the varied recreational life in Santa Monica. Golf courses abound in nearby communities.

Galleries, museums, and public art scattered throughout the city are testament to the city's commitment. Murals decorate parking structures and overpasses. Totem poles grace its parks. Handsome architectural features are preserved. Santa Monica is not a city that gives in easily to the modernization and homogenization that afflict so much of Southern California.

You can enjoy a play at the renowned Santa Monica Playhouse or at several other theaters. Symphony concerts are presented at the Civic

Auditorium. Other offerings include radio theater, poetry readings, and celebrity appearances.

Real Estate

Santa Monica is an expensive housing market. The few houses offered at less than $260,000 tend to be tiny or in need of considerable work ("fixer-uppers").

Medical Care

Hospitals in Santa Monica include the Santa Monica UCLA Medical Center and Saint John's Hospital and Health Center. Many other health-care services offer everything from emergency response to acupuncture.

When Grandkids Visit

The Santa Monica Pier has enough arcades and rides, including a roller coaster and the famous Pacific Wheel, to satisfy any young adventurer. For a less strenuous interlude, take them to a kid's concert at the Ash Grove, which is also on the pier.

Addresses and Connections

Chamber of Commerce: 501 Colorado Avenue, Room 150, Santa Monica, CA 90401–2430

Senior Services: WISE Senior Services, 1527 Fourth Street, Santa Monica, CA 94101; Santa Monica Recreation Center, 1450 Ocean Avenue, Santa Monica, CA 90401

Newspaper: The Outlook, 1920 Colorado Avenue, Santa Monica, CA 90404; Santa Monica News, 11999 San Vicente, #150, Los Angeles, CA 90049

Airport: Los Angeles International Airport is a short bus ride away. (It is much closer to Santa Monica than to Los Angeles.)

Bus/Train: The many routes of the Santa Monica Municipal Bus Lines blanket the city and connect it to Los Angeles and other nearby communities. The Tide Shuttle takes you around downtown, too. There is no train service to Santa Monica. Travelers use public transit to Los Angeles' Union Station.

Internet: http://smchamber.com
http:// www.santamonica.com

Santa Monica Weather

	JAN.	APR.	JUL.	OCT.	RAIN	SNOW
		In degrees Fahrenheit				
DAILY HIGHS	65	64	69	71	13"	—
DAILY LOWS	50	53	62	59		

The South Bay: Redondo Beach/Long Beach

A favorite resort for Los Angeles dwellers for more than a century, Redondo Beach (population 63,000) is now also an attractive residential area. The Redondo Pier is still a center for tourists and locals seeking amusements, restaurants, and markets where you can count on the fish to be fresh. One of the town's advantages is its closeness to Los Angeles—only a short bus or car trip (18 miles) away.

With almost 430,000 residents, Long Beach is America's thirty-second largest city, bigger than Pittsburgh, St. Louis, or Atlanta. Yet it is within Los Angeles County and not very well known outside Southern California. One reason is that its past was filled with oil wells, shipping, and heavy industry, unlike its glamorous neighbor whose reputation is built on orange groves and movie studios.

Long Beach's reputation was greatly improved when the retired ocean liner, the *Queen Mary,* was anchored in the harbor to serve as a floating hotel, convention center, and tourist attraction. More important, however, is that the city is the home of the prestigious Long Beach State University.

Recreation and Culture

Ocean fishing and whale-watching rank high among the maritime activities in Redondo Beach. Billing itself as a fisherman's paradise, it offers easy access to deep-sea fishing, pier fishing, and angling from a barge anchored a mile and a half offshore over two fishing reefs. Tennis courts are available in its public parks, and there are golf courses nearby in Long Beach and Manhattan Beach.

The city-operated Redondo Beach Performing Arts Center is the home of the Civic Light Opera of South Bay Cities. The numerous cultural and recreational attractions of Los Angeles are, of course, within easy striking distance.

All sorts of recreational opportunities abound in Long Beach. Its more than sixty community parks offer fishing, hiking, nature centers, and much more for people of all ages. The waterfront activities include swimming, sailing, fishing, and bicycling along the beach. Golf courses and tennis centers are available both in Long Beach and nearby.

Real Estate

A little less glitzy than some of its neighboring beach communities, Redondo Beach has apartment rentals that begin at $950 and home prices at $275,000.

Long Beach realtors list small homes (one-bath, two-bedroom) from about $100,000. Many somewhat larger homes are available from about $150,000.

Medical Care

The South Bay Medical Center in Redondo Beach is a general hospital with 203 beds, staffed by 178 physicians and 177 other health-care providers.

When Grandkids Visit

That off-shore fishing barge is a safe, convenient, and inexpensive way to introduce your grandkids to the joys of ocean fishing. Boats depart every hour from the downtown fishing pier. The barge has rest rooms, a place to eat, and free live bait.

Addresses and Connections

Chamber of Commerce: Redondo Beach Chamber of Commerce, 200 North Pacific Coast Highway, Redondo Beach, CA 90277; Long Beach Area Chamber, One World Trade Center, Suite 350, Long Beach, CA 90831–0350

Senior Services: Redondo Beach Senior Services, 200 North Pacific Coast Highway, Redondo Beach, CA 90277

Newspaper: Long Beach Press-Telegram, One Herald Plaza, Long Beach, CA 90800; *Los Angeles Times,* One Market Square, Los Angeles, CA 90053

Airport: Long Beach Municipal Airport and Los Angeles International Airport

Bus/Train: Metro Rail Blue Line terminus is in Long Beach, and the Metro Rail is part of a regional rail network connecting most of the population centers of Southern California. Long Beach Transit is the local bus system. Long Beach Runabout is free within the downtown area. Greyhound Bus Lines, Orange County Transportation Authority (OCTA), and Torrance Transit also offer service. AMTRAK furnishes train-connection bus service for Long Beach for transport via Los Angeles to the Santa Ana depot.

The Wave is a city-operated bus service serving Redondo Beach and nearby Hermosa Beach. The (Los Angeles County) Metropolitan Transit Authority also operates many bus lines throughout the city.

The southern terminus of the Metro Rail Green Line is located in Redondo Beach.

Internet: http://www.redondobeach.com
http://www.la.yahoo.com/cities/redondobeach
http://www.ci.long-beach.ca.us

Long Beach Weather

	JAN.	APR.	JUL.	OCT.	RAIN	SNOW
		In degrees Fahrenheit				
DAILY HIGHS	67	72	83	78	11"	—
DAILY LOWS	45	52	63	58		

Redondo Beach Weather

	JAN.	APR.	JUL.	OCT.	RAIN	SNOW
		In degrees Fahrenheit				
DAILY HIGHS	68	67	75	74	12"	—
DAILY LOWS	48	53	63	59		

The Orange Coast

As you follow the Pacific coastline south of Long Beach and into Orange County, the first major communities you soon encounter are Huntington Beach, Newport Beach, and Laguna Beach. Huntington Beach, with a population of 182,000, is by far the largest of these ocean-front communities. It is, in fact, one of the nation's hundred largest cities. Next, both geographically and in number of inhabitants, is Newport Beach, with 69,000 inhabitants. Laguna Beach is smallest (population 23,000) and farthest south.

Beaches in Northern California can be beautiful. They are great places for relaxing in the sun, watching the crashing waves (and sometimes wet-suited surfers), scanning the horizon for whales, and lots of other good things. But only the hardy are likely to venture into the water, which is chilled by the Humboldt Current pouring down from the Gulf of Alaska. As a matter of fact, it is not until you reach the vicinity of Long Beach that the ocean is reliably warm enough for comfortable bathing and swimming. These Orange County beachfront towns are, therefore, among the northernmost in which to enjoy a California lifestyle that includes frequent immersion in warm water.

All three (and their neighboring communities) are, predictably, magnets for refugees from cold winters who seek the amenities of a South Florida retirement with all the many California extras thrown in. And the south coast responds with a wealth of senior-oriented programs and facilities.

Recreation and Culture

All three communities are blessed with beautiful beaches. Huntington Beach has some where the conditions are just right for swimming or for just splashing around in warm, gentle waters with moderate swells. Newport Beach advertises the good surfing at its ocean beaches, but directs swimmers to the gentler waters of its bay beaches. Laguna Beach has a full range of spots for swimming, surfing, and all other water sports. Orange County is a golfer's paradise, with no fewer than twenty-nine public courses and fifteen private ones. Weekday greens fees begin at $10.

All three communities are well endowed with entertainment and cultural attractions. From Huntington Beach's community playhouse and art center, to the Newport Theater Arts Center, to Laguna Beach's summertime Sawdust Festival of art, crafts, music and entertainment, there are always lots of things to do in the immediate vicinity. Laguna Beach is home to the oldest fine arts museum in California. Newport Beach honors its maritime heritage with the Newport Harbor Nautical Museum aboard the 190-foot *Pride of Newport.*

All three enjoy easy access to the larger-scale attractions of nearby Orange County communities, including the Orange County Performing Arts Center at Costa Mesa, which features jazz, chamber music, Broadway entertainment, and dance. And then there is Disneyland, just a few miles away in Anaheim. If all this is not enough, it is a short enough trip to Los Angeles to enjoy an evening of theater, music, or spectator sports there.

Real Estate

Huntington Beach has one of the highest per capita income levels of any city in the country. It also is ranked as one of the safest cities. It should, therefore, be no surprise that real estate there commands high prices. The median value of a home is about $236,000. A recent newspaper classified section showed two-bedroom, three-bath houses beginning at about $210,000. Apartments are advertised at around $800 a month. One development renting to seniors only lists low-income units from $345 to $395 for a studio or one-bedroom. Other senior housing generally runs from about $535 to $850 for one- or two-bedroom units.

In Newport Beach, the average price of a three-bedroom tract home is $485,000, according to the chamber of commerce, which also notes that single family home prices range from $250,000 to $5.5 million.

Of Laguna Beach's 5,386 owner-occupied housing units, only 883 are valued at less than $300,000 and only about 200 at less than $200,000. There are, however, a very substantial number of rental units, including about 500 with rents of less than $500 a month and many more with rents of less than $750.

Medical Care

Huntington Beach: Columbia Huntington Beach Hospital and Medical Care Center and Pacifica Community Hospital are full-service hospitals with 133 and 109 beds, respectively.

Newport Beach: Hoag Memorial Hospital–Presbyterian and Newport Bay Hospital serve the area.

Laguna Beach: The South Coast Medical Center

All three communities are within the University of California at Irvine Medical Center.

When Grandkids Visit

Take your grandchildren to the Balboa Fun Zone, a Newport Beach highlight for more than sixty years. There are a Ferris wheel, a merry-go-round, bumper cars, video games, and oh so many places to eat the delicious snacks that will set your diet back weeks and weeks.

Addresses and Connections

Chamber of Commerce: Huntington Beach Chamber, 2100 Main Street, Suite 200, Huntington Beach, CA 92648; Newport Harbor Area

Chamber, 1470 Jamboree Road, Newport Beach, CA 92660; Laguna Beach Chamber of Commerce, 357 Glenneyre Street, Laguna Beach, CA 92651

Newspaper: *Orange County Register*, 625 North Grand Avenue, Santa Ana, CA 92711; *Long Beach Press-Telegram*, One Herald Plaza, Long Beach, CA 90800; *Los Angeles Times*, One Market Square, Los Angeles, CA 90053

Senior Services: Huntington Beach: Michael Rodgers Seniors' Center, 1706 Orange Avenue, and Senior Outreach Center, 1718 Orange Avenue, Huntington Beach, CA 92648; Newport Beach: Newport Beach Oasis Senior Center, Fifth Avenue at Marguerite Avenue, Corona Del Mar, CA 92625; Laguna Beach: Laguna Beach Senior Service Center, 384 Legion Street, Laguna Beach, CA 93651

Airports: John Wayne Airport, Long Beach Municipal Airport, and Los Angeles International Airport are all convenient to the Orange Coast.

Bus/Train: Orange County Transportation Authority provides service through Laguna Beach to Newport Harbor and Huntington Beach out toward Anaheim and Santa Ana where Amtrak and Metro Link serve the region. Greyhound also serves these communities.

Internet: (Huntington Beach) http://www.ci.huntington-beach.ca.us (Newport Beach) http://www.newportbeach.com (Laguna Beach) http://www.lagunabeach.com

Orange Coast Weather

	JAN.	APR.	JUL.	OCT.	RAIN	SNOW
		In degrees Fahrenheit				
DAILY HIGHS	64	65	72	72	11"	—
DAILY LOWS	47	52	62	58		

Ventura

The city of Ventura touts itself as "The Best-Kept Secret on the California Coast." Originally named San Buenaventura (meaning "good fortune" in Spanish), it was first settled by the Chumash, who used it both for its fertile land and its proximity to a bountiful ocean and the islands off the coast. Father Junipero Serra chose Ventura for the last mission in California in 1782 (it was completed in 1809).

The coast and the mountains border the west and the east of Ventura respectively, giving its 100,000 residents beautiful vistas and plenty of outdoor enjoyment. The lands to the north and south continue to be used primarily for agriculture.

About 70 miles north of Los Angeles and a half hour south of Santa Barbara, Ventura and the surrounding county enjoy the benefits of ocean breezes and sunny days. With an average minimum low of forty-four degrees in winter and an average maximum high in the seventies in summer and fall, Ventura has some of the best weather in the state.

The beaches bring the sunbathers, swimmers, and surfers. The municipal pier, the longest wooden pier in California, attracts commercial, professional, and amateur fishers.

Downtown redevelopment is almost finished; the revitalized area has an abundance of coffeehouses, shops, and dining that attract residents and visitors alike. San Buenaventura Mission welcomes visitors; it is still a house of worship, and it houses an educational center.

Even with the expansion of light industry, especially in the computer field, agriculture continues to play an important role in the economy and environment of coastal Ventura County. Citrus groves, as well as fields of other fruits and vegetables, dot the landscape. The citizenry, including farmers and businesspeople, strive for a better environment that still allows for economic growth and prosperity.

Local off-campus sites for the University of California at Santa Barbara and California State University, Northridge along with Ventura College have created an educational focus for the city. High-tech firms have brought a demand for highly trained employees. From this, the area has seen growth in its overall cultural experience.

Seniors have been drawn to this area because of its beauty, it affordability, and its friendliness. Ventura's cleanliness and safety are also big factors.

Recreation and Culture

The hills of Ventura are alive with the sounds of enjoyment. Hiking, bicycling, camping, and mountain climbing are available throughout the areas to the east and northeast. The Los Padres National Forest, which protects the wilderness, comes to the edge of the city. Mount Pinos, more than 8,000 feet high, has been a destination for many climbers over the years.

The bountiful beach offerings include white sands and good surf. The municipal pier is a great place to fish or to watch the sunset. Whale-watching cruises take their passengers into pods of migrating whales. Scuba diving, windsurfing, and boating are other possibilities for fun. There are boat rides to Channel Islands National Park, where diving, fishing, hiking, and camping can be found. Stop at the visitors center in Ventura Harbor for more information.

The Albinger Archaeological Museum has artifacts as old as 3,500 years. The Ventura County Museum of History and Art has exhibits on local history and also brings in touring exhibits of art. It is also known for the George Stuart Collection of Historical Figures. Old-time fire equipment can be found at the AJ Comstock Fire Museum.

Live music and theater are part of the cultural backbone of Ventura. The Duchess III in Ventura Harbor, the Ventura College Theater, and the Performance Studio at the Old Livery Arts Center offer live performances. The Ventura County Chamber Orchestra, the New West Symphony, and the Ventura Master Chorale present classical music at the Ventura Theater.

Real Estate

Two-bedroom houses are available from $155,000. A three-bedroom house runs between $200,000 and $350,000. A two-bedroom apartment median rent is $695.

Medical Care

There are two full-service hospitals and a full range of medical doctors and support staff. The major medical centers of Los Angeles are about one and a half hours away.

When Grandkids Visit

Ventura draws families for beach fun—swimming, sunbathing, and surfing. Sun is plentiful, so beach outings are possible most of the time. Bicycling and hiking can fill out the days away from the beach (see Recreation and Culture, above).

At Skate Main Street Ventura, skating is taken to new heights. An in-line-skating and skateboarding facility, its ramps and street course are rated world class. Other places to take children include museums, parks, movies, and a variety of family dining establishments.

Other cities and towns within a two-hour driving distance offer more adventures.

Addresses and Connections

Chamber of Commerce: 785 South Seaward Avenue, Ventura, CA 93001

Senior Services: Ventura Avenue Adult Senior Center/Information and Referral, 550 North Ventura Avenue, Ventura, CA 93001; Ventura Senior Recreation and Employment Service, 420 East Santa Clara Street, Ventura, CA 93001

Newspaper: Ventura City Star, 5250 Ralston Street, Ventura, CA 93003; *Los Angeles Times* (Ventura County Edition), 93 South Chestnut Street, Ventura, CA 95003; *Ventura County and Coast Reporter* (weekly), 1583 Spinnaker Drive, Suite 213, Ventura CA 93001; *Ventura Independent* (weekly), 138 West Main Street, Ventura, CA 93001

Airport: Los Angeles International Airport is about one and a half hours away, and Burbank Airport is one hour away. The Santa Barbara Airport, thirty minutes away, has local commercial services available.

Bus/Train: Amtrak and Greyhound stop in Ventura. SCAT (South County Area Transit, P.O. Box 1146, Oxnard, CA 93032) provides bus services locally with routes to the Ojai Valley, Oxnard, and other adjoining cities.

Internet: http://la.yahoo.com/Cities/Ventura
http://www.ventura-chamber.org/

Ventura Weather

	JAN.	APR.	JUL.	OCT.	RAIN	SNOW
		In degrees Fahrenheit				
DAILY HIGHS	66	68	75	75	15"	—
DAILY LOWS	44	47	57	52		

Ojai

The eastern edge of Ojai Valley rests gently against the 6,700-foot Topa Topa Mountains east of the coastal city of Ventura. The coastal mountains, with peaks as high as 4,500 feet above sea level, protect the valley's other flanks. The city of Ojai is about 15 miles east of Ventura, 85 miles northwest of Los Angeles and 35 miles southeast of Santa Barbara. Ojai has about a quarter of the valley's 32,000 residents, and has been a mecca for vacationers and retirees for decades.

Ojai is generally thought to mean "moon" in the language of the Chumash, the inhabitants of the valley until recent times. The once lively Ventura River is mostly dry these days, though there is occasional flooding from harsh winters in the mountains. But some residents have now built on the riverbed in the belief that controls upstream make it safe.

The uninhabitable lands continue to hide and protect many of the local animals and vegetation. Most of the area is part of the Los Padres National Forest. Nearby, Lake Casitas Recreation Area protects its environment while offering park access for a variety of outdoor activities.

Ojai became famous in the late 1800s. When Charles Nordoff (for whom the town was temporarily renamed until its incorporation as Ojai in 1917) wrote so glowingly of the area and its (arguably) medicinally beneficial hot springs, easterners clamored for a chance to stay at the one hotel in town. The area became a weekend vacation spot for many Los Angelenos. The fertile valley was tilled. Today there are still a few farms left with citrus and avocado groves. But many have become housing for the valley's expanding population and visitors. Vineyards have also been started, and the valley now sports a new reputation for its wines.

Ojai's climate runs from winter lows in the thirties to July highs in the nineties, with about 20 inches of rain each year. The upper valley is at 1,500 feet, while the lower is at 750 feet.

Retirees have found Ojai an exceptional place to live. Home values are reasonable, the climate and environment healthy, and the support exceptional. One of the main reasons for the excellent support is due to the work of Help of Ojai, a mostly volunteer organization providing professional services to seniors and juniors alike. Coordination and creation of programs through Help of Ojai and religious, educational, and governmental organizations in the Ojai Valley provide seniors with emergency assistance, meals-on-wheels, a senior day center amidst a parklike setting, a Caring Neighbor program, limited transportation around the valley, volunteer possibilities, security patrols—in other words, a potpourri of services and facilities to make the lives of seniors more fulfilled.

Events in the valley, such as the annual Ojai Music Festival, highlight the beauty of the Ojai Valley. The 1984 Olympic rowing events held at Lake Casitas took place in a spectacular setting.

Ojai, partially due to its ideas of natural cures, has developed a community serious in its study of alternatives in health and philosophy.

Places such as the J. Krishnamurti Foundation of America, the Krotona Institute of Theosophy, Meditation Mount, and the International Center for Earth Concerns give the community new ideas to absorb and debate.

Recreation and Culture

The blend of environment, alternative health and philosophy, and tourism combine to create a unique cultural life and recreational activism in the Ojai Valley. With each passing year, the residents develop and maintain more and more organized programs to enlighten and to raise the quality of life.

Perhaps the center for outdoor activities in the Ojai Valley is the Lake Casitas Recreation Area. The lake and its 60 miles of shoreline provide breathtaking settings for the camper and boater alike. The lake is a reservoir, and its water is filled with trout and bass, channel catfish and sunfish. There are 6,200 acres of trees for shade where camping, hiking, and picnicking occur. Fishing from shore is best done from one of the fishing docks, and rentals of boats and bikes are available, as are rides in a horse-drawn carriage. There is even an airfield for model builders and fliers.

The valley offers other enjoyments outdoors as well. Horses can be rented for guided trips or for rides on the ranch, and riding lessons are available. Two eighteen-hole golf courses are open to the public. Bicycling and bicycle rentals are available. The city created a bike and walking path through town and even experimented (unsuccessfully) with unsupervised use of free bicycles. The city now encourages the locking of bicycles left unattended.

Hiking trails will take you through the valley and into the hills. A number of parks offer a variety of activities throughout the area.

Culturally Ojai has much to offer. The historical museum gives the visitor an understanding of the various settlings of the valley. The Ojai Film Society brings classic, foreign, Hollywood, and independent films for screenings in the city.

There is a strong focus on live theater and music. The Ojai Music Festival has been an important annual event, bringing world-class musicians to perform a contemporary repertoire and rarely heard musical works. The Ojai Shakespeare Festival takes place each summer. Ojai Community Chorus performs regularly.

Illusions Theatre provides experience and entertainment for and by local children. The Ojai Children's Chorus brings children in touch with their musical talents.

Adult theater is alive, too. The Ojai Civic Light Opera had its first full season in 1997. Theatre 150 presents the acting, staging, and writing of students of Kim Maxwell Brown in an intimate forty-seat room. The Ojai Theatre Company, an established group for many years, has recently merged with the Ojai Theatre Guild.

At the Ojai Center for the Arts, the oldest continuing art center in California, performances are presented in a 120-seat theater. The center also offers dance lessons in a variety of modes, as well as lessons in voice and singing, poetry workshops, and art classes. Three public galleries at the arts center are open with changing exhibits. There are several art galleries and studios in town.

Real Estate

Two-bedroom, one-bath houses start at $135,000. A three-bedroom, one-and-a-half-bath ranch house with mountain view can be found for $219,000. The community also contains many million-dollar homes.

Medical Care

Ojai Valley Community Hospital serves the Ojai Valley. A number of alternative medical services are also available.

When Grandkids Visit

The focus of life in Ojai is on the outdoors, so there are many activities for kids to enjoy, from fishing to hiking to bicycling to picnicking. Frog catching in the streams near Lake Casitas entertains for hours. Ventura, 14 miles away, has movie complexes and ocean beach access, along with other activities. See Recreation and Culture, above, and the section on Ventura.

Addresses and Connections

Chamber of Commerce: 150 West Ojai Avenue, Ojai, CA 93024

Senior Center: Help of Ojai, 111 West Santa Ana Street, P.O. Box 621, Ojai, CA 93024

Newspaper: Ventura Star, 5250 Ralston Street, Ventura, CA 93003; *Los Angeles Times* (Ventura County Edition), 93 South Chestnut Street, Ventura, CA 93003; *Ojai Valley News,* P.O. Box 277, Ojai, CA 93024

Airport: Los Angeles International Airport is about one and three-quarters hours away; Burbank is one and one-quarter hours, and Santa Barbara is one hour.

Bus/Train: Amtrak service is available via Ventura. Greyhound stops in Ojai. South Coast Area Transit (SCAT) provides bus service among the towns of the Ojai Valley and the coastal cities, such as Ventura and Oxnard.

Internet: http://la.yahoo.com/Cities/Ojai/

Ojai Weather

	JAN.	APR.	JUL.	OCT.	RAIN	SNOW
		In degrees Fahrenheit				
DAILY HIGHS	67	74	90	82	21"	—
DAILY LOWS	37	43	55	48		

THE CENTRAL COAST

From Monterey Bay south to the beaches of Santa Barbara, one of the most beautiful stretches of seacoast in the West awaits your discovery. Lightly populated in places, the majority of the oceanfront is protected by strict coastal regulations, with free access to the public. The top portion of California's Central Coast is anchored by Monterey Bay, the bottom by Santa Barbara. These are arguably the most beautiful communities on the Pacific Coast. Often compared with the French Riviera, both areas are distinguished by sweeping shorelines, mountains towering in the background, forests, and luxury homes in lushly landscaped settings. In both Monterey and Santa Barbara, you have your choice of whale-watching, mountain biking, wine tasting, and sailing—just about any day of the year. You can enjoy museums, art galleries, great restaurants, theater, and music performances year-round. Did we mention golf? Regional golf courses are world-renowned and draw golfers from all over the globe.

The main access to the Central Coast is Highway 1, one of California's most scenic roads. This mostly two-lane pavement twists and turns as it leisurely follows the coastline and volunteers breathtaking views of the Pacific from time to time, alternating between sandy beaches and cliffs washed by rolling surf.

Long stretches of the Central Coast are all but uninhabited, notably the 100-mile length of Big Sur country. Here, between Cayucos (near Morro Bay) and Carmel Highlands (below Monterey), you'll find but a handful of hamlets, too tiny to be described as villages—some consisting of little more than a gas station and a convenience store. This is unquestionably one of the world's most spectacular and isolated coastlines.

The California Central Coast also enjoys some of the nation's best weather. Its pleasant Mediterranean climate is remarkably drier and warmer than the northern Mendocino/Redwood coast. Sunshine is plentiful and rainfall relatively rare, with a scant 12 to 15 inches a year—compared with as much as 60 inches of rain along California's northern coast. You'll seldom see a drop of rain from May until November. Winter frost occurs once every decade and snow is unheard of, so golf courses are open every day. Spring and fall provide the most glorious and sunny

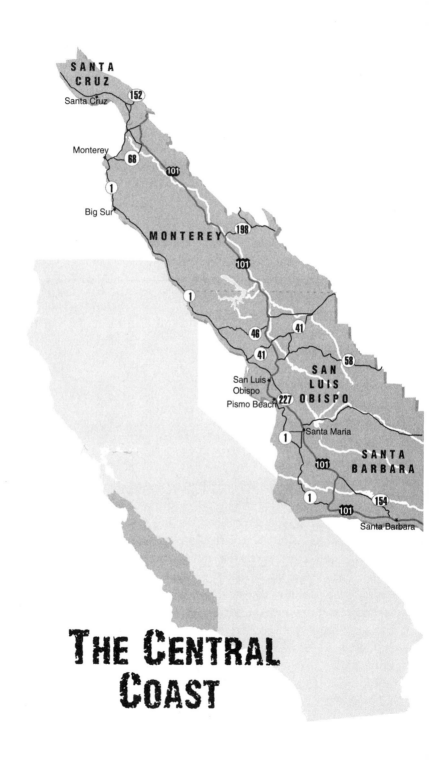

THE CENTRAL COAST

weather, saving cooler days for midsummer. The warmest days seldom reach eighty degrees, even though it could be sweltering just a few miles inland. The reason: When the summer sun heats up nearby inland valleys, the hot air rises and pulls colder air in from the ocean in the form of cool breezes and low clouds. With this natural air-conditioning, you don't need air conditioners that plug into the wall.

Santa Cruz

On the northern end of the Monterey Bay lies a stretch of sandy beaches and redwood forests that makes up the Santa Cruz area. The city of Santa Cruz, once a small fishing village, was founded in 1790 as part of the California mission system but also was known for its beach houses in the 1800s. The area actually comprises a number of smaller cities and towns as well. From the cities of Capitola and Aptos by the water to Scotts Valley and Soquel in the hills, no matter which way you look, the land and sea create a beautiful backdrop for active retirees.

The regular city resident population of 50,000 is augmented in the summer by thousands of beachgoers. During the rest of the year students come to study at the campus of the University of California at Santa Cruz, hidden in the redwoods on the hill above the city, and at Cabrillo College in Aptos. Because of these visitors, a dynamic cultural and social city life has developed.

Mainstream and art-house movies thrive here, and many restaurants and coffeehouses dot the Pacific Garden Mall, the center of downtown life. Rebuilt after a devastating earthquake in 1989, the downtown is a mixture of old buildings and new edifices designed to blend and augment the old feel of prequake downtown. With open-air cafes at which to sit and watch shoppers and tourists or to meet friends, the mall has a festive air. A weekly farmers' market and a monthly antiques fair are a couple of the many events around the city.

For those who desire a quieter life, the towns surrounding the city offer open space and a small-town feel. Seacliff and New Brighton beaches are available to swim, surf, or walk. Sailing is available from the Santa Cruz Yacht Harbor and the Capitola pier. Hikes through the mountains and redwood forests are plentiful. And to get to where you want to walk—or shop or eat or anything else you might have in mind—there is a bus system with an extensive route layout.

Santa Cruz offers its residents and visitors a sunny and warm climate for most of the year. The winter months bring cooler temperatures with an average of 29 inches of rainfall. Daytime temperatures throughout the year are in the sixties and seventies, with seasonal dips and surges, and evening temperatures in the winter can go as low as the upper thirties but stay in the fifties and sixties in the other seasons.

Santa Cruz County has a total population of about 235,000. Its residents work in agriculture, education and social services, computer technology, and other light industries. The area is also known for its encouragement of alternative technologies, philosophies, and medical practices. It is the home of the Twin Lakes College of the Healing Arts.

Healing also happens at the more than one hundred places of worship in the area. Santa Cruz is served by one local and two area newspapers as well as three weekly papers. A number of local and regional television stations on cable systems and local public and commercial radio play an important role in the cultural developments throughout the area.

Recreation and Culture

Life in Santa Cruz revolves around the environment. An early protector of open space and opponent of urban sprawl, the city, with the county and the state, has developed a number of locations for enjoyment of the land and sea.

Certainly the Santa Cruz Beach Boardwalk makes the ocean accessible, as do beaches in Capitola and Aptos, all part of 29 miles of public beachfront. San Lorenzo Park runs along the San Lorenzo River parallel to downtown. Walkers and bicyclists follow the paved trails alongside the river as well.

The UCSC campus, 2,000 acres filled with redwood forestland, is open to the public. Henry Cowell State Park north of Felton on Highway 9 offers another area in which to walk through redwoods.

On the east side of town is the small-craft harbor from which to sail, and people fish from the wharf next to the beach boardwalk area, as well as upstream on the San Lorenzo River and other creeks and streams in the mountains.

Three area golf courses are open to the public, and a number of country clubs and fitness centers have pools, tennis, and other sports. The area also has two bowling centers.

Cultural activities include the Santa Cruz Shakespeare Company, which performs three plays in repertory during the summer; the Cabrillo Music Festival; the Santa Cruz County Fair in Watsonville; and free musical concerts at the boardwalk. Because of the large student and faculty community, performances by major folk and rock artists, classical and jazz musicians, and small theater companies are plentiful.

The recently developed McPherson Museum of Art and History presents local and regional art, and both campuses in the area have galleries for the showing of student and faculty work. A number of local galleries and studios feature local art. Each year, there is a three-weekend, open-studio tour, when local artists and craftspeople open their doors to the public.

The senior center, run by the County of Santa Cruz Department of Parks, Open Space, and Cultural Services, offers a wide range of activities. From armchair travel to line dancing, and from organized mall walking to classes in tai chi chuan, the center provides a social gathering place for seniors of diverse backgrounds and cultures.

Movie theaters are in abundance, with nineteen screens within the city limits of Santa Cruz itself and another dozen in the surrounding cities. The drive-in, which doubles as a large flea market every Saturday morning, has two screens. UCSC film series are open to the public.

Santa Cruz is relatively close to the larger cities of San Jose and San Francisco. It takes about forty minutes to reach downtown San Jose and about one and one-half hours to reach San Francisco.

Real Estate

As is true for most coastal communities in California, living space in Santa Cruz and its surrounding towns doesn't come cheap. Standard housing costs for a three-bedroom, two-bath house range from $249,500 to $274,500. But retirees can purchase smaller homes and condominiums for less. The average monthly rental for a two-bedroom apartment is $825.

Medical Care

The Santa Cruz area is served by Dominican Hospital, which has its main residential and primary-care facility outside the city limits and its rehabilitation facility in the city. Within reasonable driving distances are hospitals run by Kaiser Permanente, Stanford University, the University of California, and the Veterans Administration.

Several individual doctors, medical groups, clinics, and community health centers serve the Santa Cruz area. There is also an extensive alternative medical–care community, practicing herbal, chiropractic, and Asian medicines.

When Grandkids Visit

The Santa Cruz Beach Boardwalk is a kid's paradise. The boardwalk, open seven days a week from Memorial Day to Labor Day and on weekends and holidays the rest of the year, offers rides for everyone. An extensive game floor in the main building includes everything from antique-prize grabbers to state-of-the-art electronics. There is a photo area in which you can dress in costume and a laser-tag facility. Throughout the boardwalk and out on the street there are many food concessions and restaurants. A bowling alley sits across from the boardwalk. And during the summer months there are weekly evening concerts of family-oriented oldies music.

Defying the laws of gravity, the Mystery Spot is another favorite of children. Balls rolling uphill, rising while walking on level ground, and other perspective-changing happenings keep young and old off balance.

Another treat is the Roaring Camp and Big Trees Railroad, which takes you on narrow-gauge tracks through the redwoods in the Santa Cruz hills. Music and a chuckwagon lunch are available.

Throughout the county are pick-your-own farms with seasonal fruits and vegetables. Biking and hiking trails will take you and your grandchildren into natural worlds of wonder.

Addresses and Connections

Chamber of Commerce: 701 Front Street, Santa Cruz, CA 95060

Senior Center: 1777 Capitola Road, Santa Cruz, CA 95062

Newspaper: Santa Cruz Sentinel, 207 Church Street, Santa Cruz, CA 95060; *Metro Santa Cruz,* 111 Union, Santa Cruz, CA 95060

Airport: San Jose International Airport, 25 miles away

Bus/Train: Extensive city-regional bus system, as well as Greyhound service

Internet: http://www.ci.santa-cruz.ca.us/

Santa Cruz Weather

	JAN.	APR.	JUL.	OCT.	RAIN	SNOW
		In degrees Fahrenheit				
DAILY HIGHS	61	68	76	74	29"	—
DAILY LOWS	39	43	51	47		

Monterey Peninsula

The Monterey Peninsula is a very special place. The ocean and the forested coastal scenery are always spectacular. Cresting waves surge onto the beaches or crash against granite rocks and towering cliffs. The scent of Monterey pines and cypress from thick forests freshens the air with pungent perfume. Flowers seem to be everywhere and recognize no season. (In a spirit of full disclosure, we must admit that two of this book's three authors book live in the Monterey Bay region.)

Conveniently located along scenic Highway 1, just west of Highway 101, the Monterey Peninsula sits 120 miles south of San Francisco and 350 miles north of Los Angeles. Several communities make up the Peninsula. Fort Ord and the towns of Marina and Seaside sit on the eastern side of the city of Monterey, while the towns of Pacific Grove, Pebble Beach, Carmel, and Carmel Valley flank Monterey's western edge. These cities form a loosely connected metropolitan area, with Monterey the central commercial center. Each community has its own unique identity, a distinct personality, and each caters to different economic and cultural levels.

The Monterey Bay region has a well-earned reputation for expensive, upscale housing—particularly places like Carmel, Pebble Beach, and Pacific Grove. Celebrities of all kinds make their homes here and participate in community affairs; Clint Eastwood once took his turn at being mayor of one of the towns, and you'll commonly see well-known personalities pushing shopping carts in the supermarket and dining in local restaurants. Although the Monterey peninsula has a reputation for being expensive, some communities here are quite affordable, with housing costs as low as you'll find along most of the Central Coast region. These less expensive areas are grouped around the recently decommissioned army base of Fort Ord—the oceanfront towns of Marina and Seaside.

Even though the towns along the peninsula have contiguous city limits, each has its own miniclimate. The peninsula's mountains and ocean currents create slight differences in rainfall, cloud cover, and sunshine—giving each community a slightly different habitat. While all share a Mediterranean climate with low rainfall and pleasant winters, some areas tend to catch slightly more sunshine than others. Carmel Valley, a few miles inland, will have warm, continual sunshine during the summer while the rest of the Peninsula is cloudy and cool most of the day. (Carmel Valley is one place where air conditioners are welcome in the summer.) Local residents refer to these low-hanging clouds as "fog," but newcomers who have experienced real fog—swirling low on the ground, making driving impossible—will not agree that clouds and fog are the same thing. More often than not the overcast clears in the afternoon, bestowing sunshine along the coast in preparation for a radiant sunset.

In 1602 Sebastian Vizcaino anchored at a fine harbor located near present-day Fisherman's Wharf. He named the area **Monterey**, after the Count of Monte del Rey, under whose orders he was sailing. Monterey Bay was recognized as a perfect location for a settlement. However, when the Spanish returned with a shipload of colonists, they couldn't locate the harbor. From the sea, the broad indentation of the coast doesn't appear to be a bay. It wasn't until 1770 that a Spanish expedition, under the command of Capitán Gaspar de Portola and Father Junipero Serra, arrived by land to establish a military post and a Franciscan mission. This became California's first capital—under a Spanish flag. In 1822, when Mexico gained independence from Spain, a Mexican flag flew over Monterey as a Mexican capital. Monterey next became California's first territorial United States capital on July 7, 1846, when Commodore John Drake Sloat landed U.S. troops here and declared 600,000 square miles of Mexican land to be part of the United States. Three years later California delegates convened here to draft a state constitution and requested admittance to the Union as a nonslave state. Thus Monterey became the first capital of the new state of California.

Reflecting its rich historic background, Monterey has become a showcase of old Spanish adobes and California-Mexican architecture, as well as beautifully designed Victorian and contemporary homes. Beginning at sea level, the city rises gently at first, then sharply, up tree-covered mountain slopes. Views of ocean and mountain are enjoyed from almost any part of the city. This is the heart of "Steinbeck Country," where

Nobel-Prize winning author John Steinbeck set most of his novels and short stories. This place has been immortalized by books, tales, and legends. The peninsula is colored by its cultural addition of Italian, Chinese, and Portuguese fishermen, as well as immigrants from all over the world.

As the region's commercial and cultural center, Monterey has a full range of theaters, shopping malls, and medical services. Nearby Carmel and Carmel Valley offer even higher-scale shopping, restaurants, and entertainment. Monterey's residential areas are mostly single-family homes arranged to take advantage of mountain or ocean views, with prices ranging from above average to moderately expensive. Monterey was fully developed many years ago, so few homes are modern, and replacement homes are styled to fit in with old-Monterey traditions. Tall Monterey pines, cypress trees, and mature landscaping create a special ambience for each neighborhood.

Marina and **Seaside** are affordable communities on the Monterey peninsula, which has a well-earned reputation for expensive housing. Cost-of-living statistics show the peninsula to have one of the highest in the nation. The major reason for this is housing costs. When multimillion-dollar homes in the elegant areas are figured into the cost of living, it's not surprising that statistics hit the top of the scale. However, this is somewhat misleading because the prices of food, utilities, and other everyday necessities are no higher than elsewhere in California.

The surprising thing is that the Monterey Peninsula has truly affordable communities, with housing prices no costlier than in more mundane areas of the state. Marina (population 18,000) and Seaside (population 28,300) are the two communities bordering Fort Ord, places where the overall cost of living isn't affected by high home prices. A couple of years ago the huge U.S. Army base at Fort Ord was closed; about 18,000 families were affected by the closure, including soldiers, their dependents, and support personnel. For a time, this created a buyer's market for homes near Fort Ord. To everyone's surprise the establishment of a California University at Monterey Bay and conversion of some facilities to civilian use brought in enough newcomers to prevent the real-estate meltdown some had predicted. Since most neighborhoods near Fort Ord are affordable, wellkept, and neat, with excellent shopping, sellers didn't have to lower prices significantly. Admittedly some areas of exceptionally low-cost housing may be inappropriate for retirement living—being substandard and run-down—but not far away are neighborhoods of bargain homes in a Monterey peninsula setting.

Founded in 1875 as a Methodist Church summer campground, **Pacific Grove** was divided into 25-foot lots intended for tents and small cottages to accommodate visiting worshipers. John Steinbeck's father was a minister here for several seasons. Because of the beauty of the area, with its tall Monterey pines and famous cypress trees, Pacific Grove soon attracted year-round residents who built substantial homes instead of tents; religion became incidental. Many quaint homes still sit on these 25-foot lots. Larger homes required two to four lots for a single house of any size. The result is a fascinating collection of individually designed homes, no two alike, in mature neighborhoods that give Pacific Grove a personality of its own. Its 17,500 population is proud of this personality, claiming to be "America's last hometown." The town consistently scores at the top of the list of America's safest communities.

Pebble Beach is the epitome of upscale living, and one of the most spectacular areas of the peninsula as well as one of the most exclusive. Del Monte Forest—a private community, with guarded entrances—is better known as Pebble Beach because of its world-famous golf course and lodge. The post office is also listed as Pebble Beach. Homes here are the most expensive on the peninsula, and among the most costly and elaborate in the state. Even if you can't even dream of retiring here, it's worth a drive along beautiful 17 Mile Drive as it meanders through lush forests, past stunning, multimillion-dollar estates, and gemlike ocean views. (The public is charged a small admission fee for entrance to Pebble Beach and its scenic 17-mile drive.) The population of about 6,000 is spread out on large, acreage-size pieces of forest land. A few condo developments are available, and some units can be relatively inexpensive, starting in the $300,000 range. (Remember, we said *relatively* inexpensive.)

Carmel, affectionately known as Carmel-by-the-Sea, is an overgrown village of some 5,000 inhabitants with upscale shopping and gourmet restaurants. Despite the hoopla and commercial embellishment, Carmel manages to retain a laid-back European village atmosphere. Winding tree-lined streets, lovely cottages and bungalows with flowerboxes hanging from windowsills, hidden courtyards and mature shrubbery, all combine to bestow a unique charm on Carmel-by-the-Sea. Residents are fiercely committed to preserving the town's charisma; they fight political battles over whether ice-cream stores or T-shirt shops should be allowed among the downtown's outdoor cafes, intimate shops, and boutiques. Even though tourism is rampant, downtown parking is difficult, and small cottages sell for shocking amounts, inhabitants love the special ambience of Carmel. Expect to pay $400,000 for a cottage here.

Carmel Valley is one place on the Monterey peninsula where you can count on being warm. Carmel Valley is the sunbelt of the peninsula, with an average of 283 sunny days a year. A pastoral setting of rolling ranch land, valleys, streams, and forests, the valley is hemmed in by steep and rugged mountains on the south and the high ridge of the peninsula on the north. The valley extends 26 miles inland, starting from the town of Carmel. It's a place of small horse ranches and orchards interspersed with individual homes and upscale golf-course developments. Despite its 13,000 inhabitants, Carmel Valley doesn't have a commercial section that could truly be called a downtown. Shopping, restaurants, and services are spread the 26-mile length of Carmel Valley with a couple of upscale shopping malls at one end and a small collection of businesses in the unincorporated village of Carmel Valley.

Recreation and Culture

The Monterey peninsula likes to call itself the "Golf Capital of the World." Its seventeen courses are the setting for many regional and national championship tournaments, as are the twenty courses in the county. This is the site of the world-renowned Pebble Beach course and the annual Pebble Beach Pro-Am event. Tourists fly in from all over the world and pay big money just to be able to say, "I played Pebble Beach."

Monterey area beaches are famous for the variety of sea life, swimming, and scuba diving. The water is very cold here, however, and it takes some determination to swim. Some do, some do not. (One of the authors once went in water up to his knees, a foolhardy event not likely to be repeated.) Small harbors here make boating a favorite with the sailing set.

Monterey Peninsula is rich in culture, with more than one hundred art galleries and studios. Several live theater groups, both professional and amateur, perform in Monterey and Carmel. Monterey Peninsula College has an excellent theater program and provides musical events and lectures for the public's enjoyment. The school offers a special program directed toward older students; the curriculum includes history, philosophy, art, and music. The Monterey Jazz and Blues Festivals draw aficionados from all over the world. This is also the site of the famous Monterey Bay Aquarium with numerous galleries and exhibits, making it one of the world's finest. Membership in the aquarium entitles local residents not only to free entry to the facility, but also to various social events, such as wine-tasting parties and dinners in the aquarium in the evenings.

Real Estate

Housing prices dropped from 1994 to 1996, but have recovered to slightly above the pre-slump period. Approximate home prices for three-bedroom, two-bath homes: Seaside, $147,000; Marina, $180,000; Pacific Grove, $295,000; Monterey, $300,000; Carmel Valley, $380,000; Carmel, $420,000; Pebble Beach $510,000 (up to several million).

Medical Care

The peninsula has excellent medical care, served by two topnotch hospitals. Community Hospital and Monterey Peninsula Hospital have specialists in all fields of medical practice. There are also several clinics and a large number of doctors in private practice.

When Grandkids Visit

When you take out a yearly membership in the Monterey Bay Aquarium, you are entitled to special passes for your grandchildren. These unlimited passes are free and are issued in the name of your grandkids, giving them a feeling of belonging. At the aquarium, they can pet bat rays, ogle octopuses, and touch tidepool creatures. One of the most popular attractions is the sea otter exhibit. The fascinating little critters seem to enjoy entertaining the public, diving, spinning, and playing tricks. Try to get there at feeding time, about 2:00 P.M., for the most activity.

Addresses and Connections

Chamber of Commerce: (Monterey) 380 Alvarado Street, Monterey, CA 93940; (Pacific Grove) P.O. Box 167, Pacific Grove, CA 93950; (Carmel-by-the-Sea) P.O. Box 4444, Carmel, CA 93921; (Carmel Valley) P.O. Box 288, Carmel Valley, CA 93924; (Seaside) 505 Broadway Avenue, Seaside, CA 93955

Senior Services: 801 Lighthouse Avenue, Monterey, CA 93940

Newspaper: (Monterey) *Peninsula Herald*, 8 Upper Ragsdale Drive, Monterey, CA 93940; (Monterey) *Coast Weekly*, 668 Williams Avenue, Seaside, CA 93955; (Carmel) *Pine Cone*, Fourth Avenue, Carmel, CA 93921

Airport: Monterey Municipal Airport

Bus/Train: Greyhound; countywide bus service; Amtrak in Salinas, 30 miles

Internet: (Monterey)
http://www.infomanagecom/montereybay/monterey/default. html
(Pacific Grove)
http://www.infomanagecom/montereybay/pacificgrove/default.html
(Carmel) http://www. carmelnet.com/bythec/

Monterey Peninsula Weather

	JAN.	APR.	JUL.	OCT.	RAIN	SNOW
		In degrees Fahrenheit				
DAILY HIGHS	61	65	72	71	18"	—
DAILY LOWS	42	47	55	51		

Big Sur

Beginning just south of Carmel, the Big Sur country follows a stunning coastline some 100 miles, ending below San Simeon (Hearst Castle) in San Luis Obispo County. The coast gains its name from the Big Sur River, which empties into the Pacific here. Big Sur isn't a town, and it's not really a village—it's just a few businesses scattered here and there and a few homes spotted here and there, clinging to the edge of a cliff or tucked away among tall redwoods. Henry Miller described the Big Sur Coast as "a way of looking at the world, a place of grandeur, where one is always conscious of eloquent silence—the face of the earth as the Creator intended it to look." Highway 1, recognized as one of the most beautiful drives in the world, winds through redwoods and meadows, across river canyons and creeks, with wildflowers and untouched beaches at every turn of the road.

For years Big Sur was the best-kept secret of famous and not-so-famous artists, authors, and philosophers. Isolated by gravel roads and a rustic infrastructure, residents maintained a self-sufficient colony among the redwoods, with cabins tucked away in deep canyons or perched on cliffs overlooking the ocean. They often lived without electricity or running water. With Big Sur gaining in popularity as well as population, the starving artists gave way to wealthy weekenders and affluent retirees. Some homes along the coast have sold for multimillion-dollar prices, although there are many more humble places for almost-humble prices—albeit without a view of crashing surf. Most of the coast is jealously protected from development by the California Coastal Commission. This is why so much of the shoreline is absolutely pristine, without a hint of construction or commercialism—nothing but mountains, trees, and surf.

Medical services are all but nonexistent here, with Monterey offering the nearest hospital to the north and Morro Bay to the south. Real estate cannot be categorized; oceanfront properties sell for millions, and rustic cabins for a few thousand dollars.

San Luis Obispo

Attempting to rediscover elusive Monterey Bay in 1769, the land expedition of Gaspar de Portola and Junipero Serra passed through San Luis Obispo. They were impressed with the region and recommended that a mission be founded here. Established in 1772, the mission flourished, and a town grew up around it. However, when Mexico gained independence, the missions were secularized and soon fell into disrepair. For several decades San Luis Obispo remained an isolated cattle town. Things didn't pick up until the Southern Pacific Railroad arrived here in 1894. When the railroad finally reached Los Angeles in 1901, San Luis Obispo became an important station on the line between San Francisco and Los Angeles.

San Luis (as it's called by natives) gained further stature when it became a university town. California Polytechnic State University is an integral part of the city's social life today. The school provides numerous cultural, entertainment, and sports events; students color the town with youthful enthusiasm and energy. In San Luis Obispo, the school affects the community much more than does Santa Barbara's university, partly because it's located right in the community rather than in a nearby town, as is the University of California at Santa Barbara. Today's population is nearly 42,000, not counting college students.

In many ways, San Luis is a smaller, less extravagant version of Santa Barbara. There's a conscious attempt to capitalize on the early California, Spanish mission theme—yet without the opulence and Southern California exuberance that marks Santa Barbara.

The relaxed yet intellectual atmosphere of San Luis Obispo makes it a viable retirement location for those who don't have to be able to walk to the beach. Yet the ocean is only a 13-mile drive from the town. The advantage of living away from the shore is more sunshine and more comfortable evenings, which can be shirtsleeve weather rather than the typically cool, after-dark sweater weather found in Pismo Beach and similar beach towns.

Like other university towns, San Luis Obispo enjoys a vibrant combination of services and facilities that satisfies the tastes and requirements of students and retirees alike. Interesting yet affordable restaurants, bookstores that stock more than just best-sellers, and foreign and award-winning movies that other towns would never think to present are just a few of the advantages that retirees like about living here.

Recreation and Culture

San Luis Obispo, being a much larger community than the Pismo Beach area, naturally offers more senior activities. From bowling leagues to golf tournaments, the sports sector is covered. Woodcarving, folk and square dancing, lectures, and all sorts of social activities are available.

The university sponsors a multitude of cultural events, such as plays, lectures, and concerts, many free to the public. Special events are held in Mission Plaza, a superbly developed square, complete with a woods, a meandering creek, and facilities for enjoying events such as the Mozart Festival in late July and early August and the Central Coast Wine Festival at harvest time.

Real Estate

The median price of a three-bedroom home in San Luis Obispo is around $220,000, with condominiums averaging $110,000. Condos and apartments are plentiful because of student-created demands.

Medical Care

As the health-care center for the region, San Luis Obispo has three medical facilities: Arroyo Grande Community Hospital, San Luis Obispo General

Hospital, and Sierra Vista Regional Medical Center. Several outpatient clinics and a full range of medical practitioners ensure good medical care.

When Grandkids Visit

Although it's an hour's drive north of San Luis Obispo, you must take the grandkids to the William Randolph Hearst Castle at San Simeon. The collection of art objects, segments of genuine European palaces, marble statuary, and other outlandish displays of wealth are guaranteed to leave you overwhelmed. The complex is so large that it takes several tours to take it all in.

Addresses and Connections

Chamber of Commerce: 781 Los Osos Valley Road, San Luis Obispo, CA 93402–2603

Senior Services: 1455 Santa Rosa Street, San Luis Obispo, CA, 93401–3717

Newspaper: Telegram Tribune, 3825 South Higuera Street, San Luis Obispo, CA, 93401–7438

Airport: San Luis Obispo Airport

Bus/Train: City bus service, Greyhound, and Amtrak

Internet: http://www.globalindex.com/comindex/comm_cal/s/san_luis.htm

San Luis Obispo Weather

	JAN.	APR.	JUL.	OCT.	RAIN	SNOW
		In degrees Fahrenheit				
DAILY HIGHS	64	68	72	74	13"	—
DAILY LOWS	43	48	53	51		

Pismo Beach

Once the butt of many Jack Benny jokes, Pismo Beach is today having the last laugh. People are discovering that it's not only a pleasant place to spend a vacation—it's a great place to retire. Established as a beach resort in 1887, Pismo has been bringing tourists and retirees to the Central Coast for more than a century.

Located about 200 miles north of Los Angeles, Pismo Beach is the Central Coast's only major beach area between Santa Barbara and

Monterey. This is one of California's longest and widest beaches, with 23 miles of clean sand and sweeping dunes.

Pismo Beach derives its name from the Chumash Indian word, *pimuz*, a word for the tar found in nearby Price Canyon. The Chumash used the tar to seal their canoes to make them seaworthy. In turn, the famous Pismo clam gets its name from the Chumash word. At one time, the clams almost seemed to pave long stretches of sandy shoreline. The clams were so large and plentiful that early residents used teams of horses and farm equipment to harvest the crustaceans. Until the feisty sea otters and too many clam forks thinned the mollusk population, the favorite sport here was searching through the sand at low tide to bring in a quick limit of the large, succulent shellfish. People still search for them, but today's clam diggers aren't nearly as numerous as the crowds of a few years ago.

The town of Pismo Beach is just one of the towns spread along this shore. The beach area is made up of several small cities that loosely connect to form a sprawling, lightly populated district known as Five Cities, a complex comprising the communities of Shell Beach, Oceano, Grover City, Avila Beach, and Pismo Beach itself. Arroyo Grande sits away from the shore, but is considered part of the Five Cities area. The combined population is 30,000. The town of Pismo Beach itself has about 6,000 inhabitants.

As you might expect, where there are large numbers of retired folks, you will find active senior citizens organizations. Pismo Beach supports several organizations, ranging from grandmothers clubs to a singles club for people over fifty-five. There is an active Retired and Senior Volunteer Programs chapter, meals-on-wheels, and a senior citizens ride program. You will find plenty of opportunities to get involved in volunteer projects.

Recreation and Culture

Fishing is great from the long pier that juts out past the surf in downtown Pismo Beach (no license required). Bottom fish, such as ling cod, red snapper, and sand dabs, are favorite catches. Fishing and clamming are year-round sports. Boat-launching facilities are available at Avila Beach, at the sheltered northern section.

Pismo Beach is one of the few places along the California coast where it is permissible to drive a motor vehicle onto the sand, and there are several ramps that give access to the beach. Huge, undulating sand dunes are meccas for four-wheel-drive vehicles and dune buggies. Converted Volkswagens, Jeeps, and other souped-up contraptions zip up and down the dunes like motorized roller coasters (away from the more quiet beach crowd, of course). Another favorite beach activity is horseback riding. A couple of stables rent horses for leisurely rides along the surf line. Golf is popular, with several courses in the area.

Real Estate

Housing is naturally more expensive along the cliffs or anywhere an ocean view fills your picture window. Still, for a California beach area, Pismo Beach is surprisingly affordable. Brand-new, two-bedroom condos can be had for $90,000 and up. Two- or three-bedroom homes range from $129,000 and up. Some very expensive homes sit on the cliffs of Shell Beach, homes with gorgeous views and walled privacy. Yet just a block or two back from the ocean are many modest homes with low-maintenance yards along neat, comfortable-looking streets. Numerous mobile home parks with low monthly rents dot the area.

Medical Care

Health care needs for the Five Cities complex are handled by the Arroyo Grande Community Hospital. This is a medium-size, general service facility, which is augmented by several smaller clinics scattered around the Pismo Beach area. Excellent medical services are also located in nearby San Luis Obispo.

When Grandkids Visit

Go to a bait shop near the beach and rent some clam forks and a burlap bag. Then take the grandkids clamming. This writer is convinced that Pismo clams are the tastiest clams in the entire world! Fried in butter and lightly dashed with homemade tartar sauce, they are the ultimate experience in gourmet cuisine. But they aren't plentiful, so you have to be prepared to spend time to collect a limit. Get a tide chart and go in the water at a minus low tide, and walk backward in the surf, thrusting the clam fork into the sand every 3 inches until you feel a hard shell. Then scoop it up and toss it into your burlap bag.

Addresses and Connections

Chamber of Commerce: 760 Mattie Road, Pismo Beach, CA 93449
Senior Services: 189 Windward Avenue, Pismo Beach, CA 93449

Newspaper: Five Cities Times-Press Recorder, P.O. Box 460, Arroyo Grande, CA 93430

Airport: San Luis Obispo Airport

Bus/Train: Greyhound, Amtrak

Internet: http://www.pismobeach.com/index.html

Pismo Beach Weather

	JAN.	APR.	JUL.	OCT.	RAIN	SNOW
		In degrees Fahrenheit				
DAILY HIGHS	63	67	74	73	16"	—
DAILY LOWS	41	47	57	51		

Santa Maria

Because of its large population of Chumash Indians, early Spanish Jesuits probably considered the Santa Maria River Valley for a mission site. Instead they decided to establish their missions in La Purisima, about 20 miles south, and in San Luis Obispo, 20 miles north. Until after the Civil War, the valley remained a serene place where ranchero families—along with their vaqueros, friends, and neighbors—gathered together under the large oak trees to celebrate the frequent church holidays with Spanish-style barbecues. The famous Santa Maria Barbecue grew out of this tradition, and achieved its special style when cooks began to string beef brisket on skewers to grill over glowing red-oak wood fires.

The town of Santa Maria (originally called Central City) began in 1867, when Benjamin T. Wiley, a Civil War veteran from Mississippi, discovered an overlooked stretch of public land where Mexican land-grant boundaries failed to meet. The land, about 6 miles wide and 15 miles long, is today a place of homes, businesses, and parks.

The gentle Central Coast weather—great almost every day of the year, never too hot or too cold—is responsible for bringing newcomers to Santa Maria. Those wishing to be near the ocean beaches, but not overwhelmed by them and the tourists, are finding Santa Maria a more economic alternative than either San Luis Obispo or Santa Barbara. The cost of living is as favorable as you will find until you get many hours north of San Francisco. The increasing population of retirees has stirred a minor housing boom, with several quality developments where you get an amazing amount for your housing dollars.

Downtown Santa Maria has managed to keep from surrendering to the chain stores on the outskirts of town. Although it lacks the charm of downtown Santa Barbara or San Luis Obispo, Santa Maria's center offers affordable shopping. The downtown is neat and tidy, with wide streets. A beautifully designed and fully equipped mall near the city center offers everything from Robinson's May Company to warehouse stores.

Santa Maria's city government is very retiree-friendly. The two senior centers here are well funded and provide activities and volunteer opportunities for the residents. One retiree said of her new community, "This is a place that's still small enough to feel like a community, not an urban metroplex, and you get an amazing amount of services for your money." Beneath the bustle of today's business, the quiet settlement of Santa Maria lingers. Cattle and deer still graze the green foothills, meadow larks trill their songs in the marshes, and you can almost see the ghosts of vaqueros tending a barbecue under the oak trees. It's not unlike the peaceful valley Benjamin T. Wiley found in 1867.

Recreation and Culture

With the ocean beaches just 15 miles distant, surf fishing, beach-combing, and swimming are popular pastimes. Several golf courses and numerous tennis courts are available for public play. Mountain skiing can be enjoyed with about two hours of driving time.

Culture amenities in Santa Maria include a community theater and large movieplexes. A thirty-minute drive takes you to San Luis Obispo to varied university events found there. Santa Barbara's cultural world is seventy minutes away. The Santa Maria Rodeo is a looked-forward-to event that brings people from far-flung places.

Real Estate

Housing close to downtown is very affordable, with quiet side streets, older homes, and mature neighborhoods. But most folks choose to locate in one of the mushrooming subdivisions on the outskirts of town. In fact, local people say that one of the attractions here is quality housing at affordable prices. Prices range from $60,000 to $500,000, with many between $100,000 to $120,000.

Medical Care

Santa Maria also enjoys well-funded medical care, with two hospitals taking care of health needs. Marian Medical Center has 225 beds, and Valley Community Hospital has 70 beds. The facilities are well staffed with doctors specializing in practices that focus on issues of aging.

When Grandkids Visit

Try the Santa Maria Museum of Flight, with its wide range of aviation exhibits, from early-day experiments with heavier-than-air flight to the mysterious Stealth bomber. Some of the displays are models and others are the real thing, housed in two hangars.

Addresses and Connections

Chamber of Commerce: 614 South Broadway, Santa Maria, CA 93454
Senior Services: 301 South Miller Street, Santa Maria, CA 93454
Newspaper: Santa Maria Times, 3200 Skyway Drive, Santa Maria, CA 93455–1896
Airport: Santa Barbara, 70 miles
Bus/Train: No city bus service; Greyhound
Internet: http://www. ci. santa-maria. ca. us/

Santa Maria Weather

	JAN.	APR.	JUL.	OCT.	RAIN	SNOW
		In degrees Fahrenheit				
DAILY HIGHS	63	65	72	73	12"	—
DAILY LOWS	39	43	53	48		

Santa Barbara

Along with Monterey Bay, Santa Barbara is considered one of the most desirable settings on the California coast. Indeed a lovely place, the town is poised on a narrow coastal plain rising from the Pacific and overshadowed by the steep Santa Ynez Mountains. Protected by the rugged Channel Islands, Santa Barbara's miles of prime beaches are edged with palm trees, lush lemon and avocado groves, and subtropical foliage.

Santa Barbara received an early start as a retirement and weekend getaway when it was "discovered" in the late 1880s by wealthy families escaping from booming Los Angeles. Only a 90-mile train ride from the burgeoning metropolis, Santa Barbara became an ideal place to get away from it all, a kind of "Beverly Hills north." Business tycoons, developers, industrialists—and later, movie stars—made Santa Barbara the in place for second homes. Ultimately, those elaborate weekend houses in Santa Barbara became retirement homes.

With typical Southern California flair, the newly rich built mansions and lavish homes near the beaches, in the town, and high up on the mountain slopes. Stuccoed Spanish and Moorish palaces with red-tiled roofs and swimming pools made Santa Barbara the archetype of Southern California extravagance. No expense was spared in construction or landscaping. Decorative trees and plants from all over the world graced mansions and cottages alike. Today this landscaping has matured into a virtual arboretum.

Because of its auspicious beginnings and quality architecture, Santa Barbara didn't need to follow the example of other cities by overbuilding beyond recognition and then undergoing urban renewal to correct the mess. Residents fought successfully to protect Santa Barbara's stunning, Riviera-like setting from modernization. From simple bungalows to vast, exclusive estates, Santa Barbara homes have a style, a rich heritage of Spanish, Mediterranean, Moorish and contemporary California influences. Most striking is Santa Barbara's downtown commercial district, a jewel of urban design and good taste. Buildings have low-pitched roofs of red tile, arched facades, walls stuccoed in warm earth tones, wrought-iron decorations, and delightful enclosed patios.

The presence of a major university brings Santa Barbara a wealth of cultural and educational advantages, yet the school is located in Goleta, several miles away from the city, so its influence isn't overwhelming.

Santa Barbara's population today is 87,000, not including its suburban communities. Along with the Monterey peninsula, Santa Barbara has a deserved reputation for expensive housing. However, as pointed out earlier, both places have affordable housing—if you look carefully—and you do have a wide range of neighborhoods to choose from. Listed below are several communities, both in and near Santa Barbara, that are suitable for various retirement budgets.

Goleta is the home of the University of California at Santa Barbara and the location of the region's aerospace industry. As a college town, this is one of the places to look for more moderate housing (moderate, not cheap), and rentals are plentiful. Homes are currently available from the high $100,000 range to $3 million, with a median sales price of $260,000. Condos from sell from $85,000 to $260,000. Southern California–style homes in established tract developments are the best buys. For more elaborate housing, look to the foothills or near the coast for custom, executive-style homes with ocean views. Partially because of the university, Goleta has a strong sense of community, with shopping centers and transportation throughout old and new Goleta. Goleta beach has a 200-foot fishing pier, a picnic area, and park.

The Mesa is located on the bluffs just beyond the harbor and it extends from the ocean up to the top of the ridge. In this pleasant area of single-family homes and condos, residents have views of the ocean, the mountains, and the city of Santa Barbara. The Mesa is convenient to transportation and shopping. Over the hill from the Mesa—near the Highway 101 freeway and downtown Santa Barbara—is another afford-able area. This is an area of smaller homes and duplexes, with rentals plentiful, said to be popular with first-time buyers.

San Roque is a quiet location, convenient to downtown, where the homes are a charming mixture of small cottages, classic Tudors, and replicas of Old California hacienda. Most are single-family; you'll find few rentals here.

Upper East, one of the oldest quality neighborhoods, is where the most wealthy once built their early Spanish styles alongside fancy Victorian homes. The mature landscaping and large trees create a sense of the elegance of turn-of-the-century living. Some streets have original sandstone curbs and some homes have hitching posts by the street, seemingly waiting for a horse-and-buggy carriage to tie up.

Montecito, just east of Santa Barbara, began as a fashionable health resort—a seaside village popular with the Eastern elite around the turn of the century. Today it's a place of country clubs, quaint shops, and private schools. Quiet lanes lead to secluded homes, the beach, mountain trails, creeks, and waterfalls. In short, this is a place of elegance. Thickly wood-ed hills display magnificent monuments to big money. Elegant Normandy castles and regal mansions of Italian marble are intermixed with dignified Cape Cod colonials and contemporary California ranch homes. You'll pay for the privilege of living here: Homes are currently available from $300,000 to $8.5 million, and condos from $250,000 to $1.2 million.

The Riviera is another exclusive community. With narrow, winding streets like its European namesake, the Riviera offers custom homes with views of the city, harbor, ocean, and islands beyond. Located above Santa Barbara's downtown area, the Riviera receives a maximum amount of sunlight, from early morning to late evening. Beaches, shopping, and dining are just minutes away from Riviera neighborhoods; however, public transportation does not access the winding streets.

Summerland and **Carpinteria**, east of Santa Barbara's city limits, are pleasant beach communities worthy of investigation. Summerland sits next to exclusive Montecito, and is the smaller town, with a population of 1,600. Basically residential, Summerland enjoys gorgeous views of the ocean and offshore Channel Islands. You can choose among a wide variety of large and small homes, condominiums, and small ranches. Carpinteria (population 13,800) claims to have "the world's safest beach." It's also coined the term "Silicon Beach" to honor the fast-growing high-tech computer and software businesses that have located here. The area has little trouble attracting refugees from crowded Silicon Valley firms in the San Jose area who enjoy their choices of tract or custom ocean-view homes. Just outside town there are horse ranches, as well as orange and avocado orchards.

Recreation and Culture

Santa Barbara is the regional center for culture and outdoor recreation. Numerous galleries display the work of local and international artists, and the University of California presents top-rated musical and theatrical events. Golf, tennis, sailing, and horseback riding are year-round pastimes.

Real Estate

The tradition of costly housing has endured over the years, making Santa Barbara one of more expensive places we've investigated, as well as one of the highest-quality retirement areas. The local newspaper shows some two- and three-bedroom houses renting for more than many retired couples earn. A few places can be found for around $1,000 a month, but they are described as "cottages" or "charming" (translation: cramped). Most house rentals fall into the $1,300 to $1,700 range. At $1,700 a month, that means $20,400 just for rent. In Montecito, on the eastern edge of the city, rents range from a low of $2,400 to $5,900 a month ($5,900 computes to $70,800 a year, not counting gas, electricity, and an occasional meal). Even studio apartments (translation: one room and a hot plate) rent for $500 to $600. Santa Barbara homes were being offered (spring 1998) from $195,000 to $2.5 million. Condos were selling from $100,000 to $685,000.

Medical Care

Three hospitals serve the area: Goleta Valley Community Hospital, St. Francis Medical Center, and Santa Barbara Cottage Hospital. Medical care is excellent, with all specialties covered. Santa Barbara ranks high in the number of doctors per capita with twenty-three for every 1,000 residents.

When Grandkids Visit

Everybody seems to recommend Kid's World, located in Santa Barbara's Alameda Park. Designed by children as a dreamland, it was built by community volunteers in 1993. Kids can glide down an eel, sail a pirate ship, walk inside a whale's mouth, pet a shark, clamber up to a tree house, or slink through a haunted castle. Another possibility is the Zoological Gardens and Museum of Natural History, built on the grounds of an old beachside estate. More than 700 animals live in natural habitats here. There's a domestic animal section where children can pet and feed farm animals in the zoo's barnyard.

Addresses and Connections

Chamber of Commerce: 504 State Street, Santa Barbara, CA 92702
Senior Services: 35 West Victoria Street, Santa Barbara, CA 93101
Newspaper: Santa Barbara News-Press, De La Guerra Plaza, Santa Barbara, CA 93102
Airport: Santa Barbara Regional Airport, at Goleta
Bus/Train: City bus, Greyhound, Amtrak
Internet: http://www.santabarbaraca.com/

Santa Barbara Weather

	JAN.	APR.	JUL.	OCT.	RAIN	SNOW
		In degrees Fahrenheit				
DAILY HIGHS	63	67	74	73	16"	—
DAILY LOWS	41	47	57	51		

SAN FRANCISCO
BAY AREA

THE SAN FRANCISCO BAY AREA

San Francisco is a medium-size city of about 700,000 people occupying forty-five square miles at the top of a peninsula in Northern California. That makes it the nation's fourteenth largest city in terms of population. Yet it ranks very near the top in influence, visibility, and overall importance. This is at least in part because San Francisco serves as a magnet for tourists from all over the world who flock to it year-round to enjoy its scenic beauty, gourmet restaurants, museums, music, theater, shopping, spectator sports, and countless other attractions. It is often referred to as "Everybody's Favorite City."

The 6.5 million inhabitants of scores of villages, towns, and smaller cities within the nine-county region that makes up the Bay Area share in "The City's" bounty year-round. When they go home, it is with the knowledge that they can go back to San Francisco as often as they want. Together with all the things that tourists know about, Bay Area residents have swimming, sailing, fishing, hiking, and riding to keep them physically fit, and classes, community service, and social groups to keep them mentally alert.

The San Francisco Bay Area extends from Napa and Sonoma Counties on the north to Santa Clara County on the south, a distance of approximately 70 miles, and from the Pacific Ocean on the west to a fringe of farms, ranches, villages, and small towns in Contra Costa and Alemeda Counties on the east, about 50 miles.

The San Francisco Bay Area offers more opportunity for choice than many entire countries and most states. There is an old saying that, if you don't like the weather in San Francisco, just wait a minute. It is equally true that, if you don't like the climate, you can change it by moving a few miles. In summer, while people in San Rafael, Walnut Creek, and San Jose are sweltering in ninety-degree-plus temperatures, the thermometers in the City, Half Moon Bay, and West Marin may be registering temperatures in the low sixties. Conversely, when the residents of San Francisco and Oakland are enjoying winter temperatures that seldom drop below the low forties, even at night, their neighbors to the north, south, and east may be wrapping their outdoor plants in plastic to protect them from hard freezes. The price San Francisco pays for its narrow year-round temperature change is the lack of a real summer.

Its cultural diversity is a major factor in San Francisco's attractiveness. It is a place where people of all religions and ethnic origins live together in harmony. In the main, its neighborhoods are microcosms of the area, containing a healthy mix of people who have only their general economic level and choice of lifestyle in common. But there are pockets of ethnic culture throughout the area: Japan Town, Chinatown, the largely Latino Mission District, the Philippine concentration in Daly City, African-American centers in the Filmore District and Oakland, and the fading Little Italy in North Beach. These enclaves continue to keep cultural traditions alive.

One token of the Bay Area's ethnic diversity is the plethora of festivals and celebrations throughout the year. For example, you can join in the Scottish Gathering of the Clans to listen to bagpipe and fiddle music or gape at huge men in kilts tossing around telephone-pole-size cabers as if they were matchsticks. Or you can go Greek and dance the hosapico or miserlou, eat spinach pies and baclava, and drink retsina (wine in which a baseball bat has been marinated) while you listen to bazouki music. If your taste runs to corridos (Mexican topical ballads), tacos, and enchiladas, you will find them at the many Cinco de Mayo celebrations commemorating Mexico's victory over the French in the battle of Puebla on May 5, 1862. African-American history is celebrated on Juneteenth with rodeos and barbecues marking the day when the word of the Emancipation Proclamation reached Texas. Chinese New Year, however, is the occasion of San Francisco's biggest parade, in which dozens of marching bands representing every ethnic and cultural group in the area mingle with dragon dancers and practitioners of the martial arts to illustrate that San Franciscans know how to share what is best in each other's traditions.

What sort of terrain do you prefer? Chances are it can be found in the Bay Area. Ocean beaches extend all along its western edge; hills and mountains are scattered throughout; some sections are heavily wooded; and flat farmland—some, but by no means all, of it converted to housing tracts—is still characteristic of the area's eastern and southern edges.

Because the Bay Area includes not one, but several large cities, it offers a range of urban lifestyles, including that of San Francisco, which is arguably America's most cosmopolitan. Oakland, while decidedly urban, has a distinctly different flavor. Oakland benefits from its strong African-American influence and its conviction that it represents the city of tomorrow.

Suburban communities abound throughout the entire area, offering the security of homogeneous neighborhoods where you know all your neighbors, together with the easy access to San Francisco that is their reason for being. A little farther from the center are truly small towns that embody what is still America's most traditional lifestyle.

Most surprisingly, the Bay Area, particularly in the western end of Marin and the eastern fringes of Contra Costa, still includes areas that are thoroughly rural. Working farms and ranches flourish and the standard mode of transportation is the pickup truck.

From the time that San Francisco was the base camp for the forty-niners seeking their fortunes in the nearby gold fields, its citizens have always been willing to let people find happiness in their own ways. This quality is most evident today in the refusal by most locals to condemn or shun gay and lesbian neighbors and associates. If this makes you uncomfortable, there are numerous neighborhoods both in the City and the surrounding area that are as solidly heterosexual as your hometown.

San Francisco—"The City"

No discussion of retirement in the Bay Area is complete without mention of the City itself. For a host of reasons it may be the perfect choice for at least a small number of prospective retirees who are willing and able to handle its high cost of living. San Francisco is not only one of the most beautiful and stimulating cities in the world, it is also, because of its small size and first-rate transit system, one of the most manageable. Its exceptionally even, temperate year-round climate makes it ideal for those who do not choose to struggle with extremes of heat and cold. When Mark Twain said (or is reputed to have said), "The coldest winter I ever spent was one summer in San Francisco," he was referring to cloudy, foggy days with the temperatures in the fifties—not at all uncommon there, but hardly likely to cause frostbite. There is seldom a day in winter when the midday temperature does not get up into the fifties.

Recreation and Culture

San Francisco's attractions are both too numerous and too well known to detail here. From one of the world's great opera companies to the Super Bowl–perennial 49ers, San Francisco abounds in the first-rate. And it never settles for the status quo: New museums and art galleries spring up constantly, as do new cultural centers, such as Yerba Buena Gardens, where the Museum of Modern Art, some fine new restaurants, and an ultramodern theater are located. There is not only an active theatrical scene and more movie theaters than one could easily count, but their offerings exhibit a greater range than is available in any but one or two larger U.S. cities.

Although seldom discussed as a recreation activity, dining is one of San Francisco's favorites. There are excellent restaurants in every price range and serving almost any ethnic cuisine available. If today you are tired of Burmese food, why not try Russian, Nicaraguan, or Ethiopian? Or why not something as daring as good old American country cooking? There are lots of good restaurant guides that you can consult if you visit this great city.

Within San Francisco there are many good hiking trails. The one that scales Twin Peaks leads to the tourists' favorite panoramic (360-degree) view of the city. From the one along the cliffs of Land's End, you look down at the pounding surf and across the Golden Gate at the green hills of Marin.

The activities within San Francisco's famous Golden Gate Park, ranging from museum going to trout fishing, would fill a book by themselves. In fact, you should neither visit nor consider a move to San Francisco without consulting one or more of the innumerable guidebooks that "America's Favorite City" has spawned.

Sailing can be enjoyed, both on San Francisco Bay or at Muir Lake. Fishing is also a popular activity: Surf casters line Ocean Beach on the city's western edge; boats sail from Fishermen's Wharf out into the Pacific in pursuit of salmon and other deep-water fish; and other anglers choose spots along piers, including those at Fort Mason and Fort Point, not to mention Muni Pier, not far from downtown.

Real Estate

Homes in the city of San Francisco are considered to be among the most expensive in the United States. In San Francisco it is hard to find an adequate house in a pleasant neighborhood for less than $300,000. Condos command proportionately high prices, and rentals for a one-bedroom apartment at less than $1,200 a month are scarce. These may well be bargain prices for those who can afford them, but that offers small comfort to the rest of us. It is possible, however, to live in the Bay Area and enjoy all of its riches, including those of the City, on a much more modest budget than the highly publicized San Francisco housing costs would suggest. Here is a sampling of prices in some of the more affordable and popular neighborhoods:

Richmond District. Homes start at $410,000 for two bedrooms, one bath. Condos start at $279,500 for two bedrooms.

Marina District. Homes start at $499,000 for two bedrooms. Condos start at $249,000 for one bedroom.

Noe Valley. Homes start at $350,000 for two bedrooms. Condos start at $309,000 for two bedrooms.

Rentals are in high demand in San Francisco. In the Richmond district, studio apartments can be rented for about $800 a month, one-bedroom apartments for $1,200 a month, and two-bedroom apartments from $1,500 a month. Parking, if available, may come with extra charges.

Medical Care

San Francisco's hospitals are widely regarded as among the best in the world. It would be superfluous to list here the number of beds, varieties of specialty care, hours of operation, or the other specifics that one would want to know about a smaller city. This is, without question, one of medicine's world capitals, and if the facility and physician to respond to your needs don't exist in San Francisco, they probably don't exist anywhere.

When Grandkids Visit

For a visit to a view of nature, a view of history, a view of antique technology, and a view of an ageless miracle, drive out to Seal Rock out at the western end of San Francisco. (MUNI buses run there from downtown and other neighborhoods every few minutes.) The view nature is all around you in the crashing waves, the seal-covered rocks just off shore, the wind-sculpted Monterey Pines plunging toward the ocean. The antique technology is in the Musée Mechanique, 130 coin-operated machines, mostly from the turn of the century, that move, play instruments, conduct an execution, or tell your fortune. One of the most elaborate is a miniature farm, replete with livestock, equipment, and little people. The timeless miracle is a room-size *camera obscura,* the predecessor of the photographic camera, which projects the image of its surroundings onto the four walls.

Addresses and Connections

Chamber of Commerce: 465 California Street, Room 900, San Francisco, CA 94104

Senior Services: There is no central agency or center for seniors. Innumerable churches, synagogues, and community organizations, however, conduct senior programs and offer services.

Newspaper: San Francisco Chronicle, 901 Mission Street, San Francisco, CA 94103; *San Francisco Examiner,* 925 Mission Street, San Francisco, CA 94103

Airport: San Francisco International Airport

Bus/Train: San Francisco MUNI system blankets all the City's neighborhoods with bus, trolley, and light-rail service. In addition, BART (Bay Area Rapid Transit) offers subway-type service within some parts of the city and to adjacent communities. Rail service (Cal Train) is available for communities on the San Francisco peninsula. For long-distance train service, there are bus connections to the Amtrak station in Oakland.

Internet: http://www.sfgate.com

San Francisco Weather

	JAN.	APR.	JUL.	OCT.	RAIN	SNOW
		In degrees Fahrenheit				
DAILY HIGHS	56	62	65	69	20"	—
DAILY LOWS	46	50	54	55		

Oakland

Across the Bay from San Francisco and linked to it by the Bay Area Rapid Transit system (BART), numerous bus lines, and a great network of freeways and bridges is the collection of cities, small and large towns, and villages in Alameda and Contra Costa counties referred to collectively as the East Bay. Primary among them is Oakland.

Forget what you think you know about Oakland! It gets an almost universally bad rap because of its history and because crime and school board clumsiness make better copy than quiet, tree-lined neighborhoods where people live in harmony and comfort. Gertrude Stein's oft-quoted and usually misunderstood remark, "There's no there there," wasn't meant as a reflection on the quality of her hometown. It was just her way of saying that you can't go home again.

A principal reason for choosing Oakland is that it is only twenty minutes from San Francisco. Also its housing is much more affordable. But Oakland really is, as the frequently repeated characterization would have it, "the best-kept secret in the Bay Area." A major part of that secret is that Oakland has many varied middle-class neighborhoods with pretty front yards, comfortable houses, and friendly neighbors, all within a short and easy trip to San Francisco. Another part of the secret is that you don't have to go to San Francisco to enjoy fine dining, interesting shops, beautiful parks, the latest movies, concerts, sporting events, and just about anything else you might want to do. Finally, there is the intangible, but very important, sense of community that Oakland provides. One indication that Oakland is not just about economy is that so many people affluent enough to live wherever they want have chosen Oakland, particularly its hill neighborhoods and the city of Piedmont, which is wholly contained within Oakland's borders. In this and other Oakland neighborhoods, you can find some of the most elegant (and most expensive) homes in the Bay with prices that begin at $750,000 and go straight up from there.

Nearby, in the stable residential neighborhoods that the rest of us can afford, you can enjoy a very similar quality of life. Oakland really does have something for just about everyone.

San Francisco's famous fog is a prominent and picturesque feature of its landscape. It is pleasing to the eye, but not usually to the skin. Although downtown Oakland sometimes shares in this phenomenon, just as soon as you climb a little way up the hills, you can look down from your sunny neighborhood onto the chillier regions below. Oakland's temperature is accordingly five degrees warmer year-round than San Francisco's and ranges from the fifties and sixties in winter to the seventies and low eighties in summer. Although there is usually some nighttime cooling, it seldom sets in early enough to make dinner under the stars uncomfortable.

At this point we must make a disclosure: About five years ago the author of this section and his wife, both in their sixties, having lived in San Francisco and other parts of the Bay Area for a number of years, moved to Oakland. They have never been happier and do not intend to move ever again. We think this description of our adopted hometown is accurate, but we cannot claim that it is entirely objective.

Recreation and Culture

There are three public and two private golf courses in and around Oakland. An outstanding complex of regional parks with twenty regional trails offers hikers and other nature lovers the opportunity to experience the wilderness within minutes of the city. There are various places to swim, including Lake Temescal, nestled in a peaceful glade within minutes of any part of Oakland.

In spectator sports Oakland has few peers. The Athletics (baseball), the Raiders (football), and the Warriors (basketball) are almost always in national contention. (Those of us who remain loyal to the San Francisco Giants and the 49ers are graciously tolerated.)

The Oakland Museum, the Oakland East Bay Symphony, and the Oakland Ballet are probably the city's best-known cultural attractions, but by no means the only ones. Camron-Stanford House on the shore of

Sausalito

Just across the Golden Gate Bridge from San Francisco and possessing one of the most spectacular views of its skyline, the waterfront town of Sausalito reminds many people of the Mediterranean coast. The mountainside above its busy, pleasure craft–filled harbor is sprinkled with pastel-colored houses. Its climate is gentle, and its narrow, winding streets are peaceful—once you get out of the tourist-packed downtown area.

In its time, Sausalito has been a Miwok village, a bustling, bawdy seaport, a quiet fishing center, and an art colony. The Miwoks are gone; the rowdy saloons and bordellos, too (though not for nearly so long); most artists have been driven out by rising real estate prices; and tourism has become the major industry. Yet there are few Bay Area residents who would not give an arm and a leg for a house with a view, high in the Sausalito hills where few tourists venture.

Real Estate

Most real estate ads do not mention an arm and a leg as part of the deal, but the $500,000 median price is high enough to ensure that only a favored few will have their fantasies fulfilled. The median rent is well over $900 and apartments tend to be small—designed for affluent singles.

Lake Merritt, and Dunsmuir House and Gardens on Oakland's outskirts are beautifully preserved and restored examples of gracious nineteenth-century homes available for public visits. The Morcom Amphitheatre of Roses offers spectacular floral displays from May to November, and the Alice Arts Center is home to an ensemble theater and dance companies. Put Oakland on an island, many miles from civilization, and it would still be a culturally rich community. But it isn't on an island and both San Francisco and Berkeley are only minutes away. Enough said!

Real Estate

Despite small pockets of extreme wealth (and much larger pockets of poverty), much of Oakland consists of middle-class, middle-income neighborhoods of owner-occupied, single-family homes. Many of these neighborhoods contain a healthy mix of white, African-American, and Asian-American families. Among the neighborhoods known for moderately priced housing are Glenview, Dimond, Temescal, Laurel, Fruitvale, Oakmore, Oak Knoll, Sheffield Village, and parts of East and West Oakland. Planned developments include Hiller Highlands, Ridgemont, Parkwoods, and Crestmount. If you live in Rockridge, you can walk to innumerable shops and restaurants, and what is most important to the largely commuter population, to a BART (Bay Area Rapid Transit) station. Even more convenient and more urban is a high-rise condo in Chinatown. More than any other place we know, Oakland can give you whatever you want.

Real estate prices, although not nearly as low as in the farther reaches of the Bay Area, are significantly below those in San Francisco. The recent median sales price for a two-bedroom house was $123,000. (That is probably somewhat less than you would have to pay for a nice house in a comfortable neighborhood; better figure on at least $150,000.) Condominiums, which are likely to be newer, tend to be a little more expensive, with the median price for two bedrooms slightly over $150,000.

Rentals are available in clean modern buildings close to public transportation for as little as $600 a month. One such apartment complex lists the minimum qualifying annual income for two people at $16,368.

Medical Care

Oakland is home to the Kaiser Permanente prepaid health-care system, the oldest and largest in the world. Its huge network of hospitals and health-care centers serves one of every four Bay Area residents and offers every medical service imaginable.

Summit Medical Center, with 517 beds, is Oakland's largest private nonprofit hospital. This centrally located facility offers the full spectrum of health-care services. It is especially well known for its outstanding cardiovascular care.

Alta Bates Medical Center is a 509-bed facility serving the Oakland-Berkeley area with high-quality medical care.

When Grandkids Visit

Take the children in hand and make straight for the Redwood Valley Railway on Skyline Drive, high in the Oakland-Berkeley Hills. These coal-burning miniature trains will take you and your grandkids on a thrilling scenic tour, through tunnels and over bridges, with breathtaking views of the Bay Area.

Addresses and Connections

Chamber of Commerce: 475 Fourteenth Street, Oakland, CA 94612–1903

Newspaper: The *Oakland Tribune,* 66 Jack London Square, Oakland, CA 94607

Airport: Oakland International Airport is conveniently located and can easily be reached by car or public transit. San Francisco International Airport is about thirty minutes away.

Bus/Train: Oakland is served by the AC Transit system, which operates an extremely extensive network of bus routes throughout the city and provides express service to San Francisco during commuting hours. Seniors pay greatly reduced fares.

BART is a regional transit system that links Oakland to San Francisco and to other East Bay communities. It has numerous stops in Oakland and is a fast and easy way of getting around.

Internet: http://www.oaklandca.com
http://oaklandnet.com

Berkeley

Few communities anywhere in the world are better known or have a more distinctive image than Berkeley. If ever there was a city whose life was shaped by the presence of a great university, this is it. Jam-packed with art, music, and intellectual and social ferment, this East Bay city of 105,000 probably generates more headlines than any similar-size municipalities in the world. Only twenty minutes from San Francisco, with which it is linked by highway, bus, and the speedy BART subway system, Berkeley is entirely distinct from the City and very largely self-contained.

From the funkier stretches of Telegraph Avenue, where the 1960s seem to be alive, although not very well, to the ivory towers of the University of California, Berkeley campus, the entire community is constantly at fever pitch. Nobel Prizes are a dime a dozen among the stellar faculty. Attend a play, film, or concert there and you will immediately know that you are in a Berkeley audience. Even when most of the hair is white, the eyes are brighter, the talk more animated, and the clothes more casual than anywhere else.

The list of the ten largest employers begins with the university and contains only three who are not purveyors of education or medical care. Health professionals are the largest occupational group, followed by professors and librarians. Artists, entertainers, and writers are also near the top.

Although Berkeley would not be the retirement location of choice for many of our readers, we know of some for whom it must sound like the promised land.

Recreation and Culture

The city of Berkeley boasts forty-seven local parks and playgrounds (seventeen with tennis courts), three swim centers, a golf course, lawn bowling, and an ice-skating rink. Add the facilities of the Berkeley YMCA and the huge East Bay Regional Park system just east of the city, with its countless walking trails, plus the boating facilities of the Berkeley Marina and fishing from the Berkeley Pier, and there is almost no recreational taste that cannot be accommodated.

As for the arts, six museums, three theater companies (including the distinguished Berkeley Repertory Theater), a symphony orchestra, and a ballet company are just the tip of the iceberg, since they are augmented by the huge cultural wealth of the university. And then San Francisco is just twenty minutes away.

Real Estate

Berkeley is almost as expensive to live in as San Francisco. The median home value of $234,000 is all the more discouraging because Berkeley has many poor neighborhoods with tiny run-down houses. A house comparable to one that might sell for $150,000 in an outlying area would be at least $300,000 here.

Medical Care

Alta Bates Medical Center is a 509-bed facility serving the Oakland-Berkeley area with high-quality medical care. It has a medical staff of 900, and more than 90 percent of its physicians are board-certified.

When Grandkids Visit

The Lawrence Hall of Science is the future scientist's heaven. Filled with interactive machines, exhibits, and games, this might be called the mother of all participatory museums.

Addresses and Connections

Chamber of Commerce: 1834 University Avenue, Berkeley, CA 94703

Senior Services: 1901 Hearst Street, Berkeley, CA 94709; 2939 Ellis Street, Berkeley, CA 94703; 1900 Sixth Street, Berkeley, CA 94710

Newspaper: Two weeklies, the *Berkeley Voice* (2396 Domingo Avenue, Berkeley, CA 94705) and the *East Bay Express* (931 Ashby Avenue, Berkeley, CA 94710), cover local news as do the *Oakland Tribune* and the San Francisco papers.

Airport: Oakland International is 12 miles south; San Francisco International is 20 miles west.

Bus/Train: Alameda Transit and Berkeley Electric Shuttle Transit furnish frequent and reliable bus transportation within the community and to nearby counties. The Bay Area Rapid Transit system (BART) has three stations in Berkeley and provides rapid access to San Francisco.

Internet: http://www.berkeleychamber.com
http://www.ci.berkeley.ca.us

Berkeley Weather

	JAN.	APR.	JUL.	OCT.	RAIN	SNOW
		In degrees Fahrenheit				
DAILY HIGHS	56	64	70	70	24"	—
DAILY LOWS	43	48	54	53		

Petaluma

Located at the southern end of Sonoma County, Petaluma (population 49,000) is about as far from San Francisco as most commuters want to be. But for the retiree who wants to enjoy the charms of a small city without sacrificing easy access to the big one, it is close enough. (The drive to San Francisco can take as little as forty minutes, except during rush hours when it takes much, much longer.) Petaluma bills itself as "a modern city with nineteenth-century charm," not a bad description of this river port whose downtown boasts numerous unspoiled Victorians and is surrounded by dairy ranches and hayfields.

From the last decades of the nineteenth-century until the middle decades of the twentieth, Petaluma was the home of a thriving poultry-raising industry and was known as "the world's egg basket." The unusually active cultural life the city enjoys today may, in part, be the legacy of the many Jewish farmers who had come from New York and New Jersey to farm in the West.

The chickens and the farmers are gone, but the climate that made this area so ideal for agriculture remains one of Petaluma's attractions. In winter, days are pleasant and evenings are cheery with temperatures ranging between thirty-five and sixty degrees. Summers are dry, with warm days (sixty-five to eighty-five degrees) and comfortably cool evenings.

Recreation and Culture

Sonoma County's fourteen golf courses are all within an easy drive. A weekday greens fee of $30 seems typical. Other sports facilities open to the public include swimming pools, tennis courts, and walking trails. Boating can be enjoyed on the Petaluma River, which runs through the center of town. Two live theaters offer performances year-round. Cinnabar presents innovative opera, drama, dance, and music in a number of theaters, gardens, and mansions. The Mystic Theatre headlines top performers, music, and special events. Two movie theaters, with a combined total of thirteen screens, ensure that you can see all the current films without leaving town.

Real Estate

By Bay Area standards, Petaluma is an inexpensive place in which to live. There is a large variety of affordable homes available, starting in price at around $120,000 for two bedrooms, one bath. Three-bedroom, two-bath homes range from $180,000 to $250,000. The prices vary considerably from the more economical eastern section of the town to the upscale western neighborhoods.

The year-round temperate climate cuts heating costs, and an air-conditioned house is a rarity.

The average house rental in Petaluma is about $725. The town's seven mobile home parks, three of them specifically for retirees, offer an economical housing alternative.

Medical Care

Petaluma Valley Hospital is a ninety-nine-bed acute-care facility with a twenty-four-hour emergency room. Kaiser Permanente medical plan members receive services from the Kaiser Permanente Hospital and Medical Center. A variety of self-help programs, home-care referral services, a hospice, several health maintenance organizations, and, of course, numerous private physicians round out the medical care picture.

When Grandkids Visit

Take your grandchildren on an old-fashioned paddlewheeler trip on the *Petaluma Queen*. Enjoy the calliope music while you cruise down the river. Call (415) 762–2100 for tickets and information.

Addresses and Connections

Chamber of Commerce: 799 Baywood Drive, Suite 3, Petaluma, CA 94954

Senior Services: Petaluma People Service Center, 25 Howard Street, Petaluma, CA 94952 (Information and Referral)

Newspaper: Press Democrat, 550 Redwood Drive, Rohnert Park, CA 94928; *Argus-Courier,* 830 Petaluma Boulevard North, Petaluma, CA 94953

Airport: Bus and limousine services are offered to San Francisco and Oakland airports.

Bus/Train: Golden Gate Transit buses run frequently to San Francisco, making the trip in about an hour and forty minutes. Petaluma Transit provides excellent local service, weekdays and Saturdays. Both offer 50 percent discounts to seniors. There is no train service here.

Internet: http://www.petaluma.org

Petaluma Weather

	JAN.	APR.	JUL.	OCT.	RAIN	SNOW
		In degrees Fahrenheit				
DAILY HIGHS	56	68	83	76	25"	—
DAILY LOWS	37	43	52	47		

Benicia

Although it is within commuting distance of San Francisco, Benicia (population 28,000), which is located on the Carquinez Strait at the southern end of Solano County, has far too distinguished a history and too distinctive an atmosphere to be taken for just another bedroom suburb. The city was incorporated in 1847 and named after the wife of General Mariano Guadaloupe Vallejo, one of its founders and Spain's last commandante general in California. For thirteen brief months in the 1850s, Benicia served as California's state capital, and the ornate state capitol building is still a major tourist attraction. The chamber of commerce lists thirty-nine other points of interest, all dating back to the last half of the nineteenth century and somehow giving Benicia its unique feeling of belonging to a bygone era. There is much more to the city than antique charm, however, and it richly deserves its reputation as one of the Bay Area's most comfortable places to live.

Benicia has long been known as an art colony, attracting world-renowned painters, sculptors, and workers in glass. Their studios are often open to the public and attract visitors from all over. The work of Benicia artists is also shown in restaurants, the library, and various retail establishments, and an Art in Public Places program displays pieces by some of the most famous.

Benicia is just 35 miles from San Francisco, making the non-rush-hour drive less than forty-five minutes. A half-hour bus ride takes you to a station on the BART system, which will get you to the City in an additional forty minutes.

Recreation and Culture

Because Benicia is a waterfront town, boating and fishing are high on the list of recreational activities. A public launch in the Benicia marina gives easy access to the Carquinez Strait, the Delta (a magical world of land and water at the confluence of the Sacramento and San Joachin Rivers), and the wide range of Bay Area waterways. Walkers and bicyclists enjoy Benicia's great water views on the city waterfront pathway system, which connects more than a dozen of the city's thirty parks and rest areas. A public swimming center boasts an Olympic pool for laps and racing and a standard pool for recreation.

There are facilities for tennis and other participatory sports. There are four golf courses in nearby Vallejo, with weekday greens fees ranging from $7.00 to $50.00. The Parks and Community Services Department sponsors an active senior program that includes exercise classes, crafts, and trips and tours.

A gallery and open houses in painters' and sculptors' studios, together with public access to the three outstanding famous glass-blowing studios, provide ways to share in the community's artistic riches. The Benicia Old Town Theater Group offers performances of plays and musicals; the Benicia Ballet Theater presents the *Nutcracker* each December; and Capital Candlelight Concerts sponsors a series of excellent chamber music concerts.

Solano Community College in nearby Suisun offers courses in everything from art history to arc welding.

Real Estate

Despite its high quality of life, Benicia remains a relatively affordable community by Bay Area standards. Especially good buys are Victorian-style homes within walking distance of the historic downtown area and newer homes on the surrounding hillsides. Two-bedroom, one-bath homes range in price from $150,000 to $175,000; three-bedroom, two-bath homes from $180,000 to $250,000. Four-bedroom homes are $250,000 and up. Condos are available from $50,000 for a one-bedroom unit and from $90,000 for a four-bedroom unit.

Rentals of two-bedroom apartments range from $640 to $775. Benicia has three mobile home parks.

Medical Care

Benicia's routine health-care needs are met by a large number of individual physicians and medical group centers. The nearest major hospital is in Vallejo, about 7 miles away.

When Grandkids Visit

Marine World Africa in nearby Vallejo offers everything from a shark experience (which involves walking through a transparent underwater tunnel with the finny predators swimming all around you) to gentle encounters with jewel-like birds from all over the world. Chances are you'll enjoy it as much as the kids. For information: (707) 643–ORCA.

Addresses and Connections

Chamber of Commerce: 601 First Street, Benicia, CA 94510

Senior Services: Benicia Senior Center, 1205 East Second Street, Benicia, CA 94510

Newspaper: Benicia Herald, 820 First Street, Benicia, CA 94510

Airport: Both San Francisco and Oakland's airports are within an hour's drive, and public transit will connect you with either.

Bus/Train: The area is served by both community and countywide bus systems.

Internet: http://www.ci.benicia.ca.us

Brentwood

Brentwood, located in eastern Contra Costa County 54 miles and ninety-five minutes (by car) from San Francisco, is by any definition on the outer limits of the Bay Area. But when the planned extension of the Bay Area Rapid Transit system is complete, travel time will probably be halved. This farming community (population 14,000), on the brink of becoming a commuting town, is still one of the places in the Bay Area where the old agricultural small-town lifestyle of California's central valley is preserved. Local government would like to keep it that way while encouraging development. That is a tall order, but for now, this town is well worth considering.

Brentwood is bounded on one side by the towering Mount Diablo and on the other by the waterways of the Delta.

A harvest-time flyer lists thirty-six farms, orchards, and ranches where you can buy (and sometimes pick) almonds, apples, apricots, asparagus, and so on through the alphabet. Twenty-three sites are listed for peaches alone. No wonder Brentwood's slogan is "In the Heart of Plenty."

Recreation and Culture

Because Brentwood is adjacent to the Delta, water sports loom large in its recreational offerings. But hiking, bicycling, golf, and tennis are also convenient, as are the offerings of the East Bay Regional Park District. They have activities that range from birdwalks to llama trips. An annual Cornfest offers food, music, and family fun.

For more serious cultural activities the resources of San Francisco, Oakland, Berkeley, and all the other Bay Area towns are within an easy drive. In short, Brentwood is a place to live but not to find cultural activities right down the block.

Real Estate

Housing in Brentwood is still inexpensive by Bay Area standards, but with the approach of rapid transit to the City, upscale homes in gated communities are bringing $300,000 and more (not bad for land that went for 3 cents an acre back in 1837).

Most homes in this rural farming community are located in subdivisions ten to twenty years old. Older three-bedroom, two-bath homes are available from $120,000 to $165,000. Newer ones are available from $180,000.

Medical Care

Delta Memorial Hospital and Kaiser Permanente Medical Center in Antioch (6 miles away) provide twenty-four-hour emergency medical services to Brentwood residents. In addition, a variety of health-care professionals are located in the community.

When Grandkids Visit

Your grandchildren, particularly if they are city kids, will probably be delighted to accompany you to one of the numerous farms in the area that feature pick-it-yourself harvesting of fruit or berries. Perhaps it will help teach them that work can be fun; especially if they know that grandma (or grandpa) is going to bake their pickings into a pie that they can enjoy that same evening.

Addresses and Connections

Chamber of Commerce: 240 Oak Street, Brentwood CA 94513–1337

Senior Services: Delta Community Services, 730 Third Street, Brentwood, CA 94513

Newspaper: Contra Costa Newspapers, 2640 Shadelands Drive,

Walnut Creek, CA 94598; *Clayton Pioneer*, 739 First Street, Brentwood, CA 94513–1324; *Brentwood News*, 654 Third Street, Brentwood, CA 94513–1357

Airport: Stockton Metro Airport, Metro Oakland International Airport, San Jose International Airport, and Sacramento Metropolitan Airport are within driving times of less than an hour.

Bus/Train: Tri Delta Transit furnishes bus transportation for Dimes-a-Ride (twenty cents) throughout the community. Express buses connect Brentwood with BART.

Internet: http://www.yahoo.com/Regional/U_S_States/California/Cities/Brentwood_Contra_Costa_County

Brentwood Weather

	JAN.	APR.	JUL.	OCT.	RAIN	SNOW
		In degrees Fahrenheit				
DAILY HIGHS	54	73	93	78	16"	—
DAILY LOWS	37	46	58	49		

San Mateo

The mission established in San Francisco in 1776 had a wide area to control. The land to the south was flat, great for grazing. To manage cattle and sheep, an outpost was set up part way down the peninsula, along the bay's shore. In 1783, with the help of the local Native Americans, San Mateo (Saint Matthew) was founded.

Today San Mateo is a city of 90,000 that sits at a crossroads connecting San Francisco to San Jose, and the East Bay to the coast at Half Moon Bay in the west. The city is also in the Silicon Valley, making it a part of the future of the world.

Yet, for all that, San Mateo maintains the feel of a much smaller city, with at least twenty-five parks and playgrounds within its boundaries. Many streets are tree-lined and there is a good mix of housing, from condos and town houses to single-family homes to the old large downtown houses. San Mateo is hemmed in by other cities north and south; to its east is the bay, and to the west are the open spaces of the San Francisco Peninsula Watershed and the state fish and game refuge.

San Mateo's climate is mild. Average temperatures in the rainy winters and spring run from the low forties to the mid-sixties; in dry summer and fall months, average temperatures are from the mid-fifties to mid-seventies. An average of 19 inches of rain falls upon San Mateans each year.

Recreation and Culture

San Mateo's commitment to its residents' comforts can be measured by the more than twenty-five parks and playgrounds scattered throughout the city.

Beresford Park has tennis courts, garden plots, and a community recreation center, as well as other amenities. Central Park in downtown has a Japanese tea garden designed by an architect of the Imperial Palace.

A municipal golf course is a popular site. There are private courses in the surrounding cities and in the Crystal Springs area of the watershed. Arnold Palmer designed the links at Half Moon Bay.

State and county parks are plentiful in and around San Mateo—from the San Francisco Bay side into the Santa Cruz Mountains and down to the Pacific coast. Ano Neuvo State Reserve, on the Pacific Ocean, is the place to see elephant seals, who come ashore from December to March. At other times of year, try Sweeney Ridge, a federally protected, open space for hiking near Pacifica. Skyline Ridge, a state park that was formerly the Skyline Ranch, features hiking and equestrian trails over former pastures and ridge tops and around reservoirs. Pescadero Creek Park, a county park, has an important spawning stream for steelhead trout, campsites reached by hiking only, and horseback and hiking trails. Or perhaps you'd like the rough terrain of San Bruno Mountain, where a climb to the top gives great views of San Francisco and the bay.

The county's Coyote Point and Recreation Area, on the bay, offers water sports, a marina, playgrounds, and picnicking. A state-of-the-art wildlife center and environmental museum are major attractions there, too. Fishing is good at the San Mateo Fishing Pier. Two parks have swimming facilities.

One of the important sites in San Mateo is the Bay Meadows Race Course, where thoroughbreds and quarterhorses race. A major highlight of the racing season is the running of the El Camino Real Derby, where future Triple Crown competitors are previewed.

The College of Notre Dame and the College of San Mateo are the local centers for higher learning. At the CSM, the San Mateo County Historical

Museum has special exhibits explaining the history of the area. Nearby Palo Alto is the home of Stanford University. To the north is San Francisco State University; across the bridge is the campus of California State University, Hayward; and in San Jose you'll find San Jose State University.

The Peninsula Light Opera presents Broadway musicals at the San Mateo Performing Arts Center (SAMPAC). The Peninsula Symphony also holds concerts here. Look for the works of other local groups at SAMPAC, such as the Peninsula Ballet Theater, the Masterworks Chorale, and the Tri-City Concert Association. There is also a speakers series.

The county has a number of attractions to visit. Pigeon Point Lighthouse in Pescadero, one of the tallest lighthouses on the West Coast, has tours every Sunday. The headquarters of Sunset Magazine and Books is at Sunset Gardens in Menlo Park. Sunset, known for its gardening advice, offers tours to the public.

To the south are a number of museums of interest. The Stanford University Art Gallery in Palo Alto includes a Rodin sculpture garden. Through an association with the Whitney Museum of American Art in New York City, the San Jose Museum of Art presents exhibits from the Whitney exclusively for the West Coast.

Of course, the San Francisco Bay Area is known for its art museums: the de Young Memorial Museum in Golden Gate Park, the San Francisco Museum of Modern Art just south of Mission Street near the downtown business district, and the California Palace of the Legion of Honor overlooking the Presidio (see San Francisco).

Real Estate

The average value of a house in San Mateo is $349,778, with a median value at $390,000. The average condominium price is $195,000. More than half the renter-occupied units are priced between $600 and $1,000 a month, and another 20 percent are more than $1,000.

Medical Care

The peninsula area has access to some of the finest medical care in the world. In San Mateo, the Mills–Peninsula Health Center is the local outpatient and emergency facility. In Burlingame, the Mills–Peninsula Medical Center is the inpatient care center. In Palo Alto, south of San Mateo, is the Stanford Medical Center and the Veterans Affairs hospital. San Francisco and San Jose have several first-class care centers.

With these hospitals come some of the finest physicians in the world. There is also a large alternative medicine community in the area.

When Grandkids Visit

San Mateo is kid-friendly. Most of its parks and playgrounds have special areas for children, as well as picnic spots. More specialized facilities, from ball fields to recreation centers to swimming pools to boating and sailing, are spread around town, easily accessible to most residents.

The grandchildren will also enjoy the Coyote Point Museum and Wildlife Center, which features displays, computers, and experiments. The new wildlife center has birds and many small- to medium-size animals.

In nearby Redwood City, Malibu Castle and Malibu Grand Prix make up an amusement park of a different sort. Miniature golf courses, batting cages, and arcade games delight all ages. In Palo Alto find the Hall of Barbie, an extensive collection of the dolls and accessories from nearly forty years of Barbie history.

Addresses and Connections

Chamber of Commerce: 1021 South El Camino Real, San Mateo, CA 94402

Senior Center: 2645 Alameda de las Pulgas, San Mateo, CA 94402

Newspaper: San Mateo Times, P.O. Box 5400, San Mateo, CA 94402; *San Francisco Chronicle,* 901 Mission Street, San Francisco, CA 94103; *San Francisco Examiner,* 925 Mission Street, San Francisco, CA 94103; *San Jose Mercury,* 750 Ridder Park Drive, San Jose, CA 95190

Airport: San Francisco International Airport is a few minutes north on US 101. San Jose International Airport is twenty minutes away.

Bus/Train: Amtrak stops here; CalTrain, the commuter line from San Jose to San Francisco, has three stops in San Mateo.

Internet: http://sfbay.yahoo.com/Cities/San_Mateo/

San Mateo Weather

	JAN.	APR.	JUL.	OCT.	RAIN	SNOW
		In degrees Fahrenheit				
DAILY HIGHS	58	66	73	73	19"	—
DAILY LOWS	44	45	56	53		

Pacifica

In 1769, a Spanish exploration party heading for Monterey Bay from the south missed its turnoff. Low on food, with many members of his party ill, Captain Gaspar de Portola stopped to rest, find provisions, and determine their location. Realizing that they had overshot their destination, he knew they needed to head south, but he decided to give his people an opportunity to recover. He sent out scouts to explore the area. Climbing up a ridge, Sergeant Jose Francisco Ortega made a startling discovery: "An enormous area of the sea or estuary which shot inland as far as the eye could see." It was the second discovery of the San Francisco Bay, first settled by Native Americans many centuries before. Sergeant Ortega was standing upon a hill now called Sweeney Ridge. The ridge and the land upon which his captain's party rested is today the city of Pacifica, along the coast 12 miles south of San Francisco.

A city of 40,000, mostly young residents (the median age is twenty-eight), Pacifica has a moderate climate: from the mid-forties to the mid-sixties in winter, and in the eighties from spring to fall. Winter storms cause enormous waves at high tide that splash over the rocks onto the streets in the Rockaway Beach area. Streams often threaten to flood some areas because of the storm's runoff from the hills, but such flooding rarely occurs.

Although *Pacifica* is Spanish for *peace*, the Spanish did not name the city. That was done in a contest after the 1957 incorporation of the nine small towns that make up the city. Pacifica's first mayor was a woman, Jean Fassler. In 1993, the citizens elected an all-female council.

Proximity to San Francisco and the Silicon Valley make Pacifica a great place to live. The area retains a natural beauty, marked by forests in the canyons, miles of beaches, and rolling hills. But the charm of the area relies on the vigilance of the city's council and citizens to limit land use and expansion. These limitations, and the cost of maintaining them, are questions in constant debate.

The changeable weather is celebrated at Fog Fest, held in September when the weather is warm and sunny and at its most stable. Fog for the festival comes courtesy of electric fog machines, but the real thing plays an important part in the area's attraction. Fog acts as a coolant on an otherwise warm area, its air-conditioning effect bringing relief for residents and visitors.

Another summer event, this one in July, is the Antique and Collectibles Fair. This Sunday-only street fair brings dozens of vendors and thousands of people looking to buy or sell all sorts of collectible items.

Shopping in Pacifica is limited, but over the hill in South San Francisco and Daly City are major malls with big anchor stores. It takes but a few minutes to reach them.

Recreation and Culture

The number one recreation in Pacifica is admiring the beauty of the city and its environment. Though you might be tempted to just stand and watch the waves, you may find that traveling through the hills and canyons on foot, bicycle, or horseback is too inviting to refuse.

Sweeney Ridge, where Ortega first saw San Francisco Bay, and Milagra Ridge, where cattle grazed for the Mission San Francisco de Assis (and later where bunkers were built and missiles waited to protect our western shores), are part of the Golden Gate National Recreation Area. These federally protected areas are open spaces used for hikes and nature walks.

From Sweeney Ridge the view is astounding. On a clear day, you can see Montara Mountain to the south, San Mateo to the southeast, and the East Bay hills and Mount Diablo to the east and northeast. North views go all the way to Point Reyes, with San Francisco, the Golden Gate Bridge and the Marin headlands in between. To the west is the Pacific and beyond are the Farralon Islands, 25 miles out into the ocean.

Discovery Site, the place where Ortega first saw San Francisco Bay, in the Sweeney Ridge section, has a number of approaches with different degrees of difficulty. There is also an equestrian trail. A walker may be able to see the wildlife here. (By the way, no one knows for certain who Sweeney was.)

San Pedro Creek is one of the active steelhead trout–spawning areas left on the West Coast. This large gray fish with a silver stripe and a white underside digs a hole, where its eggs are laid and fertilized, and then returns to the ocean.

San Pedro Valley County Park is great for biking, walking, and hiking. Various fitness levels are accommodated and the park lends wheelchairs designed for mountainous trails. The park trails connect to the Montara Mountain Trail, which in turn leads to McNee Ranch State Park. The county park allows horses on many trails, but bicyclists are limited to Weiler Ranch Road.

Sharp Park sits just above Pacifica. An eighteen-hole golf course is one of its amenities. The park has an archery range. Municipal Pier is a great place to fish, but any spot along the coast will do for anglers.

Rockaway Beach is good for surfing. Swimming can be done on the miles of beaches, but there is also a municipal pool.

Skyline College sits on the summit of the hill between Pacifica and San Bruno. San Francisco State University is at the entrance to San Francisco on state Route 1. Further north on SR 1 is the University of California at San Francisco, with its world-renowned school of medicine, and past that is the University of San Francisco.

The arts have support here in Pacifica. The Sanchez Art Center has sixteen studios. The thirty resident artists as well as other Bay Area artists exhibit in the center's gallery with monthly shows. This former school auditorium is being converted into a performing arts space. The Pacifica Arts and Heritage Council presents a regular music series there.

The Oddstad Theater at the Oddstad Cultural Center is the home of the Spindrift Players, who have been performing there for more than forty years. The Spindrift School of the Performing Arts offers classes in theater and music. Keyboard Productions is a nonprofit musical theater group that performs original musical productions. It also presents a New Composers' Showcase. Keyboard Productions performs at the Pacifica Community Center.

Real Estate

A two- to three-bedroom house in Pacifica costs between $168,000 and $500,000. House rentals range from $950 to $1,350; apartments rent from $600 to $850.

Medical Care

Although there is no hospital in Pacifica proper, there are excellent services in San Francisco and on the east side of the peninsula (as in Redwood City and San Mateo). Ambulance service is on twenty-four-hour call. A rehabilitation center and a physical therapy center can be found in Pacifica, as can a number of physicians and dentists.

When Grandkids Visit

Hiking, biking, fishing, swimming, and surfing are the big activities for visiting kids. The surrounding area is a wonderland filled with historical sites, beautiful views, and splendid heights. Fish at the pier or swim in the surf, and hike in hills and canyons.

Within twenty minutes of Pacifica south on SR 1 is the city of Half Moon Bay. In winter it's a great place to watch whales, and in October it is the home of the Pumpkin Festival. Farther south is the Ano Neuvo State Reserve, where elephant seals beach and swim.

North will take the kids to San Francisco. Eat in North Beach or Chinatown and take them to the Exploratorium for a day of hands-on projects and displays.

A ferry ride in San Francisco takes you to Alcatraz, the infamous prison of old, while other ferries take you to Larkspur or Sausalito and Alameda or Oakland. Ride BART for the fun of it. Visit the California Academy of the Sciences and the Steinhart Aquarium in Golden Gate Park.

Watch from the hills above South San Francisco as the planes take off from San Francisco International Airport.

Addresses and Connections

Chamber of Commerce: 225 Rockaway Beach, Pacifica, CA 94044

Senior Center: Pacifica Community Center, 540 Crespi Drive, Pacifica, CA 94044

Newspaper: San Francisco Chronicle, 901 Mission Street, San Francisco, CA 94103; *San Francisco Examiner,* 925 Mission Street, San Francisco, CA 94103

Airport: San Francisco International Airport is 7.5 miles away, over the hill near San Bruno.

Bus/Train: No train stops in the city, but access to CalTrain is available on the east side of the peninsula, and Amtrak is available in San Francisco and Oakland.

Internet: http://sfbay.yahoo.com/Cities/Pacifica/

Pacifica Weather

	JAN.	APR.	JUL.	OCT.	RAIN	SNOW
		In degrees Fahrenheit				
DAILY HIGHS	58	60	64	65	36"	—
DAILY LOWS	43	44	51	49		

Half Moon Bay

Hardly a dozen miles from downtown San Francisco, Half Moon Bay (population 9,000) in San Mateo County and its companion villages of Montara, Moss Beach, and El Granada lie between rolling, wooded hills and the dramatic ocean coast. This is a seaside area proud of its history, determined to preserve its beauty, and happy to attract new residents who will appreciate what its chamber of commerce describes as "a balanced lifestyle of rural ambience with all the comforts of the 1990s."

The attractions are many: miles of wide, sandy beaches, crashing surf and quiet lagoons; picturesque villages strung along the shore; a luxuriant redwood forest; colorful flower farms; but most of all, the feeling of tranquillity that comes from being in a place where nature comes first.

Recreation and Culture

A local hotel offers a brochure called *101 Things to Do in and around Half Moon Bay*. They range from deep-sea fishing and watching whales or elephant seals to meeting a local artist at the Coastal Arts League Gallery in one of the town's historic houses. Others (not necessarily listed in the brochure) include golfing, berry picking, bicycling, wine tasting, hiking, and horseback riding.

Music of all descriptions, from classical through jazz, folk, and rock, is performed at several local clubs. More to the point, the multiple cultural attractions of Palo Alto, San Jose, and, of course, San Francisco are only a short drive away.

Real Estate

It is not surprising, given its proximity to San Francisco and its quality of life, that the Half Moon Bay area is not an inexpensive place to live. Yet, in among the $500,000 and $750,000 houses are some condos and smaller homes at less than $250,000. Mobile homes are in the $35,000 to $50,000 range.

Medical Care

Seton Medical Center Coastside in nearby Moss Beach is a 121-bed hospital offering twenty-four-hour emergency care and other services. Mills-Peninsula Hospital in Burlingame is a major facility providing a full range of services. Stanford Coastside Medical Clinic in Moss Beach is a busy family practice.

When Grandkids Visit

There are many hillside spots from which you can watch whales during their migrations up and down the coast. But if your grandkids visit between December and April, treat them (and yourself) to a close-up view from one of the boats that glide right up beside the mammoth creatures. At any time of the year, kids of all ages can enjoy a visit to the Fitzgerald Marine Reserve, where tide pools swarm with smaller denizens of the sea.

Important Addresses and Connections

Chamber of Commerce: 520 Kelly Avenue, Half Moon Bay, CA 94019

Senior Services: TIES (Teamwork Insuring Elder Support), 225 West Thirty-seventh Avenue, San Mateo, CA 94403

Newspaper: Coast Views, 8865 La Honda Road, La Honda, CA 94020; *Half Moon Bay Review,* 714 Main Street, Half Moon Bay, CA 94019

Airport: San Francisco International Airport is about a half hour away.

Bus/Train: San Mateo County Transit District (SamTrans) has buses to San Francisco, the airport, and ommunities throughout the county.

Internet: http://www.halfmoonbaychamber.org
http://sfbay.yahoo.com/Cities/Half_Moon_Bay/Community

Half Moon Bay Weather

	JAN.	APR.	JUL.	OCT.	RAIN	SNOW
		In degrees Fahrenheit				
DAILY HIGHS	58	60	64	65	36"	—
DAILY LOWS	43	44	51	49		

Palo Alto

This upscale community (population 56,000), located about 30 miles south of San Francisco, has two principal distinctions: It is the home of Stanford University, and it is the heart (symbolically, if not geographically) of the area known as Silicon Valley, the world capital of the computer industry. It is included here because it is an outstanding place. Any readers who can afford to live there should be aware of it. For the rest of us, reading about Palo Alto and how the other half lives may make the prospect of winning the lottery a little more exciting.

Palo Alto is significantly warmer than San Francisco in summer and significantly cooler in winter, but it would be hard to describe the climate as anything but mild and pleasant year-round. To the east of Palo Alto is the southwest shore of San Francisco Bay, and to the west are Coast Range mountains (which block out the Pacific storms and give Palo Alto a much lower rainfall total than most Bay Area communities).

Stanford and its associated medical enterprises, Hewlett Packard, and other medical, educational, and computer-related organizations dominate its list of ten largest employers. Palo Alto is not a smokestack town.

The mean household income of $90,000 is expected to cross the $100,000 mark by the turn of the century. Only 4.7 percent of its residents are below the poverty level. What makes Palo Alto so special, however, is not that it is filled with rich people. Some of its neighboring communities (not discussed in this book) have an even higher percentage of wealthy inhabitants. Palo Alto's distinction lies in having what is probably the best-educated population of any city in the world. Fully 65 percent of its adults have college degrees, and 34 percent have advanced degrees. Only 14.5 percent have no college education.

A stroll through its quiet residential streets or a stop in a restaurant, bookstore, movie theater, or even a bank soon convinces the visitor that this is a community apart.

Recreation and Culture

As might be expected, Palo Alto has no shortage of recreational and cultural facilities. There are thirty-four parks, three with swimming pools; forty-five tennis courts; and 30 miles of bike lanes. And yes, golfers, there is a course in Palo Alto (and many more in the vicinity). Although few retirees are likely to make use of it, there is also a skateboard facility in one of the parks. (We hope it serves to keep skateboarders off the sidewalks.)

Palo Alto's six libraries lend more than a million books, videos, CDs, and cassettes each year. This averages to 17.4 per capita.

A couple of community theaters, three museums, numerous concert venues, demonstration and showplace gardens, and tours of everything from old mansions to the NASA Research Center round out the area's attractions.

And all this is in addition to the facilities of Stanford University, which include everything from art galleries to a linear accelerator.

Real Estate

The median value of an owner-occupied home reached $458,000 in 1990. It is certainly substantially higher today. (All Silicon Valley is undergoing a tremendous real estate boom, with prices escalating every month.)

Medical Care

If you have to get sick, Palo Alto is as good a place as any. The Stanford University Medical Center/Hospital consistently ranks high in professional assessments of U.S. hospitals. The Palo Alto Medical Foundation is one of the nation's pioneering and most highly regarded providers of multispecialty medical care.

When Grandkids Visit

If your grandchildren are interested in particle physics, take them on a tour of that world-famous linear accelerator at Stanford. They may even be able to explain it to you. If not, how about the Junior Museum, which has a variety of periodically changing exhibits on subjects ranging from carnivorous plants to paper airplanes.

Addresses and Connections

Chamber of Commerce: 325 Forest Avenue, Palo Alto, CA 94301–2515

Newspaper: Palo Alto Daily News, 329 Alma Street, Palo Alto, CA 94310; *The Mercury News*, 310 University Avenue, Suite 200, Palo Alto, CA 94301

Senior Services: Senior Center of Palo Alto, 450 Bryant Street, Palo Alto, CA 94301

Airport: Both San Jose International and San Francisco International Airports are within a twenty-minute drive.

Bus/Train: The area is served by the SamTrans (San Mateo County) and Santa Clara County Transit systems. A special bus operates between Stanford University and downtown. CalTrain is the rail system that will get you to San Francisco, San Jose, or places in between.

Internet: http://www.service.com/PAW/home.html
http://www.city.palo-alto.ca.us

Palo Alto Weather

	JAN.	APR.	JUL.	OCT.	RAIN	SNOW
		In degrees Fahrenheit				
DAILY HIGHS	57	68	78	73	15"	—
DAILY LOWS	38	45	54	48		

Los Gatos/Saratoga

North from Santa Cruz, State Route 17 rises to 1,800 feet above sea level before plummeting back down to the Santa Clara Valley. Just as the road levels off, between the mountains and the city borders of San Jose, lies the town of Los Gatos.

This wealthy community of 29,000 has an upscale downtown. After a devastating loss in the Loma Prieta earthquake of 1989, the businesses and the town were rebuilt and are again thriving. Visitors come miles to eat, shop, and enjoy the ambience of a coffeehouse.

Protected from the coast by the Santa Cruz Mountains, Los Gatos is at the same time sheltered against the valley climate inland. The climate changes semi-annually. From November to April, rainfall averages 24 inches. But from May to October, there is hardly a drop, and the sun shines almost daily. Temperatures mirror these extremes as well, averaging forty-six degrees in January and seventy-one degrees in July.

The Santa Cruz Mountains were originally home to mountain lions and wildcats, and the land of the area was called Rancho Rinconada de Los Gatos (little corner of the cats). Today the big cats are mostly gone, but the town, now well over a century old, protects the wild with a half-dozen parks of its own. Lexington Reservoir provides San Jose with water, but it also supplies Los Gatos residents with a parklike place for recreation. Neighboring Saratoga adds its own parks, open space, and trees, blending with those of Los Gatos and Monte Sereno, creating a contiguous area of protected natural lands.

Saratoga lies north of Los Gatos on state Route 9, beyond the tiny community of Monte Sereno. One of the wealthiest communities in the United States, Saratoga is just 26 miles east of the Pacific coast, 10 miles southwest of San Jose, and 50 miles south of San Francisco. Saratoga's weather mirrors that of Los Gatos: fifties to nineties from May to

October, and forties to mid-sixties from November to April, with 29 inches of rain on average from late fall to early spring.

Originally called McCarthyville after the man who planned the town, Saratoga changed its name when its mineral springs were likened to those in the spa town of Saratoga Springs, New York. The city runs from the exclusive hills to the more moderate edge of the valley. Within its boundaries are nine city parks. The area also claims six county parks and three state parks, attesting to the residents' desire to preserve the rural beginnings of the mountain and valley. Saratoga's valley floor was an expanse of fruit orchards, but development has paved them over.

Both Los Gatos and Saratoga have downtowns with upscale shopping and some of the finest restaurants in the Bay Area. Wineries in Los Gatos and Saratoga are often open for wine tasting. Saratoga also has a larger shopping area outside of downtown. The town and city areas are within minutes of several major malls in San Jose, Cupertino, and Santa Clara.

Los Gatos and Saratoga partake of the valley's riches. Within a short distance is the revitalized downtown of San Jose, the largest and most populous city in the Bay Area, whose metropolitan area offers a variety of entertainment, educational, and business opportunities.

Recreation and Culture

Although San Jose is the major focus of the Santa Clara Valley, towns and cities like Los Gatos and Saratoga have developed their own local interests. Los Gatos has an art association, a chamber orchestra, two museums, and art galleries. Saratoga has the prestigious Villa Montalvo, where major names in the performing arts can be seen in a pastoral setting next to the mansion. In addition, Saratoga has art galleries, a museum, the West Valley Light Opera, the Saratoga Drama Group, and the West Valley Masterworks Chorale.

Los Gatos holds its famous Strawberry Festival in June; Saratoga holds Celebrate Saratoga! in September. The Saratoga Rotary Art Show, held in May, is the largest one-day art show in the United States.

Horseback riding can be found, as can swimming pools, golf courses, and tennis courts. Bicycle riding is popular, with most of the parks in Los Gatos and Saratoga providing bicycle paths. The parks also offer many activities—from walking and running to, in a few parks, boating, fishing, sailing, windsurfing, and camping.

Of special interest in Saratoga is Hakone Gardens, with more than fifteen acres designed in the Japanese manner. Bamboo gardens and ponds create a calm environment for the enjoyment of the park. Weddings and some special events are held here.

Los Gatos has Billy Jones Wildcat Railroad and Carousel in Oak Meadow Park with a scenic mile-long ride on a turn-of-the-century steam locomotive. Travel over a wooden trestle and bridge connecting Oak Meadow Park to Vasona Lake Park. Near the railroad is the Bill Mason Carousel. Vasona Lake Park has many lake-based activities, and it houses the Los Gatos Youth Science Institute.

Healthy living includes exercise. In addition to the parks listed, Los Gatos Creek Trails are great for running and biking. Try the Los Gatos Creek Trail South or North, Jones Road Trail, and Sierra Azul Mid-Peninsula Open Space. Saratoga has a number of biking trails, but a popular route follows Highway 9 in the foothills. Both towns have health and fitness clubs, and Saratoga has mineral springs.

Within the Santa Clara Valley, the arts are well appreciated. The Sandose Museum of Art, which presents exhibits from the Whitney Museum of Art in New York City, plans to develop its own collection. The Stanford University Art Gallery in Palo Alto is an international treasure, and the de Saisset Museum in Santa Clara has exhibits from its permanent collection and traveling shows.

The Ira F. Brilliant Beethoven Center at San Jose State University has first editions of a number of the composer's works, plus letters and other memorabilia. San Jose also has the Tech Museum of Innovation, the San Jose Historical Museum, and Egyptian Museum and Planetarium.

San Jose Repertory is in its own theater, and there are the San Jose–Cleveland Ballet and the San Jose Opera. The San Jose Sharks hockey team plays in the San Jose Arena. Major festivals are held in downtown Guadalupe Park and at the Santa Clara County Fairgrounds.

Real Estate

The average cost of a home in Saratoga is a whopping $646,000. There are very few rental units in the city. Las Gatos is a bit more reasonable, but not much. A home costs on average $533,125. Average rent is $1,000.

Medical Care

Los Gatos has one hospital within its boundaries, Community Hospital of Los Gatos. The Santa Clara Valley offers an assortment of services at Columbia Good Samaritan and the Santa Clara County Medical Center. Kaiser offers hospital care at Santa Clara and Santa Theresa. Stanford University Medical Center is in Palo Alto, as is the Veterans Affairs' Palo Alto Health Care System, an extensive complex of programs and facilities. Alternative medicines and therapies are available throughout the valley.

When Grandkids Visit

With all the parks in the Los Gatos–Saratoga area, children can have great outdoors fun (see Recreation and Culture, above). Both communities also offer Youth Science Institutes to give children hands-on experience with nature and other areas of science. But the Santa Clara Valley offers so many special adventures for children that finding something special to do is easy.

Going south to Santa Cruz brings the kids to Santa Cruz Beach and Boardwalk on the Monterey Bay and Pacific Ocean. The famed wooden roller coaster is surrounded by other rides and attractions. Beaches stretch south through Capitola to Aptos and Rio Del Mar.

Addresses and Connections

Chamber of Commerce: P.O. Box 1355, Los Gatos, CA 95031–1355

Senior Center: 19655 Allendale Avenue, Saratoga, CA 95070; there is no senior center in Los Gatos.

Newspaper: San Jose Mercury, 1875 South Bascom, Campbell, CA 95008; *San Jose Metro* (weekly), 550 South First Street, San Jose, CA 95113–2806; *Los Gatos Weekly Times,* 245 Almedra Avenue, Los Gatos, CA 95031

Airport: San Jose International is less than 10 miles away, while San Francisco International is about 40 miles north.

Bus/Train: Amtrak stops in San Jose, and the CalTrain commuter line from San Jose to San Francisco stops at San Jose's Cahill Station. Construction plans are well under way for a light-rail service from Los Gatos to San Jose, joining a north-south route already in service. Greyhound has service from Los Gatos as well as from downtown San

Jose. Santa Clara Transit runs buses from and to Los Gatos and Saratoga from other areas of the county.

Internet: (Los Gatos) http://sfbay.yahoo.com/Cities/Los_Gatos/ (Saratoga) http://sfbay.yahoo.com/Cities/Saratoga/

Los Gatos/Saratoga Weather

	JAN.	APR.	JUL.	OCT.	RAIN	SNOW
		In degrees Fahrenheit				
DAILY HIGHS	59	71	86	76	24"	—
DAILY LOWS	37	43	54	48		

THE WINE COUNTRY

Napa and Sonoma (these are also the names of cities) are among the nine Bay Area counties. The communities dealt with in this section, however, are sufficiently far from San Francisco and sufficiently distinct in lifestyle, climate, and surroundings to require separate discussion. In addition, although some of their residents may commute to San Francisco, they are not commuter towns.

The country at the northern end of the Bay Area is famous for its wine grapes. The hillsides are blanketed with vineyards, and dotted among them are countless wineries, ranging from ramshackle old farm buildings to elegant French-style chateaux.

The wine country enjoys a Mediterranean climate. In summer, the days are hot, cooling off overnight as breezes and sometimes fog flow in from the Pacific. Winter days are crisp, but seldom cold enough to pose a danger to the vines. It is a four-season climate in which the arrival of spring is marked with an explosion of wildflowers and fall paints the foliage red, gold, and purple.

Just mention grape growing in California and most people think of the Napa Valley. Perhaps this would still be true if the area hadn't been immortalized in the Frank Loesser musical *The Most Happy Fella*. Napa County is, after all, the leading U.S. producer of grapes and home to the vineyards and wineries that turn out most of the brands that are household names. Some well-known wineries in Napa Valley include Beringer, Franciscan, and Robert Mondavi.

Sonoma is the northernmost Bay Area county and, in particular, is a popular vacation destination for San Francisco residents fleeing the City's fog-bound summers. Low, rolling hills and cloudless skies furnish a backdrop that makes you constantly aware that this is the country. Here you can experience redwood rain forests, sunny, vineyard-filled valleys, and fog-shrouded ocean beaches. With few exceptions, its villages and towns are small enough to recall a more leisurely, friendlier time. Yet this is sophisticated, culture-rich Northern California, and the opportunities and facilities for participation in sports, the arts, and education are extensive. This is prime golf country, with some world-famous courses. Wineries double as art galleries—and as concert venues, too.

THE WINE COUNTRY

Many retirees have settled in towns throughout this area and both commercial developers and local governments are eager to meet their needs and encourage others to join them. This is reflected in the multitude of programs and services noted in this section.

Napa

The city of Napa contains 72,000 of the Valley's 116,000 inhabitants. Wineries are its principal employers, and the town relates strongly to the surrounding countryside where the grapes are grown.

But man does not live by wine alone, and even in Napa people chase little white balls through green meadows, paint pictures, volunteer to help their neighbors, and do all those other things that make for happy and productive retirement living.

Recreation and Culture

Within Napa County there are two thirty-six-hole golf courses, two eighteen-hole courses, and four nine-hole courses, most of them in or adjacent to the city of Napa.

There are numerous public and private tennis complexes in the Napa area, all with excellent facilities. Lighted courts open to the public are available at the local high schools and community college.

The Napa Valley Symphony, with a tradition of fine performances for more than six decades, is one of the area's top orchestras. Several wineries in Napa and vicinity play host to visiting musical groups.

Real Estate

Napa is a community of varied real estate from condos to vineyards. There is a larger supply of affordable single-family homes than in other Napa Valley towns. Prices range from $150,000 for smaller homes to $335,000 for three bedrooms, two baths. There are fewer condos. They range in price from $150,000 to $250,000.

Medical Care

Queen of the Valley Hospital in Napa is a 159-bed full-service hospital with a medical staff of more than 150 physicians.

Nearby St. Helena Hospital has 199 beds and is a major heart center for Northern California. The Kaiser Permanente health care system maintains a twenty-eight-physician office in Napa.

When Grandkids Visit

The Napa Firefighters Museum is a delight for both young and old. Ancient engines, ladders, tools, and clothing, together with other non-fire-related items from the community's past, are exhibited, along with a collection of photographs of fire departments from around the world. Admission is free.

Addresses and Connections

Chamber of Commerce: 1556 First Street, Napa, CA 94559

Newspaper: Napa Valley Register, 1615 Second Street, Napa, CA 94559

Senior Services: Napa Senior Center, 1500 Jefferson Street, Napa, CA 94559

Airport: Both San Francisco and Oakland Airports are within a hour drive and can be reached by public transportation.

Bus/Train: Napa Valley Transit provides bus transportation to neighboring communities and to the Bay Area Rapid Transit system (BART), which serves Oakland and San Francisco.

Internet: http://www.ci.napa.ca.us

http://www.napachamber.org

Napa Weather

	JAN.	APR.	JUL.	OCT.	RAIN	SNOW
		In degrees Fahrenheit				
DAILY HIGHS	57	69	82	77	25"	—
DAILY LOWS	37	43	54	48		

Calistoga

Lying between the foothills of Mount Saint Helena and the higher Mayacamus Mountains (which are visible everywhere you go in this spa town of 4,700), Calistoga is at the northern end of the Napa Valley. Yet it is only 75 miles from San Francisco and thus within a two-hour drive of all the City's attractions.

Its name is said to derive from the founders' desire to portray it as the Saratoga Springs of California. Certainly its dozen or more spa resorts continue to make active use of its greatest natural resource: hot mineral water. The full routine consists of a mud bath followed by a mineral bath, a steam bath, a towel wrap, and a massage. It is entirely possible, however, to enjoy Calistoga without ever getting muddy or wet. Its numerous gourmet restaurants, sports facilities, and manifold shops (and, of course, wineries) make it a choice place to visit or live in.

Recreation and Culture

Golf, horseback riding, hiking, and swimming are the prime recreational activities for which retirees choose Calistoga. The weekday greens fee for eighteen holes at the Mount St. Helena Golf Course is $10.

Art in the Southwest is an annual exhibition featuring Western artists. Several galleries display the work of local artists. For theater and music, residents travel to nearby communities (see other listings in this section) or to the San Francisco Bay Area.

Real Estate

It is not terribly surprising that living in this high-style location is not inexpensive. In the Calistoga–St. Helena area, almost all residences are single-family homes. Prices in St. Helena and Calistoga range from $159,000 to $300,000 for two- to three-bedroom homes. Larger estate properties outside the cities run more than $500,000. The inventory of homes in these towns is limited.

Medical Care

Whether or not their health benefits are verifiable, the mineral springs offer comfort to the healthy and the ill alike. For more conventional medical care, Calistoga is home to several medical groups, clinics, and a women's center. First-rate hospitals are twenty to thirty minutes away.

When Grandkids Visit

Other Napa Valley communities have their hot-air balloons, but only Calistoga has gliders. There is something special about riding the thermals like a hawk as you slowly and silently descend from a high altitude, to which a small plane has towed you, to the valley floor. Your grandchildren will never forget it (and you won't, either).

Addresses and Connections

Chamber of Commerce: 1458 Lincoln Avenue, Calistoga, CA 94515
Senior Services: See Napa.

Newspaper: *Weekly Calistogan,* 1360 Lincoln Avenue, Calistoga, CA 94515

Airport: Both San Francisco and Oakland International Airports are within a hour-and-a-half drive and can be reached by public transportation.

Bus/Train: There is Greyhound service to Calistoga, and Napa Valley Transit connects the town with neighboring communities and with the Bay Area.

Internet: http://www.napavalley.com/calistoga
http://www.sonic.net/~johnfr/Calistoga

Napa County Weather

	JAN.	APR.	JUL.	OCT.	RAIN	SNOW
		In degrees Fahrenheit				
DAILY HIGHS	57	69	82	77	25"	—
DAILY LOWS	37	43	54	48		

Santa Rosa

Located 52 miles north of San Francisco, this fair-size city (population 126,000) in Sonoma County is pretty much out of the larger metropolitan orbit. That is, it does not feel like a suburb. Only a very small percentage of the workforce commutes to San Francisco. "We're part of the Bay Area almost in name only," says the president of the chamber of commerce. It appears the city is not eager to attract new residents for whom its appeal is proximity to San Francisco.

Santa Rosa is proud of its classic turn-of-the-century downtown, of its independence from San Francisco, and even of its "provincialism." Indeed, all the elements of an extraordinarily high quality of life are present in the city and the surrounding countryside.

Recreation and Culture

The weather, the diverse terrain, and the adventurous spirit of the residents all combine to provide Sonoma County with outstanding recreational options. Hiking, bicycling, camping, and just plain communing with nature are popular in the numerous state and regional parks. Swimming, fishing, boating, canoeing, and kayaking are enjoyed in coastal waters, the Russian River, and Lake Sonoma. Golfers should enjoy Santa Rosa. There are four golf courses in the city alone, with many more in surrounding communities. Weekday greens fees begin at $9.00. Tennis courts also abound.

Music lovers of all tastes, from country to classics, will find concerts aplenty. The Luther Burbank Center for the arts offers more than a hundred performances each year, many of them by name stars. There is an active theater season, and museums and art galleries abound.

Finally, for the full range of choices that only a great metropolis can supply, San Francisco is only about an hour away.

Real Estate

Within Sonoma County there is an unusually wide variation of home prices depending upon the area and the type of home, but prices are significantly lower than in other parts of the Bay Area. A smaller, older home in an established Santa Rosa neighborhood can sell for as little as $140,000. A new three-bedroom, two-bath home was advertised in mid-1997 at $135,000. Similar homes in other parts of the county sold for as much as $190,000.

Condominium prices in Santa Rosa begin at $85,000. Mobile homes situated in a park can cost as little as $10,000 or as much as $30,000.

Rentals are also well below Bay Area averages. A two-bedroom apartment in Santa Rosa goes for $600 to $800 a month, and a two- or three-bedroom house for $800 to $1,000. Because Santa Rosa is a city (rather than a small town like most of its neighbors), there is a flourishing rental market offering many choices.

Medical Care

Santa Rosa Memorial Hospital is a full-service, not-for-profit, acute inpatient and ambulatory-care hospital for the north coastal region of California. Its 225 beds include intensive and coronary care, family-centered maternity care, pediatrics, newborn intensive care, cardiology, oncology, gastroenterology, endocrinology, neurology, orthopedics, and other medical and surgical services. Its medical staff of more than 400 physicians represents every major specialty.

When Grandkids Visit

Take your grandchildren to the Snoopy Gallery and Gift Shop, which has the world's largest collection of Peanuts memorabilia—not surprising, since Charles Schulz, the comic strip's creator, is a Santa Rosa resident.

Addresses and Connections

Chamber of Commerce: 637 First Street, Santa Rosa, CA 95404

Senior Center: Santa Rosa Senior Center, 704 Bennett Valley Road, Santa Rosa CA 95402

Newspaper: Press Democrat, 427 Mendocino Avenue, Santa Rosa, CA, 95401–6385

Airport: San Francisco International Airport can easily be reached by the Santa Rosa Airporter and by Airport Express.

Bus/Train: Service within the city is provided by Santa Rosa Municipal Transit; service to nearby communities is provided by Sonoma County Transit and Mendocino Transit. There is also Greyhound service from this location.

Internet: http://www.santarosachamber.com
http://www.pressdemo.com

Santa Rosa Weather

	JAN.	APR.	JUL.	OCT.	RAIN	SNOW
		In degrees Fahrenheit				
DAILY HIGHS	58	70	84	77	30"	—
DAILY LOWS	37	43	51	47		

Sonoma

The town of Sonoma (population 9,000) is the site of the northern-most of the missions established by Padre Junipero Sera. The eight-acre plaza laid out by General Mariano Guadalupe Vallejo as its center continues to give Sonoma the look of a handsome colonial Mexican town. It is over this plaza that the Bear Flag of California independence was first raised, and a feeling of a world somehow separate from the rest of modern America still hovers about the place.

The inviting restaurants and diverse shops around the plaza are certainly major elements in the town's attractiveness, but a few blocks' walk in any direction is required to understand why Sonoma has so long been a favorite of retirees. Here is the kind of quiet, convenient, dignified living that so many of us hope for when our working days are finished.

Recreation and Culture

The town of Sonoma is in the heart of some of the world's finest grape-growing country. Its best wines compete on an equal footing with France's finest. Touring the innumerable wineries in the immediate vicinity is a favorite occupation of tourists, although its charms might begin to fade after a while. Not to worry! There is enough golf, tennis, swimming, and tennis year-round to keep even the most energetic busy and happy. Greens fees at the golf courses in the town range from $12 to $40. Public tennis courts abound. The nearby Lake Sonoma is a great spot for swimming, fishing, and boating.

Although the town itself has few concert venues, they abound in the county, as do art galleries and museums. The many attractions of San Francisco and the Bay Area are less than an hour away.

Real Estate

There is a surprising variety of affordable homes in Sonoma. As in many of the California towns, the most affordable homes are older and an easy walk to shopping and parks. There are small homes and condos available from $110,000 for two bedrooms. Three-bedroom homes start from $175,000. Larger homes with five acres or more start at $850,000.

Medical Care

Sonoma Valley Hospital is nearby. There are also two large medical centers, as well as numerous medical practitioners.

When Grandkids Visit

The Mission, General Vallejo's home and servant quarters, and the barracks of the general's troops are all open for inspection, presenting a fascinating picture of life in old (early nineteenth century) California.

Addresses and Connections

Chamber of Commerce: 651A Broadway, Sonoma, CA 95476

Senior Services: Sonoma County Council on Aging, 264 East Street, Sonoma, CA 95476

Newspaper: Press Democrat, 427 Mendocino Avenue, Santa Rosa, CA, 95401–6385

Airport: Both the San Francisco and Oakland Airports are within a hour drive and can be reached by public transportation.

Bus/Train: Service to nearby communities is provided by Sonoma

County Transit. The Sonoma Airporter goes to San Francisco International Airport.

Internet: http://www.vom.com/chamber

Sonoma Weather

	JAN.	APR.	JUL.	OCT.	RAIN	SNOW
		In degrees Fahrenheit				
DAILY HIGHS	58	72	90	80	29"	—
DAILY LOWS	36	41	50	45		

Healdsburg/Cloverdale

Although it is only 75 miles north of San Francisco, Healdsburg (population 10,000) in Sonoma County feels as if it were a thousand miles and at least a century removed. Taking its flavor from the traditional Spanish-style plaza, it is still a small town in the early California mold. *Newsweek* said it well: "Easy vibes, rolling vistas . . . The sunlit fantasy of California is as distinctive as the scenery. Though just a memory in places like Los Angeles and San Francisco, the dream thrives in Healdsburg."

One of Healdsburg's assets is its setting: at the confluence of three valleys and surrounded by low mountains and hills. The vineyards around Healdsburg produce some of the best wine grapes in California—some would say in the world. The Russian River winds through and around the town on its way to the Pacific. The river, in addition to its contribution to the scenic beauty, is an important recreational resource, offering swimming at numerous public and private beaches, as well as canoeing.

The moderate climate features warm summer days with cool evenings, and mild winters with occasional frost but no snow. Grapes love it, and so do most people.

Lying about 11 miles north of Healdsburg, Cloverdale (population 5,600) has as its motto, "Where the Vineyards meet the Redwoods." It is, indeed, at the top of the Alexander Valley, where the rolling hills begin to give way to higher mountains. Without many major recreational or cultural attractions of its own, what it offers is easy access to all the resources of northern Sonoma County—fishing, boating, camping, hiking, concerts in the vineyards—and, of course, those of its neighbor, Healdsburg. Since San Francisco is only an hour and a half away, day trips to enjoy its cultural riches are possible, and weekend visits even easier.

Until a few years ago, U.S. Highway 101 ran through the center of the town. When a bypass was completed, Cloverdale became a much quieter place. Among the steps the community took to replace the resulting loss of revenues was the construction of a handsome downtown plaza. There were also concerted efforts to attract new enterprises. One result is that a Del Webb planned adult community has recently been built there. (Del Webb is the oldest and largest developer of planned adult communities.) In addition to providing another housing option, this major development is likely, over time, to enhance the area's attractiveness to retirees by increasing the availability of senior services.

Recreation and Culture

There are more than fifteen public and semiprivate golf courses in the area, with weekday greens fees ranging from $10 to $45. Canoeing is popular, and there are ample public facilities for tennis and swimming—both river and pool. Boating and fishing are available on nearby Lake Sonoma, and fishermen can also be found along the banks of the Russian River. The scenic back roads around Healdsburg are a cyclist's dream, and hiking trails abound in nearby state and county parks.

Cultural attractions available to Healdsburg residents fall into three categories: those for which one must travel to San Francisco; those within the region—particularly in Santa Rosa (15 miles away); and those that are part of the town's own rich cultural life. Attractions in the first two categories are described elsewhere in this book. Right in Healdsburg there are numerous art galleries and showings in wine-tasting rooms. The Healdsburg Cultural Arts Council promotes many visual and performing events. The Raven Theater and Film Center has a community performing arts room. The Healdsburg Museum is a repository of the history of the town and surrounding area. A community chorus and community band are among the groups that can be heard at the outdoor Sunday concerts, held summers in the town plaza.

With more than sixty wineries and tasting rooms within a few minutes' drive, you could spend many happy afternoons comparing cabernets and chardonnays. But three wine tastings is usually enough for one day, and, with more than two outings a week, that activity would probably lose some of its savor. So that should take care of one summer's schedule. The next year you might start over again with sauvignon blancs and zinfandels.

Real Estate

In this popular area homes range from $125,000 to $1.5 million. There are a handful of two-bedroom homes in the lower range. Most available homes have three bedrooms and range in price from $170,000 to $365,000. Many homes priced over $275,000 have views of the hills or valleys. Four-bedroom homes start at $350,000.

Condos begin at $110,000. Two-bedroom apartments can be rented for $600. There are two mobile home parks. Healdsburg has three planned adult communities and a forty-unit apartment complex with assisted living.

Real estate prices are significantly lower in Cloverdale than in Healdsburg, with the median price of homes at $178,000. Rentals of apartments begin at $375, and houses at $700.

Medical Care

Healdsburg General Hospital is a full-service, forty-nine-bed, acute-care facility providing twenty-four-hour emergency care.

When Grandkids Visit

To keep your grandkids entertained and get in some exercise at the same time, rent a canoe from Trowbridge Canoe Trips (800–640–1386) and paddle down the Russian River. No white water, but great scenery—maybe you can persuade the grandkids to paddle while you lean back and take it in.

Addresses and Connections

Chamber of Commerce: 217 Healdsburg Avenue, Healdsburg, CA 95548

Senior Services: Senior Center, 133 Matheson Street, Healdsburg, CA 95448

Newspapers: Healdsburg Tribune, 5 Mitchell Lane, Healdsburg, CA 95448;(Santa Rosa) *Press Democrat,* 427 Mendocino Avenue, Santa Rosa, CA 95401–6385

Airport: There is public transportation to the San Francisco International Airport by the Santa Rosa Airporter.

Bus/Train: Services are provided by Healdsburg In-City Transit, Sonoma County Transit, Golden Gate Transit, and Greyhound Bus Lines. There is no train service here.

Internet: http://www.hbg.sonoma.net/hburg_body_list12.html

Healdsburg/Cloverdale Weather

	JAN.	APR.	JUL.	OCT.	RAIN	SNOW
		In degrees Fahrenheit				
DAILY HIGHS	58	72	90	72	42"	—
DAILY LOWS	38	45	53	49		

Western Sonoma: Sebastopol/Bodega Bay

Sebastopol (population 7,750) is definitely a wine-country town, set in prime vineyard territory just 50 miles from San Francisco and 8 miles from the Pacific shore. The fruit most Californians associate with this town, however, is not the grape, but the apple. The huge orchards surrounding Sebastopol are not only the foundation of the area's economy but the dominant theme in its civic life. The annual Apple Blossom Parade in April and the Gravenstein Apple Fair in August celebrate the commodity in the production of which Sebastopol leads the state.

Describing itself as a "quintessential country town," Sebastopol strives to attract light industry and high-tech business such as computer software design. It stresses environmental quality and is proud of its scholars, musicians, and artists, as well as of its engineers and entrepreneurs.

Sebastopol's location, equidistant from Sonoma County's urbanized Highway 101 corridor and its wild, dramatic ocean coast, allows it to enjoy the best of two contrasting worlds. Its temperate but definitely four-season climate is ideal for those who are bored by year-round uniformity but who can do very nicely without snow.

The coastal village of Bodega Bay (population 1,000) finds itself in the wine-country section because of where it is rather than what it is. Fishing and dairy farming replace grape growing as the pillars of the economy. Warm winters and cool summers are the climatic attractions. Although the town is on the shore of Bodega Harbor, a mile or two from the ocean, the sound of surf smashing against the rocky hills is never far off. If you have seen Alfred Hitchcock's *The Birds,* you have an idea of what the area looks like (although the site of the film is Bodega, a couple of miles away from the larger community of Bodega Bay).

To stand on Bodega Head while dozens of varieties of sea birds glide by or skitter up and down the beach, or to watch the migrating whales pass close offshore, is to lose all consciousness that a busy city is less than 70 miles to the south.

The Pomo and Coastal Miwok Indians were here first. In 1775, Lieutenant Franciso Bodega y Quadra anchored his ship in the bay, to which he gave his name. In the early part of the nineteenth century, Russians established a colony nearby in Fort Ross and built a port on Bodega Bay to ship produce and supplies to their Alaskan settlements. They left when settlers, alerted to the area's attractions by Bodega, poured in from Mexico.

Recreation and Culture

In and around Sebastopol there are opportunities for hiking, bicycling, golf, tennis, horseback riding, swimming, and boating. The weekday greens fee at the Sebastopol Golf Course is $12.

Nearby theaters and a state-of-the-art multiscreen movie house developed from an old apple brandy distillery are major sources of entertainment. Seasonal events include a rodeo parade and barbecue, Shakespeare in the Park, a Celtic Festival, and, of course, the apple-flavored parade and fair mentioned above.

Real Estate

Real estate prices reflect the attractiveness of Sebastapol to young families and retirees alike. Many of the affordable homes are within walking distance of shops and restaurants. Homes range in price from $125,000 for a small two-bedroom, one-bath home to $1 million for a secluded six-bedroom, six-bath estate. The ample inventory of three-bedroom, two-bath homes ranges in price from $200,000 to $400,000; four-bedroom homes start at $400,000.

In Bodega Bay two-bedroom homes are priced from $158,000 to $198,500. Three-bedroom homes range in price from $198,000 to $400,000. There are no condos in either Bodega Bay or Sebastapol.

Medical Care

Palm Drive Hospital provides twenty-four-hour medical care. A number of alternative health practitioners augment the numerous primary-care and specialist physicians who serve the community.

When Grandkids Visit

You can entertain your grandchildren and, at the same time, teach them the important lesson that fruit and vegetables aren't manufactured in the back of the supermarket. Take them on a farm trails tour and let them join you in picking everything from sweet corn to strawberries (and, of course, apples). Along the way you can visit farms that specialize in such rare items as carnivorous plants, llamas, and peacocks. Exercise restraint, though: Some airlines will not allow you to check full-grown llamas with your baggage, and if you buy one, your grandkids might have to leave their souvenir with you when they fly home.

Addresses and Connections

Chamber of Commerce: Sebastopol Area Chamber of Commerce and Visitors Center, 256 South Main Street, P.O. Box 178, Sebastopol, CA 95473

Senior Services: Sebastopol Senior Center, 167 North High Street, Sebastopol, CA 95473

Newspaper: *Sonoma West Times & News*, P.O. Box 521, Sebastopol, CA 95473

Airport: Sonoma County Airport (thirty minutes), San Francisco International, Oakland International.

Bus/Train: Sonoma County Transit, Golden Gate Transit (to San Francisco); there is no train service available.

Internet: http://www.sebastopol.org\~apples
http://www.seb.org/comm/comm_info.htm

Bodega Bay Weather

	JAN.	APR.	JUL.	OCT.	RAIN	SNOW
		In degrees Fahrenheit				
DAILY HIGHS	54	64	85	73	50"	—
DAILY LOWS	32	37	47	39		

Sebastapol Weather

	JAN.	APR.	JUL.	OCT.	RAIN	SNOW
		In degrees Fahrenheit				
DAILY HIGHS	58	70	84	77	30"	—
DAILY LOWS	37	43	51	47		

SACRAMENTO VALLEY

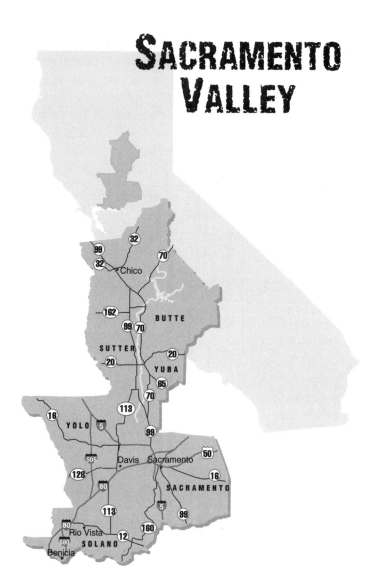

THE SACRAMENTO VALLEY

Imagine a land so flat that if it weren't for friction, a ball rolled from one end to the other more than 100 miles away might never slow down. Imagine a land where the roads can be built in a straight line for miles and miles, asphalt shimmering in the heat, and the eye can gaze without obstruction all the way to the horizon. Then imagine this land filled with peach and apricot orchards, almonds and walnuts, apples and asparagus, grass sod and cotton, and broccoli and tomatoes. Imagine almost two million people residing, working, playing and loving this land. Greetings from Sacramento Valley!

The valley follows the path of the Sacramento River, which starts up north in the mountains south of the California-Oregon border and runs all the way to San Francisco Bay. Warmth, fog, and sun characterize the climate; rain comes during the winter, but the agriculture benefits from the watershed of the Sierra Nevadas to keep crops growing year-round.

The southern valley is the area of the California Delta, represented in this section by Rio Vista. Located to the northeast of San Francisco Bay, the marshland known for its tule grass (and the winter fog of the same name) was drained years ago, and the population has settled in small towns dedicated to the quieter life of the Sacramento River. Boating, fishing, and hunting are the sports of the area; agriculture, natural gas, and shipping are its commerce.

The central part of the Sacramento Valley is best known for the city of Sacramento, the capital of California. This metropolitan area has grown from a small town at the edge of gold country to a major agricultural, industrial, governmental, and financial center.

The Sacramento area also includes the surrounding cities both within and beyond its metropolitan area. Davis, a university town less than a half hour away, is an example of another lifestyle in central Sacramento Valley. Here bicycles rule the streets and the academic life pervades the community in both style and content.

The northern part of the Sacramento Valley is another 90 or more miles north, in Butte County. Here, on the edge of the foothills of the Sierra Nevada, lies the city of Chico, another college town with a strong agricultural presence. An older and more established city than Davis, far from a major metropolis, Chico has developed into the financial, agricultural, industrial, cultural, and historical center for the area.

Sacramento

Sacramento, in the valley of the same name west of the foothills of the Sierra Nevadas, owes its existence to gold when thousands of prospectors came in search of their fortunes. After the rush ended, the city, having become the capital of the state by being where the action was, became the focal point of agriculture as well as politics. Sacramento was the terminus of the pony express and the transcontinental railroad. With World War II, the state's focus turned south, but as long as Sacramento is the capital, Sacramento will be an important place.

The development of new crops, the timber industry, military bases, the delta, and the deep-water channel of the Sacramento River have combined to extend the city of Sacramento beyond its limits; it now encompasses a large metropolitan area. The "Big Tomato" or "River City," as Sacramento has been called, has an ethnically diverse population of 385,000 in the city proper and 1.7 million in the metropolitan area.

Hot and dry in summer (often more than one hundred degrees), cool and wet in winter, and mild in spring and fall, Sacramento lies 90 miles northeast of San Francisco and 385 miles north of Los Angeles.

The business and politics of the most populous state of the Union centers on the Capitol Mall area. Decisions that affect the 32 million people in this state, as well as more than 230 million others nationwide, and, in some ways, the other 5.5 billion or so on the planet, emanate from the legislative and executive rooms of the Capitol, its gold dome a reminder of its past history and future glory. If it is true that California is the testing ground for new ideas that eventually will become the norm for the nation at large, then many of the new ideas get their initial validation here.

History can be seen elsewhere in Sacramento. Old Sacramento, railroads, and steamboats on the American River help give that feel. But the modern metropolitan life is the life lived by most residents—from good schools to clean water, from meeting the mortgage to getting to work. Overall this is a good city in which to live.

The city has more than 120 parks covering 2,000 acres. The older parts of downtown Sacramento have huge old trees lining the streets. Sacramento is known as "The City of Trees." The county of Sacramento also maintains 10,000 acres of parkland in the metropolitan area.

Recreation and Culture

Warm and dry weather brings people outdoors. The American River Parkway is an extensive river habitat running from Old Sacramento to Folsom Lake. It has 23 miles of bicycle, walking, jogging, and equestrian trails along the river's banks. Small boats are acceptable, as is fishing. White-water rafting on the American River is a well-established adventure.

Del Paso Regional Park has the Haggin Oaks golf course, one of thirteen in the Sacramento area. A trapshooting club is in the park, as are acres of horseback-riding and hiking trails. Discovery Park, on the opposite shores of the American River from Old Sacramento, is centrally located for city residents and has a small-craft launch. The Shepard Garden and Arts Center is in McKinley Park, along with tennis courts, a swimming pool, and other amenities. William Lan Park houses the Sacramento Zoo, Fairytale Town, Funderland, a pond, picnic tables, and a nine-hole golf course. There are even theater productions here during the summer.

CalExpo, the fairgrounds of Sacramento, is the home of Waterworld USA and the Paradise Island Fun Center. The California State Fair is held here each summer.

Regionally, Ancil Hoffman Park in Carmichael houses the Effie Yeaw Nature Center, a seventy-seven-acre plant and animal habitat along the American River. There is a golf course here, too, along with picnic areas.

A performing arts facility, a small lake, and a swimming pool can be found at Elk Grove Regional Park in Elk Grove. The 18,000-acre Folsom Lake State Recreation Area near Folsom has camping, a marina, and bicycle, equestrian, and hiking paths, as well as horse rentals. All kinds of boating activities take place on the lake, as do fishing and swimming. On a smaller scale, try Gibson Ranch County Park in Elverta, where a farm atmosphere is maintained, with picnic facilities, swimming, horseback riding, bicycling, fishing, and hiking. Horse-drawn hayrides are also offered.

Rancho Seco Regional Park, operated by the Sacramento Metropolitan Utility District, has a 165-acre lake for swimming, fishing, sailing, kayaking, windsurfing, and paddle boating. Hike and bike on this 400-acre property.

Old Sacramento State Historic Area, the original settlement of the Gold Rush days, has been reconstructed or renovated. It is a lively entertainment and shopping area, especially for visitors.

On the edge of this historic area is the California State Railroad Museum, with restored locomotives and cars and huge displays on the history of railroading and model railroads. There are also the Discovery Museum, with hands-on exhibits, and the California Military Museum.

The American River runs alongside the historic area. Take a riverboat cruise or a steam-train ride, launch a boat, or take a water-taxi ride. Special events here include the Sacramento Jazz Jubilee, Pacific Rim Street Fair, and Festival de la Familia, among others.

Among Sacramento's other museums are the California State Indian Museum, with displays of Native American culture, and the California State Capitol Museum, which features a variety of media displays that tell the story of California's government and history. Visit the Wells Fargo History Museum, which has other historical artifacts.

The performing arts are also plentiful. Best of Broadway brings the best out of local performers as they sing and dance to Broadway tunes. Chautauqua Playhouse and Eagle Theatre, the Sacramento Community Center Theater, the Sacramento Theatre Company, the Sacramento City College Actors' Theatre, the California State University at Sacramento Theatre Arts Department, and the Sacramento Light Opera Association all have regular performances around the metropolitan area.

Musically, the Sacramento Opera Association, the Sacramento Traditional Jazz Society, the Camellia Symphony Orchestra, and the California Wind Orchestra contribute to an active music scene. Dance is presented by the Sacramento Ballet and local ethnic dance groups. Sacramento has art galleries around the city. The second Saturday of each month is reserved for simultaneous openings. The Crocker Art Museum has Old Masters oil paintings and traveling exhibits.

California's wine country is in nearby Napa Valley. Apple Hill is an hour away on State Route 50. Trek out to the Gold Country for a reliving of California history, including the Marshall Gold Discovery State Historic Park in Coloma. Ski in winter and sail in summer at Lake Tahoe.

Real Estate

Downtown Sacramento has a very diverse selection of homes, some of which are in very charming, long-standing neighborhoods. Prices range from $200,000 to $500,000. The more expensive homes have interesting architectural detail and extra amenities, such as pools. Deluxe three-bedroom, two-bath townhouse units are priced from $225,000. Newer homes are available in suburban communities such as Roseville, Citrus Heights, and Fair Oaks.

The median price of houses in the greater Sacramento area is $111,325. The median rental is $462.

Medical Care

With a population of 1.7 million, there are many full-service hospitals, doctors, and other medical personnel to serve the communities. The University of California at Davis Medical Center is a top-rated teaching and research hospital, and health maintenance organizations and private providers have facilities throughout the area. Alternative medical practices are also available.

When Grandkids Visit

The problem in Sacramento is not what to do with grandchildren, but how to keep them home! There are parks, bicycling, hiking, boating, fishing, and picnicking throughout the region.

Add these ideas to those listed in Recreation and Culture: Safetyville USA, a place for safety training for preschoolers through third graders; Roseville Telephone Museum, displays of early technology; Hays Antique Truck Museum in Woodland; factory tour of Herman Goelitz Candy Company, makers of Jelly Belly and other candies; Discovery Museum Learning Center in Sacramento; rides on the Sacramento and American Rivers.

Addresses and Connections

Chamber of Commerce: 1301 Seventh Street, Sacramento, CA 95814–5403

Senior Services: Senior Connection, 5105 Manzanita Avenue, Carmichael, CA 95608

Newspaper: Sacramento Bee, Box 15779, Sacramento, CA 95852–0779

Airport: Sacramento Metropolitan Airport offers full-service passenger and freight service to the world.

Bus/Train: Amtrak stops in Sacramento, as does Greyhound; Regional Transit provides around-town service and connects the many towns and cities of the metro area by bus and light rail. Downtown Sacramento has free shuttle service.

Internet: http://www.ci.sacramento.ca.us
http://usacitylink.com/sacramento

Sacramento Weather

	JAN.	APR.	JUL.	OCT.	RAIN	SNOW
		In degrees Fahrenheit				
DAILY HIGHS	54	73	93	79	19"	—
DAILY LOWS	40	49	60	53		

Davis

The city of Davis, in Yolo County, lies 13 miles west of Sacramento and 72 miles east of San Francisco. Originally created as a farm cargo and passenger stop during the construction of the transcontinental railroad, "Davisville," as it was called until the early 1900s, became the home of the Davis Farm School, and, later, the University of California at Davis. Davis has since grown to a vibrant city of 53,000 people. Even so, it maintains a small college-town ambience.

Situated on and around the original Davis ranch, the city has become a center of academic excellence and environmental consciousness. The development of the university together with its resident faculty and staff has brought a demand for ongoing cultural pursuits. The student population has focused the city on alternative lifestyles, especially in the areas of transportation and health. A mild-to-hot and relatively dry climate that often goes over 100 degrees offers residents year-round conditions for outdoor activities.

The Davis Senior Center provides many services, including help for home repair, medical equipment, legal assistance, health screenings, transportation, tax help, and other vital information. Support groups for those in different health-care situations are available, as is a respite program for caregivers. Community groups encourage involvement in city life by all generations.

Farmers' markets are held twice per week. Dining options in Davis range from student fare to more formal settings. Entertainment from community theater to film to concerts keeps residents busy, as do the events in nearby Sacramento.

Recreation and Culture

In this city of 53,000 there are an estimated 50,000 bikes. Bicycle paths crisscross the town and the campus. Seven parks and additional greenbelt and open spaces, as well as the campus itself, provide not only beauty but great places for walking. A city brochure maps out a self-guided bicycle tour of historical sites, and another charts a public-art walking tour.

There are four public pools, a municipal golf course, and, within a short distance of town, places to fish. Fitness centers, indoor and outdoor sports, dance, drama, and services for persons with disabilities are also available.

Real Estate

In 1992, sale prices ranged from $130,000 to $700,000 for a house and $70,000 to $250,000 for a condominium. A two-bedroom apartment costs between $550 and $1,100 per month, and a two-bedroom house costs between $695 and $1,700, on average.

Medical Care

Sutter Davis Hospital is a full-service facility serving the city. The University of California Medical Center, in Sacramento, is internationally known for its research as well as its state-of-the-art facilities, services, and medical staff. Kaiser Permanente and other health maintenance organizations (HMOs) are located in the Sacramento area.

Healthy living has created a health-conscious community that includes all types of prevention and healing philosophies.

Animals also have access to great care. The UC Davis Veterinary School provides top-rate health services for pets.

When Grandkids Visit

There are diversions for all ages in and around Davis. The Explorit Science Center presents hands-on exhibits designed to bring children and adults a better understanding of science. The California Raptor Center also is in Davis. It rehabilitates injured birds of prey and has educational programs. UC Arboretum is a campus attraction. There are movie theatres, the Davis Musical Theatre, and UC Presents.

Check out Rainbow City, an innovative and creative playground in Community Park. Play structures were designed by the children of Davis and built by volunteers.

Addresses and Connections

Chamber of Commerce: 228 B Street, Davis, CA 95616

Senior Center: 646 A Street, Davis, CA 95616

Newspaper: Davis Enterprise, 315 G Street, Davis, CA 95616; *Sacramento Bee,* 613 G Street, Davis, CA 95616; *Newsbeat,* 227 E Street, Davis, CA 95616

Airport: The major regional and national airport is Sacramento Metropolitan, about 20 miles away. Locally, there is a small airport for light aircraft.

Bus/Train: Several local and regional services, such as YoloBus (serving Davis and other Yolo County towns), Unitrans (with routes throughout Davis), TAPS (the on-campus shuttle), and Davis Community Transit (providing door-to-door service), make getting around the area inexpensive and easy. There is also Amtrak passenger train service, as well as Greyhound bus service for connections from Davis.

Internet: http://www.city.davis.ca.us

Davis Weather

	JAN.	APR.	JUL.	OCT.	RAIN	SNOW
		In degrees Fahrenheit				
DAILY HIGHS	54	74	97	79	17"	—
DAILY LOWS	37	46	57	49		

Rio Vista

Small-town rural life is, for many, the only way to live. The California Delta, an area of land and waterways from a point south of Rio Vista northeast to Sacramento and from Antioch southeast to Stockton, is filled with small towns along the Sacramento and San Joaquin Rivers. Rio Vista, along the Sacramento, may just be where you want to be.

The Chinese settlers of the delta called the Sacramento River "The Big River." It is a fishing paradise and a boating haven. It is also the pipeline for the agricultural products of the Sacramento Valley as the crops head to markets around the world.

Originally most of the area was unusable marshlands, filled with tule (*TOO-lee*), a local plant that had taken to the swampy area. Today the word makes most Californians think of the tule fog, a thick blinding fog that can cover the valley quickly. But tule was a source of food and material for Native American settlers. Eventually, with the building of levees and the dredging of the riverbed the marshlands became usable for agriculture.

Rio Vista was first settled 2 miles to the north of its present location, but a flood in 1860 destroyed the town. Rebuilt on higher ground, the town looks out across the river toward the Montezuma Hills. Rio Vista is the protector and promoter of the delta's agriculture and natural gas. Its resident population of about 4,000 consists of boat enthusiasts, hunters, fishers, farm owners, other workers, and retirees. That population is expected to quadruple by 2015.

The delta's weather is like that of most places inland: Average low temperatures are about forty in winter and mid-fifties in summer; average high temperatures in winter are in the mid-fifties, with summer highs in the mid-eighties. About 16 inches of rain falls annually, and there are good winds from the west-northwest.

Rio Vista is about 20 miles from the larger cities of the delta, about 50 miles from Sacramento, and 65 miles from San Francisco. The distance helps Rio Vista offer residents and visitors an easygoing lifestyle.

Recreation and Culture

When Humphrey the Whale got lost in 1985 and followed the Sacramento River northeast instead of heading west out of San Francisco Bay, he made it to Rio Vista. It might have been its waterfront charm, but more likely it was its clean, fresh water that made Humphrey stop his trip upstream. After all, humans may need fresh water, but whales need the briny sea. Humphrey headed back downstream and out to sea soon after, happy to get back to the salt water he knew so well. Today, Humphrey is remembered in Rio Vista with a statue. But the good life— including the fresh water—that Humphrey saw is still going on.

The river is a wonderland of freshwater fish, wild birds, and other animals, and a great place to play. Outdoor recreation activities include boating, fishing, hunting, sailing, kayaking, canoeing, waterskiing, Jet

Skiing, windsurfing, and camping. Rio Vista's latest claim to fame is boardsailing. Considered one of the top five locations in the world for wind-powered water activities, the city is the home of the Rio Vista Windsurfing Association. The International Speed Slalom of boardsailing is held in Rio Vista. Boarders refer to the area as "Rio," and praise it highly.

It took three attempts to establish the striped bass in the waters of the delta; Rio Vista celebrates every year with a three-day Bass Derby festival. But the fishing goes on year-round, with locals and visitors testing their skills beside, above, and in the river. In December, Rio Vista is known for its Christmas parade of lighted boats. The Coast Guard Auxiliary has its own Admiral's Day Parade, too.

The Rio Vista Museum exhibits local memorabilia of Rio Vista and the surrounding delta communities. The Western Railway Museum west of the city has railroad artifacts on display. Historic trains are used for rides, and, in the spring, special May Flower train rides are available.

The Dutra Museum of Dredgers, a private collection, tells the history of sidedraft clamshell dredging, a quick and inexpensive technique that was key to water control and agricultural success in the area. The museum is open by appointment only.

The Brannan Island State Recreation Area, just 3 miles from Rio Vista, offers year-round activities. Picnic areas and campsites are available, and the visitors center has displays on the wildlife and history of the delta. Fishing and swimming are major activities, and there is a public launch for boats.

Solano County Sandy Beach Park south of Rio Vista has, as its name says, a sandy beach for swimming. Campsites, picnic and barbecue areas, and RV facilities are available. Boating, windsurfing, Jet Skiing, and waterskiing are popular. On land, volleyball courts and horseshoe pits, along with the sandy beach, keep people occupied.

Summerset Homes, a gated retirement community on the edge of Rio Vista, is built around an eighteen-hole golf course. A second course is planned.

The city has six parks of its own, besides the state and county parks. The Delta Marina, though privately owned, has 275 berths and the largest guest dock in the delta. The marina offers all the modern amenities expected of a complete facility.

Real Estate

Rio Vista offers many affordable single-family homes. Two-bedroom, one-bath homes start at $110,000, and three-bedroom, three-bath homes are available from $200,000 to $250,000. The cost of a house in Rio Vista averages about $185,000. Average rental for a two-bedroom apartment is $500 per month.

Medical Care

Doctors practice locally, and there are two local emergency centers. But for more complicated or specialized health care or hospitals, residents must go elsewhere. Emergency and nonemergency service is available to take residents to Lodi (12 miles), Antioch (20 miles), Vacaville (25 miles), Fairfield (24 miles), or Sacramento (50 miles). Kaiser Permanente is in Antioch, about 20 miles away.

When Grandkids Visit

Water-based activities will be a big part of your grandchildren's visits in Rio Vista. Most of the activities listed above in Recreation and Culture can include the kids.

The city also has a state-of-the-art library downtown. Within an easy drive are urban activities in Antioch, Lodi, and other delta cities. Sixty minutes away are Sacramento to the northeast and Oakland/San Francisco to the west. A day trip could be planned to Vallejo, the site of Marine World Africa, USA, a theme park. In a little over two hours you can be skiing in the Sierras. Everything seems reachable from Rio.

Addresses and Connections

Chamber of Commerce: 75 Main Street, Rio Vista, CA 94571

Senior Center: 41 Main Street, Rio Vista, CA 94571

Newspaper: River News-Herald and Isleton Journal, 21 South Front Street, Rio Vista, CA 94571; *Ledger Dispatch*, 1650 Cavallo Road, Antioch, CA 94509; *Lodi News-Sentinel*, 125 North Church Street, P.O. Box 1360, Lodi, CA 95241

Airport: Rio Vista Municipal Airport is for commercial freight and small planes. To fly regionally or nationally, Sacramento Metropolitan is 50 miles away, and Oakland International is 60 miles away, about an hour in either direction.

Bus/Train: Amtrak stops in Suisun City, 22 miles away, and in Davis and Sacramento. Antioch is the terminus for BART, the Bay Area Rapid Transit system. Rio Vista Transit connects Rio Vista with Vallejo, Vacaville, and Fairfield.

Internet: http://www.riovista.org/

Rio Vista Weather

	JAN.	APR.	JUL.	OCT.	RAIN	SNOW
		In degrees Fahrenheit				
DAILY HIGHS	53	69	86	76	16"	—
DAILY LOWS	40	49	57	63		

Chico

Instead of turning off Highway 99 North to go to Paradise, stay on the route to reach Chico. The flatlands of the Sacramento Valley are set off by the splendor of the nearby mountains. Just 60 miles away is Mount Lassen, which towers over the area at more than 10,000 feet. Thousands of acres of almond orchards and other agricultural lands surround the city.

Located just west of the foothills of Butte County, Chico offers a college-town life for the retiree. California State University, Chico has become a regional center for thought and activity. Like Santa Cruz and Davis, CSU, Chico and Butte College have had significant effects on the city's life with their populations.

Chico has about 50,000 residents, a portion of whom make up the 15,000 students who attend classes on campus. The city started after General John Bidwell, who had made a fortune in the Gold Rush days, purchased land and built a house. Bidwell donated the land upon which CSU, Chico now sits for a teachers college. His widow, in the late 1800s, donated the land that is now Bidwell Park, one of the largest municipally owned parks in the United States.

Recently named one of the ten best bicycling cities in the United States by *Bicycling* magazine, it is easy to live a car-free life on this valley floor. According to the magazine, the city has publicly stated its desire to be the country's most bike-friendly community by the year 2000.

A moderate to hot climate (winter averages forty-five degrees, with minimums in the mid-thirties; summer averages seventy-eight degrees, with maximums in the mid-nineties) makes Chico an outdoor wonderland. Though almost everything is available in the city for most of the year, you must go into the foothills and farther to the Tahoe area for snow.

Recreation and Culture

Chico is well suited to the active retiree. Bidwell Park offers paved trails, making walking and bicycling easy. More trails exist around the city. Parks seem to be everywhere, so the abundance of shade trees creates a calm ambience.

Bidwell Park is a state historic site. There is a visitors center next to the Bidwell Mansion. The park has three distinct areas. Upper Bidwell Park is mostly wilderness with about 25 miles of trails for bicyclists, horseback riders, and hikers. Another 10 miles are for hiking only. Swimming holes abound for great cooling-off places in the heat of summer. Middle Bidwell Park has a recreation area with baseball diamonds and picnic and playing areas; a natural swimming hole; and scenic walking paths along Horseshoe Lake. Foot and bicycle paths wander through oak groves in lower Bidwell Park, where you'll also find a playground, pool, and picnic areas. Chico Creek Nature Center, also in lower Bidwell Park, is the place to learn about the park ecology and the Chico area.

A number of public murals are scattered throughout the city. (Get a map from the Greater Chico Chamber of Commerce.) The oldest mural, "The Space Walker," was painted in 1977, and another, "Robin Hood," commemorates the fiftieth anniversary of the filming of *The Adventures of Robin Hood,* starring Errol Flynn, in 1937. Other famous films shot (at least partially) in Chico include *Gone with the Wind, Thirty Seconds over Tokyo* (with Spencer Tracy), and *Magic Town* (with Jimmy Stewart).

There are a relatively large number of music venues, most of them coffeehouses and clubs. CSU, Chico also has music and dance concerts. Downtown City Plaza has a gazebo where summer Friday night concerts are held, as are impromptu musical performances.

Theater has become a major scene in Chico. Several theatrical companies perform all over town. Chico City Light Opera and the Chico Creek Theatre Festival join the CSU, Chico Theatre Arts Department as regular sources of an evening's live stage productions. The CSU, Chico Performing Arts Center has two theaters, a recital hall, and extensive support facilities.

CSU, Chico also supports the visual arts with the Janet Turner Print Gallery, the Third Floor Gallery, and the University Art Gallery. Off-campus there are a number of studios and galleries open to the public. Of note is the Chico Art Center, a teaching center and gallery by and for local artists.

The Chico Museum exhibits artifacts from the area's history as well as traveling exhibitions. The Archaeology Museum is on campus; the National Yo-Yo Museum at Bird in Hand is on Broadway with displays on the history and types of yo-yos.

Chico has a community band and a community orchestra, the Bidwell Generals Chorus, and the Chico International Folkdancers. The Butte County Bird Club, Altacal Audubon Society, and many other groups admire and protect the flora and fauna of the northern Sacramento valley.

A U.S. Department of Agriculture Research Service Center was established here in 1904 to see what types of plants from around the world could flourish in the northern Sacramento valley. The pistachio and kiwi are now players in the agricultural industry in the Butte County area. Now known as the Genetic Resource Center, it offers self-guided tours of the property, which is at its most colorful in spring and fall.

Elsewhere in the area, visit the Covered Bridge Gardens, featuring daylily gardens, and the Plant Barn, for poinsettias. The almond orchards south of Chico bloom in February—a truly magnificent sight.

Real Estate

There is a good supply of homes for sale in Chico. Prices of condos and smaller homes start at $50,000. Two-bedroom homes are available beginning at $85,000, and three-bedroom homes from $90,000. The median price of a home in Chico is $121,000.

Medical Care

Two general hospitals serve the Chico area: Enloe Memorial Hospital, a Trauma Level II center for the six-county area that also has cardiac, cancer, and outpatient centers; and Chico Community Hospital, an acute-care facility with emergency care and a specialized respiratory center.

When Grandkids Visit

Bidwell Park is the first place to take the kids for biking, hiking, and picnicking. When they tire of that, try the Bidwell–Sacramento River State Park, where boating, kayaking, and fishing will while away the hours.

Explore the cork forest, one of a number of botanical adaptability experiments by John Bidwell, near Cedar Grove. Close by is the Chico Creek Nature Center where children can learn about Bidwell Park and visit the Living Animal Museum. Children's Park is downtown. Community Park is Chico's largest sports area, but Oak Way Playground also offers many sports facilities.

Addresses and Connections

Chamber of Commerce: 300 Salem Street, Chico, CA 95928

Senior Center: Janet Levy Center, Building D, First and Ivy Streets, Chico, CA 95929

Newspaper: Chico Enterprise-Record, 400 East Park Avenue, Chico, CA 95928; *Chico News and Review*, 353 East Second Street, Chico, CA 95928–5469

Airport: Commercial passenger service to San Francisco is available at Chico Municipal Airport.

Bus/Train: Amtrak and Greyhound have depots in Chico; Chico Area Transit System (CATS) is the local transit system; Chico Clipper serves seniors and the handicapped with door-to-door service. Butte County Transit offers service among the Butte County city areas.

Internet: http://www.chico.ca.us

http://bs.yahoo.com/Regional/ U_S_States/California/Cities/Chico/

Chico Weather

	JAN.	APR.	JUL.	OCT.	RAIN	SNOW
		In degrees Fahrenheit				
DAILY HIGHS	54	72	95	79	26"	—
DAILY LOWS	36	44	61	48		

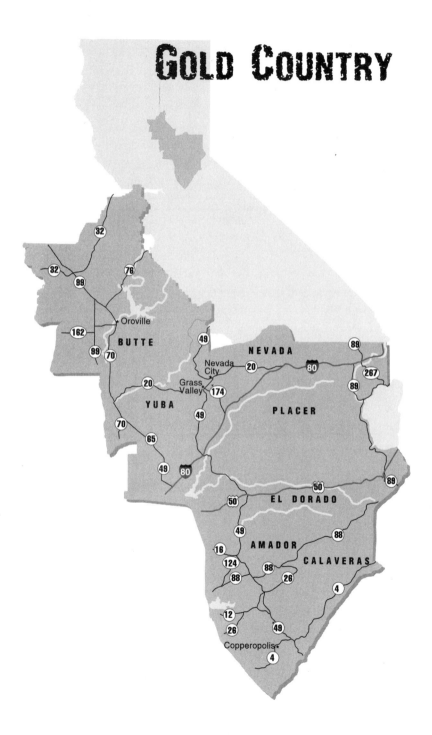

THE GOLD COUNTRY

When the eastern portion of the United States was being settled by colonists from England and Europe, the western part of the continent was still in the very earliest stages of exploration. In 1768, when the King of Spain ordered the colonization of what is now California, the eastern seaboard was already well established and civilized. At that time, Easterners lived in cities adorned with graceful public buildings; they enjoyed brick homes with polished wood floors and glass windows. While cities like New York, Philadelphia, and Boston had opera and theater, horse-drawn street cars, running water, and all the accoutrements of civilization, California colonists were still clearing land for cattle ranches and living in rustic villages of adobe houses.

By 1848, when the United States took possession of the region from Mexico, California settlements were small and scattered, mostly villages connected with the old Jesuit missions or cattle ranches owned by Mexican Californiano families. Monterey and San Francisco were about the only places with more than a few hundred residents. Los Angeles and San Diego were villages. Few buildings from those pre-gold days remain.

Back East, unless a building or event isn't 200 or 300 years old, people tend to pay it little attention. Not so in California: Any home built before 1900 is valued as an antique—before 1850, as a priceless historical monument. California's most fascinating and best-known historical sites date from the period just after the discovery of gold in 1848.

The phenomenon known as the Gold Rush brought eager people from all over the world to instantly populate California in their frantic haste to become rich. Unlike those in the East, California's population centers didn't appear first on the coast and later grow inland. The major California towns and cities were built miles from the ocean, along a long, narrow belt of land where rich gold deposits promised wealth and success. This region became known as the Mother Lode.

When the news spread, gold fever infected the eastern and southern states, and, in fact, the entire world. People left their jobs, their farms, and their homes in a mad scramble toward certain wealth. Some traveled by covered wagon or horseback; others sailed around South America.

Some even walked, carrying their possessions in backpacks. Fortune hunters came from Australia, Chile, and Europe to join in a frenzy of prospecting. Eager miners attacked streams with gold pan and sluice box to fill their pockets with gold nuggets. History records few instances of such a sudden, massive, and dramatic population shift. The population grew so quickly that two years after the discovery of gold, the California territory had enough population to qualify for statehood.

Settlements in the Mother Lode grew the fastest. In 1852, just four years after the discovery of gold, the town of Grass Valley was the seventh largest in the new state, larger than Los Angeles, San Diego, or Oakland.

Tent settlements and rude mining camps sprang up near the mines and soon became real towns—with paved streets, brick buildings, theaters, newspapers, saloons, jails, and an occasional church. Violence was met by vigilante committees and the hangman's noose. People from all social walks of life joined in the frenzy: rough miners, skilled tradesmen, merchants, even college professors and preachers. Influential writers such as Mark Twain and Bret Harte have endowed us with eloquent details of what it was like to be alive in those days.

Although historical sites in Gold Rush country are mere upstarts compared with those in most eastern cities, their emotional impact is greater. The romance and drama are a mere 100 to 150 years removed. A conservative Connecticut farmhouse dating from 1656 somehow fails to evoke the excitement of an 1856 Gold Rush assay office where miners brought ore samples and nuggets, or a newspaper building where publishers once penned editorials that evoked challenges to duels.

When gold claims finally played out, miners and prospectors drifted on to other enterprises. They deserted the Mother Lode for rich farming valleys or to swell the population in the now fast-growing coastal cities. Suddenly abandoned, many Mother Lode locations became virtual ghost towns. This abandonment preserved old buildings and communities in time-capsule form and saved them from modernization. Our heritage is a fascinating glimpse of life as it was during California's most romantic era. Fortunately, the state vigorously preserves these sites as a charming part of California's past: the country of Bret Harte, Mark Twain, and John Fremont.

Today the Mother Lode country is about as far from the stereotypical image of California as you can get. Instead of palm trees, sunny beaches, and Hollywood glitter, the charm here is semirural living in the Sierra Nevada foothills. Quaint, historic towns with narrow streets and buildings of native stone and brick seem to harmonize with modern subdivisions and golf developments silhouetted by green-clad mountain backdrops.

From rolling hills studded with black oaks and manzanita to the majestic peaks of the Sierra Nevada, the Mother Lode encompasses a unique scenic wonderland. Here you find not only a true four-season climate, but seasons that vary depending on altitude. From mild winters and hot summers in Jackson and Angels Camp to deep snowpack and cool summers in higher altitudes, you have a wide menu of climates and seasonal colors.

The Mother Lode encompasses a 300-mile stretch of rolling-to-rugged country that runs from Downieville in the north to Coarsegold in the south. It takes in nine counties—Madera, Mariposa, Tuolumne, Calaveras, El Dorado, Placer, Nevada, Sierra, and Amador. Then, 100 miles to the northwest, another area of historic gold mining towns covers several more counties—Butte, Siskiyou, Tehama, Shasta, Trinity, and Lassen. Although not part of the Mother Lode, this area has produced large quantities of gold to enrich the country.

By the way, the '49ers didn't get all the gold. They left enough to keep hundreds of weekend prospectors and amateur miners working at their dredges and sluice boxes. With most of the countryside in public land and national forest, you'll have plenty of opportunity to try your luck. A favorite family outing is to take a picnic lunch and a couple of gold pans and spend the afternoon working one of the many creeks and streams that traverse hills covered with oak, pine, and cedars. Some people do quite well, but you can expect them to be very close-mouthed about where they found their private bonanzas. Others are ashamed that they aren't skilled enough with a gold pan to find much gold, so they lie about how much they find. (That's what I do.)

Amador County

Squarely in the heart of the Mother Lode, Amador County is a perfect example of what the Gold Rush region is all about. A dozen charming small towns and villages are scattered through the county's 568 square miles of rolling foothills with their live oaks and pine trees.

Amador County straddles historic Highway 49, the original stage-coach trail that connected the bustling mining towns from northern to southern regions. It was the richest of the gold mining districts. Amador County's mines accounted for more than half of all the gold harvested along the Mother Lode.

Historic Highway 88 is the second famous road crossing Amador County. Originally the main route across the Sierra, it was known as the "Carson Emigrant Trail." Crossing the high Sierra at Carson pass, this old stagecoach and wagon trail winds down the mountain slopes on its way toward San Francisco Bay. Highway 88 is often described as the country's most scenic highway; and its beauty is overwhelming. The pavement winds past romantically named places such as Tragedy Springs, Maiden's Grave, and Inspiration Point—through Pine Grove and Volcano and many other sites steeped in Gold Rush history. The roadway crosses Highway 49 at Jackson. This intersection might be described as the exact heart of the Mother Lode country.

In western mountain locations, climate varies with altitude, and in Amador County the altitude varies widely. Lower elevations start at 200 feet and climb all the way to more than 9,000 feet. Magnificent views of snow-covered peaks, mountain lakes, and meadows are everywhere. With low summer humidity, even the hottest days are bearable. Winters are short and mild (January afternoons are usually close to sixty degrees), and the area enjoys a true spring and a colorful fall season.

Years ago fascinating towns like Jackson, Sutter Creek, Fiddletown, and Plymouth were bustling and prosperous—many times their present-day size. Drytown, now a wide spot on Highway 49, was once neither so quiet, so tiny, nor so dry. At its prime, it was a roaring mining camp that boasted twenty-seven saloons. Loaded with relics of the past, each of these towns takes pride in maintaining and restoring its historic old buildings.

Founded as a Gold Rush camp in 1848, **Jackson** is the county's largest town, with a population of 3,900. It became the county seat when Amador County was established in 1854. An intriguing example of Mother Lode history, the downtown is meticulously preserved in the tradition of the Gold Rush days. Brick and hand-hewed stone buildings adorned with iron shutters and wrought-iron balconies in the style of the mid-1800s line the narrow streets. Yet the town's newer sections display modern ranch-style homes as California-looking as you might expect to find anywhere. Like other Mother Lode towns, Jackson is proud of its restored old brick and Victorian frame houses, with all modern conveniences added. Housing costs are below national average, and below what you would pay in the larger California cities. Because of mild winters, mobile homes are a practical lifestyle here, with five mobile home parks in the county.

There are a number of other places in Amador County where gold country retirement is a viable option. The following are some possibilities. (Small farms or wooded acreage outside these towns and villages would make fine living choices, too.)

One of California's smallest incorporated municipalities, **Amador City** boasts a population of 212. Located on Highway 49, the community was named for Jose María Amador, who mined the creek in town in 1848–49. Just a mile or so from Jackson, the town has little in the way of a business district; residents depend on Jackson for shopping.

Located on the northern edge of the county on Highway 49 near the El Dorado County line, **Plymouth** is the site of the Amador County Fairgrounds and the annual county fair each July, considered by many to be one of the best county fairs in California.

The town got its start in 1856, when Adam Uhlinger dug a winery into a hill here. This is one of the oldest wineries in the state. The Empire Store building is an interesting structure remaining from mining days, along with the Methodist Episcopal Church, the first in the region. Plymouth's present-day population is 832.

Sutter Creek was named for famed gold discoverer Captain John Sutter, an early pioneer who arrived in 1844 and established a lumber mill with whipsawing pits. The town of Sutter Creek started as a camp just south of this site. The community became a supply center for quartz mines in the 1850s. Today's population is a little more than 2,000.

Sutter Creek's historic Main Street, with its original mining-era buildings, is a favorite with tourists because of its antiques stores and bed-and-breakfasts, as well as its mining-camp ambience, so typically Gold Rush era that it would be suitable as a movie set. On either side of the business district (actually part of Highway 49), numerous older homes await renovation; newer, contemporary houses are tucked away on tree-shaded lots and acreage.

Historians believe that **Drytown** may have been the first gold camp established in the area shortly after the discovery of gold in 1848. Named for Dry Creek, which carried water only in winter, Drytown was the first location in the county where gold was panned in any quantity. An 1856 history referred to "the old adobe in Drytown"—a building still standing—which may be the oldest dwelling in the county. Drytown's old schoolhouse is also believed to be one of the county's first. Most housing is scattered around the vicinity of the small business district, on heavily wooded properties.

Fiddletown, founded in 1849, is an old mining settlement located 6 miles east of Highway 49, up Fiddletown Road from Plymouth. During the height of the Gold Rush, Fiddletown had the largest Chinese settlement outside San Francisco. For some reason the local people didn't like the name "Fiddletown" and renamed it "Oleta" in 1872. The decision was reversed in 1932, so it's Fiddletown once again. Historic sites include the Chew Kee store, where Chinese artifacts and relics are displayed.

In 1855 Albert Leonard built an inn amid a pine grove and, of course, named the town of **Pine Grove**. About 100 years ago, the original Pine Grove House was replaced by the Pine Grove Hotel, which is still standing. The Pine Grove Community Church and School was constructed in 1869. Another historic site, built in 1879, is the Pine Grove Town Hall, still used as a gathering place for community and social events.

Recreation and Culture

As the geography of Amador County varies, so do the climate and landscape. The lower altitudes have mild winters and hot summers, while the high-Sierra region has cool summers and snowbound winters. This variety allows a wide range of outdoor recreational opportunities, from year-round golfing and fishing to snow sports in the winter.

Real Estate

Throughout Amador County the cost of housing is below California averages. Older homes in the small towns and villages bring the average selling prices down. Owner-occupied, single-family homes are the rule, with occasional modern developments for those with money and a hankering for something upscale.

Medical Care

As a result of the growing need for better facilities in Amador County, the Sutter Amador Hospital has been undergoing new construction and improvements. Twenty acres have now been purchased on a knoll directly across Highway 88 from the current facility, and construction of a new $30 million hospital is under way. The new 93,000-square-foot hospital will offer nearly all single rooms, technologically advanced equipment, and many new outpatient services and programs. Currently the eighty-nine-bed facility provides twenty-four-hour emergency services.

When Grandkids Visit

You are obligated to take your grandchildren panning for gold. Throughout Amador County you'll find creeks where you can set up a picnic spread while the children fill their gold pans with water, sand, and gravel. The trick is to swirl the mess around until the gold settles to the bottom. The grandkids will receive the thrill of a lifetime when they see that first trail of glittering gold dust. Well, that's the way it's supposed to work, but even if they don't find any gold, you'll have fun trying and you'll enjoy a picnic on the creek bank in the shade of a large oak tree.

Addresses and Connections

Chamber of Commerce: 125 Peek Street, Jackson, CA 95642

Senior Services: 229 New York Ranch Road, Jackson, CA 95642–2147

Newspaper: Amador Ledger Dispatch, 10776 Argonaut Lane, Jackson, CA 95642

Airport: Sacramento Airport, 45 miles

Bus/Train: No local bus service; Greyhound in Jackson

Internet: (Jackson) http://www.cdepot.net/map/jackson.html
(Amador City) http://www.cdepot.net/map/amadorc.html
http://www.amadorcounty.com/chamber/amadorcity.htm
(Plymouth) http://www.cdepot.net/map/plymouth.html
(Drytown) http://www.cdepot.net/map/drytown.html
(Pine Grove) http://www.cdepot.net/map/pinegrove.html
(Fiddletown) http://www.cdepot.net/map/fiddle.html

Amador County Weather

	JAN.	APR.	JUL.	OCT.	RAIN	SNOW
		In degrees Fahrenheit				
DAILY HIGHS	53	66	91	74	18"	8"
DAILY LOWS	31	40	56	44		

Grass Valley/Nevada City

In the summer of 1849, a party of emigrants searching for straying cattle discovered a luxuriant grassy stretch of land lying between pine-clad hills. What else to call it but Grass Valley? The following spring prospectors began arriving. Soon the little settlement started to resemble a real town. But the big rush started in October when a prospector named McKnight located a quartz ledge embedded with rich streaks of gold, the famous Gold Hill Ledge. According to local accounts, this discovery "caused wild excitement in the camp." It marked the first time gold miners realized that riches were to be found in underground quartz as well as in stream beds. With the new discovery, the towns of Grass Valley and Nevada City were under way. Grass Valley soon became one of California's largest cities.

Although both Grass Valley and Nevada City lost population after the turn of the century, the towns never came close to abandonment like most mining towns. Even during the Great Depression, Grass Valley streets and hotel lobbies bustled with mining activities. One traveler of 1933 pronounced Grass Valley "the only city in the United States where you had to wire ahead for reservations." Today Grass Valley has about 10,000 inhabitants; Nevada City, 3,000. A century and a half of gold mine activity has yielded more than $100 million in precious metal.

Nevada County, where Grass Valley and Nevada City are located, is perched in the foothills of the Sierra Nevada Mountains at an average elevation of 2,500 feet. While light snow may fall a few times a year, it rarely lasts long, and the rainfall is a little more than 30 inches a year. The surroundings vary from rolling hills to snow-covered Sierra peaks with plentiful forests of oaks, pines, cedars, and firs. The region's historical legacy is expressed in carefully preserved Gold Rush architecture throughout Nevada County. White churches with steeples and buildings of ancient red brick are shaded by century-old sugar maples and liquidambars that early settlers brought with them from New England.

Full of charm and small-town atmosphere, Grass Valley and Nevada City offer residents a variety of interesting shops and businesses. The two towns support more than 220 retail establishments and professional services, as well as a diverse group of restaurants and historic buildings. At every turn there is something to discover: unique shops, a winery, museums, old churches, a restored theater, a historic hotel, a charming bed-and-breakfast inn, a brewery, a fine restaurant.

Gold mining technology, for which Nevada County was famous, has been replaced by twenty-first-century high technology. Facilities here design and build digital video, multimedia, control and robotics equipment, as well as perform medical data processing. More than 1,000 hardware and software professionals in more than thirty high-tech companies call Nevada County home, earning it the nickname "Silicon Valley of the Sierras."

Nevada City, by the way, has an exceptionally active senior center, with activities and volunteer opportunities galore. The Gold Country Telecare network keeps folks in touch by phone for problem solving, assistance, and counseling. Telecare volunteers are available for seniors who can't afford to hire a handyman to fix a leaky faucet or to repair porch steps. Legal and tax questions are covered by other volunteers, and still others make sure seniors don't miss shopping, recreational activities, or an appointment with the dentist.

Before you settle on a gold mining location, you must see 'em all! Scattered around the countryside in the Grass Valley–Nevada City area are any number of smaller communities, historic places like **Rough and Ready**, Gold Run, or Colfax, away from town but only a few miles from shopping. Rough and Ready was founded by miners led by Captain A. A. Townsend, who served under "Old Rough and Ready" Zachary Taylor. Today a quiet residential village, the town had its brief flame of publicity when it seceded from the Union. It happened this way: Residents, outraged at a special mining tax the government had imposed, in protest seceded from the Union on April 7, 1850, and declared the town of Rough and Ready to be an independent republic. The new republic lasted until the Fourth of July celebration, when Old Glory returned to its place on the flagpole, and a good time was had by all. Several buildings still stand from that date, including the interesting W.H. Fippin Blacksmith Shop.

Early settlement of the **Penn Valley** area occurred in the mid-1800s, due primarily to its location on a freight wagon route that connected Nevada's Comstock district with the Mother Lode. Freighter service made the valley an important transportation stop. Older farm buildings coexist with modern homes in a historical, pastoral atmosphere. Residents report a low incidence of crime—neighbors know each other here.

Situated just north of scenic Highway 20, the village of **Washington** was settled in 1849 and soon became a bustling town with hotels, restaurants, and supplies for several thousand miners. Prospectors found lots of gold in the South Yuba River and Poorman's Creek. Mining claims were considered poor if they did not pay an ounce per day per man. Today, Washington is a quiet town with typical Gold Rush era buildings and convenient proximity to nearby recreational activities, such as camping and gold panning.

Recreation and Culture

From Thanksgiving to May (as long as there's snow) there are half a dozen top-rated ski resorts within an hour drive of Grass Valley and Nevada City. You can be skiing before lunch and be out of the snow and home for supper before dark.

A number of theater companies, including a cabaret-style dessert theater, offer year-round fare running from Shakespeare to contemporary works. The Foothill Theatre Company is in its twentieth season. The Twin Cities Concert Association, the oldest classical musical organization in the area, specializes in professional chamber music programs with guest artists. The Nevada County Arts Council sponsors programs like the Sierra Festival of the Arts and fine arts and crafts shows.

An exciting development for the region is the new Sierra Community College campus. Opened in August 1996, the school is likely to figure prominently in future continuing education and community involvement.

Real Estate

Along the winding, narrow streets of Grass Valley and Nevada City, you'll find lovely restored and original examples of Victorian and early twentieth-century homes, while subdivisions of newer homes appear on the outskirts, with more contemporary designs. The variety of homes available in Grass Valley and Nevada City ranges from vintage miners' cottages to million-dollar estates with panoramic views. Prices for existing homes begin at $79,000, with median prices around $155,000.

Medical Care

Sierra Nevada Memorial Hospital takes care of health needs in the western parts of Nevada County. The facility is proud of its new outpatient center and cancer center; an urgent care unit was added recently. The W.C. Jones Memorial Hospital in Grass Valley, housed in an old Victorian home, has served as the community's hospital for sixty-five years. For the eastern, higher portions of the county, medical needs are met by the Tahoe Forest Hospital in Truckee. This is a seventy-two-bed multispecialty hospital, with outpatient and home-care service.

When Grandkids Visit

Take the kids to the Empire Mine, now a state park, so they can see where almost six million ounces of gold were brought from the mine's deep shafts and passageways. They can watch videos of how the gold was mined and then hike the park's 10 miles of trails. If they'd rather look for gold, within a few miles from town there are three placer locations open to the public. There all of you can learn the technique of separating nuggets from gravel, then later go prospecting on your own.

Addresses and Connections

Chamber of Commerce: Grass Valley, 248 Mill Street, Grass Valley, CA 95945; Nevada City, 132 Main Street, Nevada City, CA 95959

Senior Services: 11350 McCourtney Road, Nevada City, CA 95959

Newspaper: The Union, 11464 Sutton Way, Grass Valley, CA 95945

Airport: Sacramento Metro Airport, 58 miles

Bus/Train: Greyhound; local bus transportation in and about Nevada City to Grass Valley through the towns and into rural areas. There is no available train service here.

Internet: http://www.ncgold.com
http://www.nccn.net/

Gold Country Weather

	JAN.	APR.	JUL.	OCT.	RAIN	SNOW
		In degrees Fahrenheit				
DAILY HIGHS	53	66	91	74	18"	8"
DAILY LOWS	31	40	56	44		

Calaveras County

On the southern edge of the Mother Lode, triangular-shaped Calaveras County was known as the "golden triangle" because of its rich yield of glittering metal. Around $500 million was taken from the mines in Mokelumne Hill, San Andreas, Angels Camp, and other towns in the county. The largest gold nugget ever found in the United States was discovered at the Morgan Mine at Carson Hill. It weighed 190 pounds! Small wonder early-day prospectors and miners were convinced that somewhere, nearby, lurked the undiscovered source of all this wealth, a fabulous mother lode of solid gold, enough to make everybody in the world rich.

The name Calaveras (Spanish for *skulls*) comes from the name the Spanish explorer Gabriel Morega gave to a river flowing through the region. The county extends from the grassy plains of the San Joaquin Valley easterly through rolling foothills and historic Mother Lode communities, up into the high country at the crest of the Sierra Nevada Mountains, at over 8,000 feet. Calaveras County encompasses quaint historic towns, wine country, and sequoia forests. Within a range of 50 miles, weather conditions change from deep-snow skiing to grape-growing warmth.

Unlike most California counties, Calaveras has no major population centers. Commercial, shopping, and business districts are scattered throughout the county, with few communities having more than 2,000 residents. But because the distances between towns aren't great, there are plenty of services within an easy drive from any point. Choices for retirement here range from small farms on oak or pine hills to historic homes in old Gold Rush towns, conventional homes on large lots, and upscale developments complete with golf and country-club amenities.

Mark Twain spent the fall of 1865 in **Angels Camp**, working a claim on nearby Jackass Hill. He made regular visits to the saloon at Angels Camp Hotel, where miners swapped tall tales. This is where he developed the story that made Angels Camp famous: "The Celebrated Jumping Frog of Calaveras County." Today the peaceful town of 3,000 comes alive every May as thousands of contestants (and their frogs) from all over the country attend the Jumping Frog Jubilee. During this celebration Angels Camp treats more than 15,000 visitors to a rodeo, concerts, and arts-and-crafts exhibits.

Angels Camp, although not the county's largest town, is the only incorporated city in Calaveras County. The main industry is tourism, which boasts such attractions as caverns, a golf course, a beautiful lake, and a marina where houseboats are rented.

After you've lived in California a while, you'll become tired of seeing T-shirts and bumper stickers saying "San Andreas, it's not my fault." But for some reason, tourists visiting San Andreas can't pass up the chance of pretending to be clever. Actually, the town of **San Andreas** has no relationship at all with the famous San Andreas Fault. The town acquired its name in the early days of the Gold Rush when some Mexican miners named the camp after their patron saint.

While Angels Camp is famous for its jumping frogs, San Andreas is known for its two infamous bandits: Joaquin Murieta and Black Bart. Murieta acquired a Robin Hood image, robbing from the rich and giving to the poor, while Black Bart robbed from the rich and sensibly kept it for himself—living a dual life as a leading San Francisco socialite and gourmet.

With an altitude of a little more than 2,000 feet, the region around **Murphys** is a perfect place for vineyards. The low-mountain climate and soil closely approximate several renowned wine regions in France. Early-day prospectors from Europe introduced the art of wine making, and during the Gold Rush era Calaveras County became the state's second largest producer of wine. Within a few miles of downtown, seven wineries are bringing fame to Calaveras County.

The population here is about 2,500, actually not much below its peak in the 1850s. Murphys is just 9 miles east of Angels Camp, and the two towns share commercial and cultural connections.

During the Gold Rush era, **Arnold** was a mere logging camp. Today, however, because of the popularity of nearby Big Trees State Park and the breathtaking beauty of the region, Arnold has grown to a town of more than 7,000 inhabitants. Sitting at an altitude of 4,000 feet, this is actually high Sierra country, but not so high that snow becomes a problem. Entirely surrounded by the Stanislaus National Forest, Arnold and nearby Avery are becoming popular retirement places, providing all services as well as world-class recreation.

Gold was found in **Mokelumne Hill** in 1848, and it soon became one of the richest spots in the Mother Lode. Fortunes were made from claims confined to sixteen square feet. It quickly grew to a city of 15,000 and became famous for being one of the most violent and bawdy towns in the Mother Lode. Today Mokelumne Hill's population is around 2,000, and its reputation is for peace and quiet.

After the discovery of copper in 1860, the area around **Copperopolis** became the one of the most important copper ore producers in the United States. During the Civil War, the mines here produced 19 million pounds of copper. In the early days of mining, ore was carried by cart to Stockton, then by riverboat to San Francisco Bay where it was loaded onto sailing ships for the trip around Cape Horn to Wales or Boston for smelting.

Some of the buildings that still stand here were built in the 1860s of brick hauled from Colombia, where buildings were torn down by miners to get at the gold-rich dirt underneath. The historic old structure with iron doors at the south end of town is an old armory that served as the headquarters for Union troops during the Civil War.

Today Copperopolis' population is less than 2,000, and the town is quiet and unassuming. Lake Turloch, a few miles from downtown, has become a retirement haven, with several developments along its shores. From an inexpensive cluster of houses and mobile homes on one side of the lake to upscale, master-planned communities on the other, the choice of housing is ample. Residents are proud of their championship golf course, which is open to the public.

Recreation and Culture

The recent opening of Greenhorn Creek, home of WPGA winner and Hall of Famer Patty Sheehan, brings another world-class golfing venue to the area, joining Saddlecreek at Copperopolis and Forest Meadows near Murphys. Several lakes, including the immense New Melones Reservoir, offer exceptional fishing and all types of water sports. The

Stanislaus National Forest has more than 800 miles of river, streams, and tributaries that are home to many types of trout, salmon, and bass.

Calaveras Big Trees State Park, a short drive from any town in the county, provides a wealth of recreational opportunities. Along with two magnificent groves of giant sequoia trees, the park has more than 6,000 acres of pine forest with hiking and bicycling trails and picnic areas. The magnificent sequoias range in size to 325 feet in height, 24 feet in diameter, and are believed to be up to 2,000 years old. You've no doubt seen pictures of an automobile driving through a tunnel in a sequoia tree. This is where those photos are taken.

About 20 miles up the highway from Arnold, Bear Valley provides topnotch skiing throughout the winter and often well into spring.

For continuing education, Sonora has a two-year community college. (Sonora is 16 miles from Angels Camp; 38 miles from San Andreas.) Although the population of the towns here is small, Calaveras County is becoming appreciated for its dedication to the arts with year-round music festivals, arts and crafts fairs, and local theater. The Calaveras Arts Council sponsors indoor and outdoor events ranging from symphony to global dance, including "Music in the Park," an evening concert series offered at various parks throughout the county for summer family entertainment.

Real Estate

The historic towns of Jackson, Sutter Creek, and Pine Grove offer excellent values. In Jackson, inventories of homes are limited. Townhouses start at $110,000. Homes range in price from $80,000 to $295,000. Houses in Pine Grove are selling from $109,000. In Sutter Creek newer homes are available from $110,000 to $260,000; older places are more affordable.

Medical Care

The Mark Twain St. Joseph's Hospital in San Andreas provides twenty-four-hour, full-service emergency care and operates clinics in Angels Camp, Valley Springs, and Arnold. Sonora Community Hospital also has twenty-four-hour, full-service emergency care. This hospital operates a series of family medical centers in Angels Camp, Arnold, and Copperopolis. Other hospitals serving Calaveras County are in Sacramento and Stockton.

When Grandkids Visit

Your grandchildren will enjoy a visit to one of the several caverns in Calaveras County. One cavern has an immense gallery, so large it could hold the Statue of Liberty. The caves are wonderlands of crystalline stalactites and stalagmites and contain lakes up to 200 feet deep. One cave offers a 180-foot rope rappel as a way to get to the bottom of the caverns—for those with the courage.

Addresses and Connections

Chamber of Commerce: P.O. Box 115, San Andreas, CA 95249

Senior Services: 956 Mountain Ranch Road, San Andreas, CA 95249–9713.

Newspaper: Amador Ledger Dispatch, 10776 Argonaut Lane, Jackson, CA 95642–9465; *Calaveras Press,* 1177 South Main, Angels Camp, CA 95222; *Sierra Sentinel News,* 2784 Shirewood Lane, Arnold, CA, 95223

Airport: Sacramento Metro Airport, 50 miles

Bus/Train: Greyhound; no local bus service

Internet: (Calaveras County) http://www.calaveras150.org (Copperopolis) http://www.hton.com/copperop.htm

Calaveras County Weather

	JAN.	APR.	JUL.	OCT.	RAIN	SNOW
		In degrees Fahrenheit				
DAILY HIGHS	53	66	91	74	20"	6"
DAILY LOWS	31	40	56	44		

Oroville

In 1848, shortly after gold was discovered at Sutters Mill, General John Bidwell found gold in a gravel bar in the Middle Fork of the Feather River. This discovery attracted the inevitable hordes of miners to the scene. Miners called their tent town Ophir City—later to be known as Oroville—and it quickly grew into a real town with brick buildings and businesses supplying the miners' needs. Before the gold supplies were exhausted, as many as 10,000 Chinese lived here, working first in the gold fields and then on railroad construction.

Nestled in a bend of the Feather River at the base of the Sierra Nevada foothills, Oroville today has 13,000 residents and serves an area several times the size of the city limits. The town center is surrounded by pleasant tracts of homes and is conveniently situated near Lake Oroville, with its 15,000 acres of blue water encompassed by oak-covered hills. This Sierra foothill's unique Mediterranean climate nurtures orange groves as well as orchards of olives, peaches, pears, plums, kiwis, and nuts. The original "mother orange tree," the direct ancestor of today's California seedless oranges, is still standing after 142 years. It was brought here as a seedling in 1856, and cuttings from the tree spawned the generations that created California's first citrus industry. The tree is carefully tended by the community for its historical significance.

Downtown Oroville features many historic buildings, some dating to the Gold Rush days. The center is well known for its many antiques stores as well as shopping convenience. Around the old Courthouse Square are several heritage murals depicting scenes from the Gold Rush era, including a Wells Fargo stagecoach holdup by Black Bart.

For rural retirement in tiny, authentic Gold Rush villages, nearby Cherokee and Oregon City are charming locations. Although gold mining was big in Cherokee, which had one of the state's largest sluice mining operations, the area was a major source of diamonds, with more than 200 stones of commercial quality discovered here.

Recreation and Culture

Long a favorite with outdoorsmen, the rugged Mother Lode country around Oroville appeals to anyone with an appreciation of California's Sierra foothills. Wildlife flourishes amid abundant trees and along the forks of the nearby Feather River and Lake Oroville with its unspoiled shoreline. *Bassmaster* magazine recently ranked the lake as California's best fishing spot. Houseboating is popular here, where there are 167 miles of coves, inlets, and places to fish or tie up for the night. In addition to the enormous Lake Oroville State Recreation Area and numerous parks maintained by the city, you'll have your choice of three golf courses within the greater Oroville area.

Butte College, a two-year community college a few miles from downtown Oroville, has an enrollment of 11,000 and offers a wide variety of classes in continuing education. California State University, Chico is twenty-five minutes away and offers a full range of courses.

Real Estate

There are many attractive smaller homes near the center of Oroville. Two-bedroom, one-bath homes start as low as $80,000, and three-bedroom, two-bath homes are priced from $100,000. Several nice subdivisions offer upscale living near the lake.

Medical Care

Oroville Hospital is a modern 153-bed facility with a twenty-four-hour emergency center, including helicopter service. An air ambulance from UC Davis medical center can reach Oroville Hospital within minutes. Oroville has more than seventy physicians and twenty dentists, plus several other health specialists.

When Grandkids Visit

Take your grandchildren to the Lake Oroville Visitors' Center, where they can learn the history and resources of the area. The center has more than thirty films covering the history of the Gold Rush era to the construction of the dam. The kids might also be interested in seeing the Feather River Hatchery, where more than 10 million salmon and steelhead trout fingerlings are released into the river every year. Being there when the sprint-run or fall-run salmon begin arriving is a special treat. The magnificent fish can be seen through special view windows as they climb the fish ladder to reach the hatchery.

Addresses and Connections

Chamber of Commerce: 2255 Del Oro Avenue, Oroville, CA 95965
Senior Services: P.O. Box 5554, Oroville, CA 95966
Newspaper: *Oroville Mercury Register*, 2081 Second Street, Oroville, CA 95965
Airport: Sacramento Metro Airport, 60 miles
Bus/Train: Oroville Transit and Butte County Transit; Greyhound
Internet: None available.

Oroville Weather

	JAN.	APR.	JUL.	OCT.	RAIN	SNOW
		In degrees Fahrenheit				
DAILY HIGHS	54	73	98	79	24"	5"
DAILY LOWS	37	46	68	53		

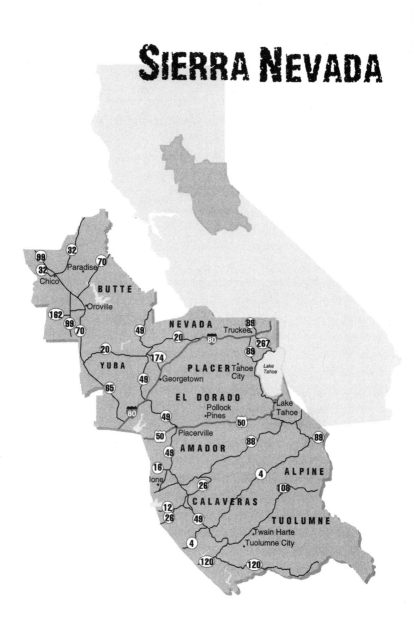

SIERRA NEVADA

BUTTE
Paradise
Chico
Oroville

NEVADA
Truckee
Tahoe City
Lake Tahoe

PLACER
Georgetown

EL DORADO
Pollock Pines
Lake Tahoe

YUBA

Placerville

AMADOR

ALPINE

CALAVERAS

TUOLUMNE
Twain Harte
Tuolumne City

99 32 70 162 70 20 174 49 65 80 50 49 16 12 26 49 4 120 120 89 267 89 80 20 49 50 88 4 108 26

THE SIERRA NEVADA

One of the nation's major mountain ranges lies within California's borders. The legendary Sierra Nevada features year-round snowy peaks, granite pinnacles, eight national forests, and two of the most beautiful national parks on the continent. The expansive Sierra Nevada range stretches approximately 400 miles, from Mount Lassen in the north to the Mojave Desert in the south. When Spanish explorers first entered the region, they were so awed by the jagged, frosted row of peaks that make up the spine of the mountain range that they described the sight as a *sierra nevada*. In Spanish, *sierra* means "sawtooth" and *nevada* means "snowy." Snow-covered sawtooth is an apt description.

This is California's year-round mountain playground. Every month of the year, tourists travel here to fish, ski, gamble, or simply to enjoy the breathtaking panorama of the Sierra Nevada. Yosemite National Park is one of the country's scenic marvels, rivaled only by Yellowstone in number of astonishing vistas. Kings Canyon, Lassen Volcanic, and Sequoia National Parks, plus a host of other marvelous wonderlands, draw visitors from all over the world who travel thousands of miles to marvel over the beauty. Yet these places are a just a short drive for tens of millions of Californians who take full advantage of the Sierra's proximity for summer and winter enjoyment.

After spending many vacations in the Sierra Nevada and taking occasional weekend trips to the mountains throughout the year, people find it natural to think about retirement in the Sierra region. After all, this is where they spent some of the most enjoyable moments of their lives; why not live here? Why drive back and forth to enjoy retirement?

Not all the Sierra Nevada country lives up to its snow-covered nomenclature. True, one of the most popular places in the mountains, Lake Tahoe, catches an unbelievable amount of snow over the course of a winter, but most of the places where folks choose to retire sit at lower elevations, where snow falls two or three times during a winter. Daytime temperatures in moderate altitudes are too warm for the snow to stay long on the ground. It disappears within a day or two. January, the coldest month of the year, ranges between fifty to sixty degrees at noon in most lower Sierra locations. You'll encounter frequent shirtsleeve days, with temperatures reaching the high sixties or low seventies. For those of you who want real winter conditions, a few minutes' drive up the highway will satisfy those desires—and then you can return to the dry comfort of home as quickly as you left it.

An astonishing number of people choose the loftiest region for retirement, the part known as the "High Sierra." (Perhaps it is astonishing only to those (like this writer) who detest cold weather. One reason for this popularity is that high Sierra property can easily be rented during whatever season, so retirees have the option of doing part-time Sierra retirement. Those who like to ski might rent their places for the summer while they spend the season at the beach. Others, who prefer fly-fishing and hiking, will abandon the winter high country to bake in the Palm Springs sun.

When considering property in the higher elevations of the Sierra Nevada, you need to be conscious of a few conditions specific to snow country. First of all, be aware that there are numerous microclimates throughout the mountains. In the Lake Tahoe region, for example, snowfall can vary greatly from one neighborhood to the next. Real estate people and residents can point this out to you. Of course you'll check to see that the home is well insulated, with dual-pane windows, and all of those standard cold-weather precautions; but there's more. Think about the slope of the driveway; will you be able to get in and out when there's a light snowpack? And how will the snow cast off from the roof? (If it unloads in the driveway or blocks the front door, you could be shoveling more snow than you counted on.) How many steps will you have to keep clean? Will you be satisfied with the sun exposure? What about off-street parking? In some neighborhoods, it's illegal to park inside the snow stakes at the curb. A final consideration might be whether your new home is convenient to tourist attractions so it can easily be rented when you desire a vacation away from vacation land.

Lake Tahoe

When John C. Fremont and his survey party camped at Lake Tahoe in 1844, they named it Mountain Lake. After several name changes, the Indian name *Tahoe,* or "big water," was formally adopted by residents.

Lake Tahoe was on the shortest route for the wagon trains from the east traveling to the California Gold Rush. With the silver discovery in Virginia City, Nevada, in 1859, the lake became a favorite playground for miners traveling between the gold fields of California and the silver fields of Nevada.

In *Roughing It,* Mark Twain had this to say about Lake Tahoe: *"Three months of camp life on Lake Tahoe would restore an Egyptian mummy to his pristine vigor and give him an appetite like an alligator. . . . The air up there in the clouds is very pure and fine, bracing and delicious. And why shouldn't it be? It is the same air the angels breathe."*

Just a short drive from Carson City and Reno, up a wide, four-lane highway, the Lake Tahoe region is an absolute jewel among California retirement possibilities. This beautiful, forested lake setting straddles the line between Nevada and California, with the lake as its centerpiece. Tall pines, rugged granite cliffs, and wild backcountry complete the scenario. The lake's water is said to be over 99 percent pure and of such brilliant transparency that the bottom is clearly visible at depths of 100 feet. The lake's deepest point is 1,645 feet. At 6,228 feet above sea level, Lake Tahoe is the third largest alpine lake in the world, with a surface area of 193 square miles. Its incomparable beauty, delightful climate, and unlimited recreational advantages place it among California's top natural wonders.

Snow is an important part of Tahoe's winter; that's one reason many people choose to retire here. In fact, the average annual snowfall is 18 feet! That's right, 216 inches of snow (not everywhere in the region, only in certain areas). If there isn't at least a six-foot pack on the ski slopes, skiers feel cheated. From anywhere in town it is a matter of minutes to a ski lift, a joy to those who enjoy the sport.

However, don't get the idea that deep snow stacks up on the ground and stays until spring, as is the case in places like Montana or New Hampshire. Daytime temperatures in this area almost always are above freezing, even in the coldest months. Often it gets warm enough to ski in shirtsleeves. Snow stays around at the higher elevations on the ski slopes, but at the lake level snow typically falls in isolated, heavy storms that dump up to 3 feet in one night. Then the weather will turn sunny for days or even weeks, quickly melting the snow until the next storm.

One nice thing about the Tahoe region is that if you get tired of snow, a half-hour drive takes you out of it. You can be skiing at Incline Village in the morning and browsing through Carson City casinos in shirtsleeves that same evening. In the summer residents look forward to warm days with occasional afternoon thunderstorms and cool, clear nights.

Besides skiing, why do folks consider Lake Tahoe retirement? "Living here is like being on permanent vacation," says a friend who owns a lakefront cottage near North Shore. Like many residents, he bought his home several years ago, in anticipation of retirement. He rented out his place by the day or week at premium rates to regular visitors—vacationers, skiers, and gamblers—and by the time he was ready to retire, a good portion of his retirement home had been paid off. The deductions and depreciation as a rental also helped ease his tax burdens. Long-term rentals here, however, are usually at rates somewhat higher than in most California urban areas. That can be expensive and worth it only if you cannot consider living anywhere else because you love Lake Tahoe so much. Many people living there feel just that way.

South Lake Tahoe is the lake's most populated residential area, and, as you might guess, it's located on the southern edge of the lake. Homes are spread lakeside for several miles and also are dispersed back in the forested sections away from the lake. Set in the El Dorado National Forest, much of the land is pure wilderness. Businesses, shopping, and commercial establishments of all descriptions abound near the lake, making this a real city with all the accoutrements, including heavy traffic.

The big attraction for some is Lake Tahoe's collection of casinos, beginning just across the state line in Nevada. Glittering and glamorous, they provide topnotch entertainment and gourmet restaurants at affordable prices. Casinos are enjoyed even by those who know better than to gamble away their grandkids' inheritance. In addition, many jobs—full-time and part-time—are created by the gaming industry. (Ever notice how casinos prefer to say "gaming establishments" instead of "gambling joints?" We all know the casino is going to win, so they're correct; it's a game, not a gamble.)

Lake Tahoe is located 204 miles from San Francisco and 49 miles from Reno. It is easily accessible from San Francisco and Sacramento via Interstate 80. Driving times from the Tahoe region to the San Francisco

Bay Area vary, but given normal traffic conditions and clear roads, most folks figure on spending between three and four hours travel time, depending on the weather. Reno is less than an hour away. Motorists always carry tire chains in winter months, but they're only needed during snowstorms.

North Shore is the name given a dozen small towns, villages, and neighborhoods lining Lake Tahoe's northern edge. Among others you'll find Tahoe City, Kings Beach, Tahoe Vista, and Meeks Bay. These places are preferred by those who want to avoid the hustle and bustle of South Lake Tahoe. An additional advantage is proximity to the ski resorts of Squaw Valley and Alpine Meadows.

The population of **Tahoe City** is only about 1,000, but the town is the center of half a dozen unincorporated neighborhoods on either side. Older cabins, cottages, and houses sit alongside quality upgrades and newly built homes. The nicer ones sit on the lake shore, but they rarely appear on the market. Prices here range from $110,000 to $300,000, with some lakefront places priced in the seven-figure range. These communities include Lake Forest, Dollar Point, Cathedral Forest, Tahoe Woods, and Tahoe Park.

A few miles south of Tahoe City, **Tahoma** is a place of low- to moderate-priced homes. Many older homes and summer cabins are being upgraded now that streets are being widened and paved. Next to Sugar Pine Park and Bliss State Park, this area has much to offer for its price range: from $70,000 to $150,000.

On the top of the lake, next to the Nevada state line, **Kings Beach** has the North Shore's best values in housing. Prices range from $100,000 to $200,000; most homes fall within the $115,000 to $150,000 range. Nearby Brockway has higher-priced places, as high as $1 million.

Although situated in Nevada, **Incline Village** is part of the Lake Tahoe complex. The most popular residential neighborhood here is Agate Bay, where you'll find moderate to high-priced homes in wooded settings. Prices range from $130,000 to $250,000 or higher for a lake view. Close to skiing and gambling, homes here have good rental histories, so prices in Nevada are usually higher than for equivalent homes in California. The Incline Village area is in demand for those seeking residence in Nevada for tax purposes. (Nevada doesn't have a state income tax.) However, income from another state may be subject to taxes under that state's tax codes. California, for example, requires you to pay nonresident taxes on income earned in California. Specific questions should be referred to your personal tax adviser before you make decisions based on taxes.

Thirteen miles from the lake and conveniently situated on Interstate 80, the town of **Truckee** is nevertheless considered part of the North Shore complex. Its downtown has an Old West appearance, and the residential areas have plenty of older, affordable homes as well as beautiful, newer places tucked away in the pines. Those who want to have peace and quiet yet still be close to gambling will find casino action just across the state line, at Crystal Bay.

Nearby is famous **Donner Lake,** where, in October 1846, the ill-fated Donner Party tried to alter its planned course from the "Emigrant Trail" to a shorter route through the Truckee area. Severe weather, including massive snowstorms, trapped the group in the mountains. The disastrous delay on their trek west is well known in the history of the Old West. A monument to the Donner Party's heroic battle with the elements and hunger stands today at the east end of the lake. Today several new residential developments are under way here, with most homes within walking distance of the lake. House prices range from $115,000 to $1.1 million. Condos run from $29,000 for a studio to $260,000 for a two-bedroom town house on the lake.

Recreation and Culture

The Tahoe basin is one of the most complete winter sports areas in the United States. Nineteen alpine ski resorts lie within the basin, including the well-known areas of Alpine Meadows, Northstar at Tahoe, and Diamond Peak. Squaw Valley, famous for its 1960 Winter Olympic Games, is located here. In addition to the alpine ski areas, there are numerous areas for cross-country skiing, snowboarding, or sledding. For summer fun, there are golf courses, tennis courts, river rafting, hiking, and boating on the lake.

Real Estate

Starting in the early 1990s, California underwent a recession of sorts, mostly due to downsizing in the defense industries. Depending on the location, real estate values dropped from 5 to 20 percent, as distressed properties went on the market. However, properties in the Sierra Nevada region—around Lake Tahoe in particular—held their values quite well. When other California real estate was stagnant, the Sierra Nevada region was appreciating a few percentage points every year.

Medical Care

Health needs are met in the lake's South Shore by Barton Memorial Hospital in South Lake Tahoe. The North Shore lake area is served by Tahoe Forest Hospital in Truckee; a seventy-two-bed, multispecialty hospital with outpatient and home-care service. It serves a wide area of the Sierra Nevada region and even the Gold Rush country of Grass Valley and Nevada City.

When Grandkids Visit

You'll find endless forms of entertainment for children, including beach and boating activities in the summer and ski resort activities in the winter. If you want a special summer treat, take them for a mile-long tram ride up to the top of Heavenly Valley, a full 2,000 feet above the lake level. That puts you at over 8,000 feet, with a wonderful panorama of Lake Tahoe's blue water below. Squaw Valley has a cable car ride to the top with a view of the lake and the ski area of Squaw Valley. If the grandkids visit in the winter, then of course you'll take them to one of the resorts and treat them to beginning ski or snowboard lessons.

Addresses and Connections

Chamber of Commerce: Incline/Crystal Bay, 969 Tahoe Boulevard, Incline Village, NV 89451; North Lake Tahoe, P.O. Box 884, Tahoe City, CA 96145; Truckee/Donner, 12036 Donner Pass Road, Truckee, CA 96161

Senior Services: 3140 Lake Tahoe Boulevard, South Lake Tahoe, CA 96150

Newspaper: North Tahoe-Truckee Weekly, P.O. Box 49, Tahoe Vista, CA 96143; *Tahoe World,* P.O. Box 138, Tahoe City, CA 96145

Airport: South Lake Tahoe Airport, shuttle; Reno International Airport, 55 miles

Bus/Train: Greyhound Bus Lines, and Continental Trailways, Amtrak at Truckee; some local bus services

Internet: http://www/virtualahoe.com/Community/

Lake Tahoe Weather

	JAN.	APR.	JUL.	OCT.	RAIN	SNOW
		In degrees Fahrenheit				
DAILY HIGHS	36	50	79	51	8"	216"
DAILY LOWS	16	26	43	31		

Low-Altitude Sierra Living

The heaviest concentration of high-Sierra population is clustered around Lake Tahoe. Most other truly high-altitude towns tend to be quite small, often villages—sometimes simply clusters of homes with just a gasoline station and convenience store making up the business district. Many homes in these higher elevations are abandoned when heavy snow sets in. There's a good reason for this: On many high-country roads, snow plows stop operating after the season's first heavy snowfall.

The vast majority of mountain retirement homes are therefore found in the lower-altitude regions of the Sierra Nevada. Folks here are willing to trade a cold, snowbound winter for a mild, four-season climate yet still be close enough to the high country to enjoy it within a half-hour drive. Throughout the length of these lower-altitude mountains, you'll find small towns, varying in size from several hundred to several thousand residents, where retirement is very practical. Combining the convenience of small-town living with forest settings and affordable housing, these places are also convenient to larger cities. Fresno, Stockton, Sacramento, or Bakersfield are within an hour or so drive; residents need add only an hour or two and they can be in the big-city complexes of Los Angeles or San Francisco. Two major routes into the high Sierra country, Highway 50 and Highway 108, have several towns that deserve mention. From these roads, many interesting towns fan out through the mountains. Below are listed several of our favorites.

High along the road toward Lake Tahoe, at an altitude of 4,000 feet, the community of **Pollock Pines** is aptly named; tall pine trees are everywhere. Narrow roads wind through the pines, past cabins and elaborate homes, most occupying large pieces of forest land. A minor construction boom is under way in and around Pollock Pines, as people from the San Francisco Bay Area build second homes for later use in retirement.

Halfway between Sacramento and Lake Tahoe, Pollock Pines is about as high in the Sierra Nevada as you can get without encountering severe winter weather. The region gets several healthy snowfalls every winter, but it's too warm here for snow to stick around very long. Summers are delightful, always several degrees cooler than Sacramento, which can be stifling.

Even without a true downtown or town center, Pollock Pines has an adequate collection of stores and a nice shopping area. And there's a theater devoted to melodrama; local residents write and produce the plays. Medical needs are taken care of in Placerville, at Marshall Hospital, 14 miles distant.

Georgetown, about 16 miles north of Highway 50, is another retirement town that combines gold mining history and low Sierra Nevada environment. Georgetown's small main street is lined with fascinating old buildings dating from the mid- to late 1800s. Tourism is an important part of the economy. This is the terminus of the famous "Rubicon Run," a long and arduous four-wheel-drive event that ends with half the vehicles strewn among the granite boulders of the incredibly rough trail. The survivors celebrate in Georgetown with steak dinners and many drinks as they swap experiences.

Most residences are away from the town center, with large lots and a mixture of hardwood and evergreen trees shading the homes. The population here is small, only about a thousand inhabitants, with many more scattered about the outskirts. Since the altitude is several hundred feet below Pollock Pines, winters are much less snowy, with one or two short-lived blankets every season.

As Highway 108 wends its way toward the high Sierra, it passes through or near several towns at lower elevations that are popular retirement locations. As the highway gains altitude, gnarled oaks and other hardwoods give way to low evergreens. Then evergreens take over as a way of announcing that you're leaving the gold country for the Sierra Nevada. This contrast between the Sierra Nevada and the Mother Lode region is dramatic.

The first resort community east of the foothills is **Twain Harte.**

Located about a mile off Highway 108, it has everything from golf and swimming to shopping and gourmet dining. And since it's only about 10 miles from Sonora, heavy-duty shopping can be found nearby. Until 1924 Twain Harte was simply a crook in the road with one farmhouse set in a pristine forest where deer, bear, elk, and smaller animals roamed. Then a man named Alonzo Wood and his wife, Keturah, remodeled the farmhouse into an inn and named it after Wood's favorite authors, Mark Twain and Bret Harte.

Today the town is a thriving community of an estimated 5,000 full- and part-time residents. Despite its quick growth, Twain Harte has managed to maintain its forest setting and quiet residential neighborhoods. The homes and businesses found here are shadowed by tall evergreens. And in Twain Harte the community spirit is strong.

Sitting about 10 miles off Highway 108, **Tuolumne** is well off the tourist trail. Unlike Twain Harte, where a busy highway runs along the edge of town, Tuolumne sits at the end of a paved road. Also unlike Twain Harte or nearby Soulsbyville, its business district can hardly be described as dynamic. Tuolumne is a place for everyday living, not commerce. The population is between 2,000 and 3,000 people, many of them living outside the town proper. You'll find few upscale residences here; this is a place for economical real estate and low-income rentals.

A few businesses still do well in the town center, but many stores have become private residences. The community's small downtown area is reminiscent of the 1950s, with a large park where bands play on summer evenings, a baseball field, a swimming pool, horseshoe pits, and a veterans memorial hall. Community spirit is high, with a large number of retirees organizing clubs and social activities. A large area of vacant lots has been converted to community gardens, with residents tending individual plots, raising flowers and fresh salad vegetables. They like to say Tuolumne is a well-kept secret.

Tuolumne wasn't always so quiet. Businesses thrived when the 348-acre historic West Side Lumber Company adjacent to town was still in business. It closed in 1962 and was later destroyed by fire. The town may be on the verge of new prosperity, however, with the development of the Cherry Valley Golf and Country Club on the site of the old lumber company property. A new development of homes on acreage-size parcels is also under way.

Recreation and Culture

Towns and villages in the lower environs of the Sierra Nevada take full advantage of the outdoor recreation opportunities available to both the Mother Lode and the high Sierra regions. Residents are famous for organizing social and cultural events, with repertory theaters, festivals, and other social activities enthusiastically supported by the community. These activities are supplemented by regular presentations of cultural events in Placerville and Sonora.

The Central Sierra Arts Council sponsors many annual events, including Friday evening "Concerts in the Park" during July and August. It is responsible for the highly successful Annual Bach Festival in October. The Mother Lode Art Association displays work throughout the region and at special shows. Columbia College offers cultural programs, including a jazz concert series featuring nationally acclaimed artists.

Real Estate

The most inexpensive housing is found in Tuolumne. In addition to older homes that sell for fixer-upper prices, there are at least two facilities with subsidized rentals for those who qualify for low-income housing. Soulsbyville, on the other hand, has an impressive amount of upscale housing in a forest setting. Twain Harte has a mixture of low-cost and upper-end homes for retirement.

Medical Care

Tuolumne has two medical facilities, unusual for a small community. Tuolumne General Hospital has 80 beds, and a Tuolumne branch of Sonora Community Hospital has 99 beds. In Sonora itself, Sonora Community has two hospitals, with a total of 127 beds. Placerville has the 114-bed Marshall Hospital to take care of medical needs for Highway 50 communities.

When Grandkids Visit

The local Native American Mi-Wuk tribe hosts the "Mi-Wuk Acorn Festival" each September at its Tuolumne Rancheria. Visitors can enjoy colorful Native dances, see authentic woven baskets and crafts, sample Native American food, and visit a roundhouse where tribal councils are still held. One of the foods featured at the festival is acorn porridge, one of the staple dishes of Native Americans throughout California. Once you taste it, you'll realize why you never see it on restaurant menus: It tastes like acorn porridge.

Addresses and Connections

Chamber of Commerce: (Pollock Pines) 6532 Pony Express Trail, Pollock Pines, CA 95726–9549; (Tuolumne County) 222 South Shepherd Street, Sonora, CA 95370–4734

Senior Services: 5581 Gail Drive, Pollock Pines, CA 95726

Newspaper: Mother Lode News, 119 Theall Street, Sonora, CA 95370–5798; *Mountain Democrat,* 1360 Broadway, Placerville, CA, 95667–5902

Airport: Sacramento, 43 miles

Bus/Train: No local bus; Greyhound; no train service available

Internet: http://hgreen.edcoe.k12.ca.us/placerville.html

Pollock Pines (Low-Altitude Sierra) Weather

	JAN.	APR.	JUL.	OCT.	RAIN	SNOW
		In degrees Fahrenheit				
DAILY HIGHS	52	63	89	73	20"	35"
DAILY LOWS	33	40	60	48		

Paradise

On the extreme northeast edge of what can be considered the Sierra Nevada region, the town of Paradise sits at the upper end of the Mother Lode. Thus it combines Sierra Nevada living with gold country experience. The Feather River Canyon, famous for its rich harvest of shining metal, runs through here. Weekend prospectors are still gleaning gold from the river's gravel beds.

Scattered above the canyon, on a place called Nimshew Ridge, is a collection of little villages and mining camps that sprang up in the 1860s. The camps had vivid names, such as Dogtown, Toadtown, Poverty Ridge, and Whiskey Flats. At Dogtown (now Magalia) a prospector uncovered a fifty-four-pound gold nugget back in 1859. Several large nuggets weighing up to nine pounds each turned up later, but after the Dogtown nugget, everything else seemed anticlimactic.

Before long, folks grew tired of explaining why they lived in Whiskey Flats or on Poverty Ridge, so they agreed to form one town and call it something more romantic. What could be more romantic than "Paradise"? Modern-day retirees believe the town was aptly named; they've found their paradise here.

Today, Paradise and nearby Magalia share a particularly scenic location as well as a reputation for being one of the most popular retirement destinations in Northern California, perhaps in all the state. Almost half the residents are over fifty-five years old, and the percentage of the population who are retired is probably higher than in any other city of its size. At first glance it's difficult to believe there could be 35,000 people living within the widespread city limits of Paradise because so many homes are built back from the roads—they're half-hidden from sight in a forested, parklike setting. More than 1,500 mobile homes are located here, most on individually owned residential lots—a popular alternative housing for retirement living.

Heavily wooded, at an altitude of 2,000 feet, Paradise sits below the snowbelt yet mercifully above the Sacramento Valley's smog level. (Actually there isn't much smog in the valley except in the fall, when farmers burn the rice fields.) This higher altitude also means ten-degree lower summer temperatures than the valley floor below. Tall pine trees shade homes beneath their thick-leaved branches, keeping air-conditioning needs to a minimum.

Around these parts, higher elevations (over 4,000 feet) are generally covered with snow most of the winter. When winter rains fall on Paradise, it's a good bet that snow is falling in Stirling City, some 20 miles away and 1,000 feet higher. Being below the snowbelt doesn't mean that Paradise is snow free. When conditions are right, Paradise's rain turns to snow. At this altitude snow doesn't come down in small flakes and particles; it forms large puffs—sometimes the size of golf balls. Very soft and fluffy, the white stuff piles up incredibly fast. Because of its expanded bulk, what would be a 4-inch snow in Stirling City quickly becomes 12 inches in Paradise or Magalia with the same precipitation. Old-timers tell of 3 feet of snow falling overnight. This type of snow melts quickly, however, the moment the sun comes out and warms things up. Even in the coldest months, afternoons are usually warm enough that most people need to wear only a light sweater to feel comfortable. And because the weather is like this, golf courses are open year-round.

Local contractors take care to build homes without disturbing the trees any more than necessary. Building lots are large, usually a quarter to half an acre, sometimes several acres. With low housing density and lots of forest, Paradise is a sanctuary for wild animals, since hunting is prohibited in town. Deer and raccoons saunter about town insolently, as if they were taxpayers.

Adequate shopping facilities, with several tastefully done shopping complexes, make for convenience. Cable TV is available, and so is that ultimate mark of civilization: pizza home delivery.

This large population of retirees means plenty of organized activities and clubs. In addition to the local branch of the American Association of Retired Persons (AARP) organization, there is a Golden Fifties Club, a retired teachers association, a senior singles club, and a couple of senior citizens political action coalitions.

Paradise is a peaceful and safe place, scoring very high on our personal safety charts. Many local police officers, like retirees, have relocated here from Los Angeles. When Paradise organized its own police force, the city recruited in Southern California. One police officer interviewed said, "What a difference! Here I spend my time helping people instead of dealing with criminals."

The early-day miners didn't exhaust the gold. Today residents make a hobby of searching for one of those fabulously large nuggets for which the region is famous. Panning efforts by the experienced usually yield at least some "color" in the gold pan. Winter storms send waters surging through the river and creek canyons—always washing more gold from the hillsides, ready to be found in the spring. Weekend miners report finding nuggets in the quarter-ounce to half-ounce range, occasionally in the ten-ounce range. One of the authors found a half-ounce nugget at Nelson Bar, just a few miles from downtown Paradise.

Although very small compared with Paradise, **Stirling City** is a truly high-mountain community of historic presence with a population of around 500. It's an interesting place to visit, even if you choose not to retire here. Not being a place of gold, Stirling City got its start in 1901 from Columbus Barber, owner of Diamond Match Company. Barber wanted a source of wood for his matches, but he found the wood too soft, so he built a sawmill and began producing lumber instead. When the mill closed in 1958, the town fell on hard times, and real estate became a buyer's market supreme. Numerous folks have found this a picturesque and quiet place for retirement. Stirling City is, however, very rustic; it's a place for those who might like to restore one of the many turn-of-the century homes.

Recreation and Culture

Eight golf courses are within a short drive of Paradise. Of course, trout fishing in the Feather River is also tops on many recreation menus in the warmer months. Then it's skiing in Stirling City when there's snow. Since the forest begins right in town and becomes more dense as you approach the nearby Plumas National Forest, deer hunters are in their individual paradise. Some of the most wild and scenic country in California is found 20 miles from home. Oroville Lake brings ducks and geese within gunsight for shotgun enthusiasts.

For continuing education classes, most residents drive 14 miles to Chico State University. Butte Community College is just a few miles from town, between Paradise and Oroville. The Paradise Auditorium is often used for adult education classes; a recent class was in gourmet cuisine. During June Paradise hosts a monthlong arts festival with guest soloists in concert and plays and ballet by regional performing groups. Little-theater performances are presented at Theatre on the Ridge.

The big celebration, however, is Gold Nugget Days, commemorating the discovery of gold here in the 1850s and the huge nuggets that made Nimshew Ridge famous. Every April three days of celebration include a parade, a carnival, and gold panning contests. Most men in town grow beards for the event; prizes go to the best. Well-known male residents who fail to sport beards are subject to fine or "going to jail" (spending a few minutes in a jail-like parade float).

Real Estate

Because almost half the population lives on fixed incomes, housing costs and rents haven't been pushed to the ridiculous highs of some other parts of California. Home prices start at around $60,000 for a modest place and run to more than $200,000 for something with a spectacular view of the Feather River Canyon below Nimshew Ridge. Rentals for two- to four-bedroom homes range from $310 to $650 a month, with mobile homes (on residential lots) renting for $250 to $400. Mobile home parks are plentiful, and space rents are quite affordable.

Medical Care

As a normal response to a large retiree population, health care is unusually good. The 109-bed Feather River Hospital provides twenty-four-hour emergency-room service, a fully equipped acute-care hospital, and a 22-bed skilled nursing facility. There are also two convalescent hospitals, three medical care centers, and several residential care and guest homes.

When Grandkids Visit

Take the grandchildren to Lime Saddle Marina and see about renting a patio boat for the day. This is a great way to combine a fishing trip, a picnic, swimming, and just loafing in one glorious day of outdoor enjoyment. If you want to stay overnight, you can dock in a cove or inlet. Houseboats are available to rent, and they come complete with a kitchen, bedroom, and a back porch that looks out over the water.

Addresses and Connections

Chamber of Commerce: P.O. Box 1423, Paradise, CA 95967
Senior Services: 877 Nunneley Road, Paradise, CA 95969–4707
Newspaper: *Paradise Post*, 5399 Clark Road, Paradise, CA 95969
Airport: Chico Airport, 20 miles
Bus/Train: Butte County Transit in Oroville; bus shuttle to Sacramento Airport
Internet: http://207.213.170.225/paradise/index.html

Paradise Weather

	JAN.	APR.	JUL.	OCT.	RAIN	SNOW
		In degrees Fahrenheit				
DAILY HIGHS	52	71	92	85	48"	18"
DAILY LOWS	32	45	61	50		

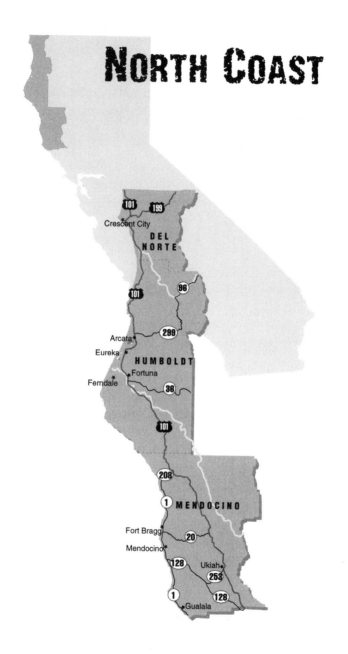

NORTH COAST

Crescent City

DEL NORTE

Arcata

Eureka

HUMBOLDT

Fortuna

Ferndale

MENDOCINO

Fort Bragg

Mendocino

Ukiah

Gualala

101 195 101 96 299 36 101 208 1 20 128 253 128 1

THE NORTH COAST

Most people are familiar with the way Southern California's semi-tropical paradise contrasts with Sierra Nevada alpine meadows. And, of course, there's Mojave Desert's harsh, dry, sagebrush landscape contrasting with the lush fields of flowers and vegetables in the interior valleys. Most people have also heard of the pine and hardwood forests of the northern portions of California. But for many newcomers the biggest surprise comes from California's Mendocino/Redwood Coast region. In many ways, Humboldt and Del Norte counties are mirror images of the Maine and Massachusetts coasts (only not so cold in the winter). California's north coast resembles her New England counterparts so closely that Hollywood routinely uses the region for movie locations instead of traveling back east to New England. The town of Mendocino, a picturesque village perched on a bluff above the Pacific, was the movie location for *The Russians Are Coming, the Russians Are Coming, Summer of '42, Same Time Next Year,* and *Dying Young,* all of which had New England settings. For more than ten years, fans of Angela Lansbury's television drama, *Murder, She Wrote,* watched the program opening with an exterior shot of Jessica Fletcher's Cabot Cove home, supposedly somewhere in New England. But the house seen on TV is actually located at 45110 Little Lake Street, Mendocino, California.

This Cape Cod look didn't come about by accident. The Mendocino coast's history dates back to California Gold Rush days when fishermen and loggers from New England found the region very much to their liking. They brought New England–style architecture with them and, in fact, shipped many homes around the tip of South America and reassembled them here. Small wonder the region is sometimes referred to as "Cape Cod Shipped 'Round the Horn." Logging and fishing were early industries and continue to play a part in today's economy.

Although the coast may be reminiscent of Massachusetts, the ocean's sheer beauty can be more universally appreciated here. Because of California's insistence on public ownership of beaches (beach access cannot be denied) and the state's strenuous efforts to restrict construction on the water's edge, the Pacific Ocean is much more accessible than the Atlantic. Almost every yard of Atlantic coastline is privately owned, and the views are restricted. More often than not, the privilege of gazing at the ocean is granted exclusively to those fortunate enough to own ocean-front property. You can drive for miles and seldom catch a glimpse of the water. In California, beach panoramas and coastal scenes belong to everyone. Furthermore, the population is a fraction of that along the heavily settled New England coast. Instead of one town or village over-lapping the other, Northern California spaces its settlements apart by miles of green fields, forests, and ocean cliffs.

Another feature that makes Mendocino/Redwood Coast unique is the juxtaposition of ocean, mountains, and redwood trees. You can gaze out on a magnificent shoreline, with the thundering Pacific crashing against a rocky shore—then do an about-face to take in the majesty of the tallest trees in the world, with the Trinity Alps looming in the background. The region's trademark is a profusion of ancient redwood trees (*Sequoia sempervirens*). Direct descendants of trees that thrived when dinosaurs walked the earth, these magnificent giants are found today only on the northern Pacific coast and in certain mountainous regions of China. You'll walk in the shade of trees that were already a thousand years old when Columbus was bumbling about the Caribbean, thinking that he'd found India. Standing proudly through drought, fire, and storms, the trees seem to be almost indestructible. John Steinbeck once wrote, "The redwoods, once seen, leave a mark or create a vision that stays with you always. It's not only their unbelievable stature, nor the color which seems to shift and vary under your eyes. No, they are not like any trees we know; they are ambassadors from another time."

If you are members of that class that hates hot summers and cold winters, you'll find your Shangri-la here. Frost is all but unheard of; forty degrees is just about as cold as it ever gets in January. Highs in January—in Eureka, for example—average fifty-three degrees, but the July and August highs often don't even reach seventy degrees! Compare that with your hometown's average July temperatures. Every night of the year you will sleep under blankets; an air conditioner would be a waste of money.

Gualala

After you cross the Golden Gate Bridge going north, U.S. Highway 1 winds around through some of the most peaceful and rural landscapes to be found anywhere. A few miles north of San Francisco, the communities become small, neighborly, and uncrowded. The only large town on the entire Mendocino/Redwood coast is Eureka, and even here the population is less than 30,000.

The southern edge of this coastal wonderland is a series of picturesque villages and towns scattered along the coast, interspersed with forest and grazing land—sleepy and laid-back, just as they should be. From south to north, these are the villages of Gualala, Anchor Bay, Point Arena, Manchester, Irish Beach, Elk, Albion, Little River, Mendocino, Caspar, Fort Bragg, Cleone, and Westport. If you prefer warmer weather, a short drive inland takes you to Comptche and the wine- and apple-growing Anderson Valley towns of Philo and Boonville.

The region isn't as well known for its wine-tasting rooms as the Napa-Sonoma wine country, but five family-owned wineries are in operation within 11 miles of each other. It makes for an interesting setting: the Pacific Ocean on one side and coastal mountains on the other. The traditional industry here has always been lumbering, which appears to be in a permanent state of depression all over the West. The second industry is fishing, also with its ups and downs; most fishing is done for sport today. Since neither industry hires new workers, jobs became scarce for a while and younger people were leaving for the cities. Housing became exceptionally affordable. However, the slack has been more than taken up by retirees and others moving here. Lumbering and fishing pursuits have been replaced by service jobs. To the north, the first community that can properly be considered part of this Mendocino/Redwood Coast region is the town of Gualala.

The espresso bar in Gualala (qwa-LA-la) sells a commuter mug to tourists—the slogan on its side reads, "Gualala, California, No Fast Way to 101." And that seems to sum up what Gualala and the surrounding communities of Sea Ranch and Point Arena are about. With a minimum driving time of two and one-half hours to San Francisco and one and one-half hours to Ukiah or Santa Rosa, these communities depend upon themselves and the beauties of local nature for the structure and activities that keep them occupied.

That isn't to say that life is not full in these towns along the Sonoma-Mendocino coastline. One resident said, "The first thing you learn here is to not volunteer. Of course, by the time you learn it, it's too late." But that, she said, is what living in a community like Gualala is all about.

Indeed, that seems to be the area's feeling. Volunteering for Gualala Arts, the heart of the community's cultural life, brings many of the locals together, as does the library in Point Arena, a branch of the Mendocino County library system.

The town is located just north of the mouth of the Gualala River. Its name comes from the Pomo Indians, who called the area *qh-a'la-oli*, meaning "water-coming-down-place." Point Arena's protrusion into the Pacific acts as a protector of the area's coast, creating a calmer and slightly warmer oceanside by deflecting the Alaskan current westward. That difference made it a place for settling; at various times in the past 200 years, the Russians and Spanish inhabited the land until the United States took over. Until the 1960s, Gualala was a mill town where loggers brought their felled redwoods. Today the mills are gone, but an artist's colony helps keep the area's economy strong.

Recreation and Culture

Gualala Arts began years ago when local artists started to exhibit their works by hanging them on the redwood trees. Today the group has a gallery store (The Dolphin), and it has just opened the Gualala Arts Center, a cultural focal point for northern Sonoma and southern Mendocino communities. Chamber concerts, folk music presentations, and film series are regularly scheduled, and the Symphony of the Redwoods performs twice a year. Recent renovations at the movie theater in Point Arena make the evening out more comfortable. There are a number of good restaurants along the coast and wineries in the Anderson Valley and Lake Valley areas. Farther away, but still accessible, are two casinos on Native American land.

The beautiful coastline with its mountain backdrop not only catches the breath of the residents, it draws them close. Its ruggedness makes swimming in the ocean impossible, but there are a series of regional beach areas designed for walking, searching tidepools, hiking, and observing. Swimming is done at "The Hole" on the Gualala River. Surf fishing is plentiful, and fishing at the Point Arena public fishing pier is a regular event. There is a public golf course at Sea Ranch and tennis at various clubs in the area.

Real Estate

A two- or three-bedroom, two-bath house in Gualala costs between $200,000 and $250,000. In Point Arena, prices range from $150,000 to

$200,000. Houses in Sea Ranch are available in the same price range.

Medical Care

Gualala and its surrounding area are not places to move if you are not in generally good health. Since the county provides little public transportation, you must be able to get around the area on your own: walking or driving. Although primary medical care is provided locally, you must travel to the hospitals in Fort Bragg and Ukiah for additional care. Medical emergency cases are usually flown by air ambulance to Santa Rosa, where there are state-of-the-art hospitals. Many residents say that they would consider moving from the area if their health deteriorated.

When Grandkids Visit

Outdoor activities are the biggest attraction in the area. There are plenty of regional parks along the coast for walking, but the water is too cold for swimming without a wet suit. The winds are strong, so kite flying is a great activity. Surfers can be found riding the waves at the Point Arena pier where others cast their lines. Canoes, kayaks, and bicycles are available to rent, as are horses owned privately at Sea Ranch.

Two movies are shown daily at the recently renovated theater in Point Arena, and events are held regularly at the Gualala Arts Center, in Point Arena, and in Fort Bragg. The Point Arena Lighthouse and Museum is open to the public.

Addresses and Connections

Chamber of Commerce: There is no chamber of commerce in Gualala.

Senior Center: 140 Main Street, Point Arena, CA 95468

Newspaper: The Observer, 38500 Highway 1, Gualala, CA 95445; *Santa Rosa Press-Democrat*, Box 910, Santa Rosa, CA 95402

Airport: There are small airports in Ukiah and Gualala, but to fly any distance, it is necessary to depart from Santa Rosa or San Francisco International Airports.

Bus/Train: Bus service is provided by Mendocino Transit Authority. Daily buses from these communities to Santa Rosa, as well as daily local services, are available, but these buses run only once a day in each direction.

Internet: http://www.yahoo.com/Regional/U_S_States/California/Cities/Gualala

Gualala/Sea Ranch/Point Arena Weather

	JAN.	APR.	JUL.	OCT.	RAIN	SNOW
		In degrees Fahrenheit				
DAILY HIGHS	56	59	66	66	41"	—
DAILY LOWS	39	42	50	46		

Mendocino/Fort Bragg

Two towns, only about 10 miles apart, form the population centers of the Mendocino Coast: Fort Bragg and Mendocino. Fort Bragg, a lumbering and fishing community, is the largest, with a little more than 6,000 residents. Its no-nonsense business section makes it the place where people come for necessary services and shopping. It's an exceptionally clean and attractive town, more modern in appearance than Mendocino.

Mendocino is much smaller, an unincorporated village of approximately 1,100 residents—although there are more than 8,000 people living in the surrounding area. It sits high on a bluff, surrounded on three sides by the Pacific Ocean, and is popular with tourists and those looking for beautiful seascapes. Many businesses here deal with art in one form or another. Mendocino has attracted a community of artisans, evident by the many art galleries and boutiques in the town.

Mendocino, Fort Bragg, and nearby villages are popular with those looking for quality living in a rural, cool (but not cold) climate. The cost of living here is a bit higher than the statewide average, partly because of the transportation involved in bringing goods and services to the area, and partly because of its popularity as a place to live. Unemployment is also higher because of the seasonal nature of the job market.

Recreation and Culture

A branch campus of the College of the Redwoods brings continuing education to the community. It's specially known for its fine woodworking courses, sought after by hobbiest and artist alike. The communities here are proud of the colony of artists and artisans whose work is exhibited in numerous galleries, featured both in Fort Bragg and Mendocino.

Community theater is produced by the Mendocino Theater Company, regional theater by Warehouse Repertory Theatre, and musicals and reviews by the Gloriana Opera Company. Fine local musicians perform at the Fort Bragg Center for the Arts, Opus Concerts, Symphony of the Redwoods, and the July Mendocino Music Festival.

Real Estate

Mendocino housing prices are not as expensive as you might expect, but they aren't at bargain levels because the quality is above average. Small homes begin in the $175,000 range, with upper-end places selling around $400,000. Rents range from $400 to $900. Housing costs in Fort Bragg are in line with local wages, thus less expensive than Mendocino. Home prices typically start in the $130,000 range, with very nice places going for $350,000 and up. Mendocino rents range from $600 to $1,200, with ocean-view properties $1,200 plus. Both communities are attracting retirees as well as artisans, many coming from the San Francisco and Los Angeles areas.

Medical Care

The Mendocino Coast District Hospital in Fort Bragg is a fully licensed, fifty-four-bed, acute-care, nonprofit community hospital. The hospital has more than thirty physicians on staff representing many medical specialities. The hospital operates an ambulance service with air service for emergency transfer.

When Grandkids Visit

Kids will enjoy a ride on the Skunk Train, which features seventy-year-old passenger coaches and an authentic steam engine puffing and chugging along. You'll all enjoy the scenic 40-mile trip through redwood groves, on bridges across the Noyo River, and through two tunnels.

Addresses and Connections

Chamber of Commerce: 490 North Harold Street, Fort Bragg, CA 95437

Senior Services: P.O. Box 686, Fort Bragg, CA 95437

Newspaper: Fort Bragg Advocate News, 450 North Franklin Street, Fort Bragg, CA 95437–3210; *Mendocino Beacon,* P.O. Box 225, Mendocino, CA 95460

Airport: No local air connections

Bus/Train: Local bus service along the coast and to Ukiah for connections with Greyhound

Internet: http://www.mendocinocoast.com/

Mendocino/Fort Bragg Weather

	JAN.	APR.	JUL.	OCT.	RAIN	SNOW
		In degrees Fahrenheit				
DAILY HIGHS	55	59	64	63	39"	0.2"
DAILY LOWS	40	43	49	47		

Ukiah

Not exactly on the sea coast—actually about 40 miles from the ocean—Ukiah is definitely part of the North Coast country. Surrounded by mountains, redwoods, and wineries, Ukiah has much to offer retirees. A central location for Northern California—110 miles from San Francisco, 150 miles from Sacramento, and 160 miles from Eureka—Ukiah offers access to a variety of day trips while making life comfortable for its residents.

The climate in this valley is mild. Temperatures are moderate, with warm days and cool nights most of the year. Unlike the towns along the coast and in the coastal mountain range, Ukiah gets little or no morning or evening fog.

The forests of redwoods are dense and thick. Many of the trees are protected by the state and federal governments. Rows of grapevines growing in the fields are a testament to the fertility of the land.

Unlike Santa Rosa, which is still a bedroom community to San Francisco and continues to outgrow its infrastructure, Ukiah is free of the metropolitan area lifestyle and relatively stable in its population of 15,000. The unincorporated area grows at a pace of about 3 percent, and at present another 20,000 people live in that part of the valley.

Recreation and Culture

Ukiah has all the trappings of a city—restaurants, movies, concerts, theater, and a museum—yet maintains the air of a smaller town. The downtown houses and buildings look pristine.

A wide variety of outdoor activities is provided by Lake Mendocino, nearby mountains and forests, and city, county, and state parks. To the north of the city, Lake Mendocino has many campsites and picnic areas. Walking and hiking trails take you into the low mountains. There are two boat-launching ramps, a marina, and a protected beach for safe swimming.

The city of Ukiah and the county of Mendocino have developed several parks closer to home. Each one is different, and all offer a variety of activity sites, including a swimming pool, tennis courts, playing fields, basketball and volleyball courts, and walking, running, and hiking trails. There is a municipal golf course, a driving range, a skating rink, and a bowling alley, as well as health and fitness centers throughout the area.

The Sun House–Grace Hudson Museum features the works of Grace Carpenter Hudson, exhibits on Pomo Indian history and culture, and other artifacts and objects from the Carpenter-Hudson family collection. The Pomo Cultural Center near Lake Mendocino provides a more detailed view of the Native Americans who lived and prospered the valley area until the European-American settlements.

Ukiah is rich in local artistic talent. The Mendocino Ballet, Ukiah Symphony, Ukiah Players Theatre, Ukiah Community Concert Association, Ukiah Civic Light Opera, and the local colleges keep the area's residents in touch with cultural life from around the world.

To round things out, there are movie theaters, six local radio stations, and cable television. Restaurants offer many different types of food, and there are cafes and coffeehouses. And, for those who like to gamble, two casinos are within driving distance on Native American land.

Lastly, there are the wineries of the Ukiah and Anderson Valleys. Routes 101 and 128 afford the wine enthusiast a pleasure romp through both large and small vineyards that offer their products for tasting.

Real Estate

Ukiah has a good supply of homes available from $100,000 to $350,000. Three-bedroom homes with views or extra land start at prices of about $200,000. Homes rent for an average of $800, and apartments are available from $550 up.

Medical Care

The area is served by the Ukiah Valley Medical Center, with doctors and staff in twenty-one specialties. For more complicated health situations, Santa Rosa hospitals are about an hour away. For alternative and holistic solutions to health care, the Ukiah–Santa Rosa area has many offerings as well.

When Grandkids Visit

The outdoors is the thing in the Ukiah Valley. Lake Mendocino is a regular stop for the grandkids, as well as the local parks with their variety of sports and game activities. Bicycling is also available. Movies in theaters and on tape are available for indoor entertainment, along with more physical fun at the bowling alley. The museums are an attraction, too. Trips to the coast offer different views and more areas to explore. And in two hours you can be in San Francisco for a day trip to its many sights.

Addresses and Connections

Chamber of Commerce: 200 South School Street, Ukiah, CA 95482

Senior Center: 499 Leslie Street, Ukiah, CA 95482

Newspaper: Ukiah Daily Journal, 590 South School Street, Ukiah, CA 95482; *Santa Rosa Press-Democrat,* 427 Mendocino Avenue, Santa Rosa, CA 95401

Airport: Ukiah has a small general aviation airport, but for commercial flights, locals travel to Santa Rosa for a short commuter flight, then on to San Francisco or Oakland.

Bus/Train: The Mendocino Transit Authority offers both regular bus service throughout the day and Dial-A-Ride, a door-to-door service. Greyhound links Ukiah to the world by bus.

Internet: http://www.ukiah.ca.us
http://relo-usa.com/california/ukiah/

Ukiah Weather

	JAN.	APR.	JUL.	OCT.	RAIN	SNOW
		In degrees Fahrenheit				
DAILY HIGHS	58	70	92	78	38"	—
DAILY LOWS	36	42	55	46		

Fortuna

Fortuna was established in the late 1800s as a farming and lumber community. Its growth was slow and steady, without the proliferation of Victorians that marks Eureka, Ferndale, and other Mendocino/Redwood towns. With plenty of open space and ample land for new housing, Fortuna has matured gracefully; its scenic, rural atmosphere makes for a pleasantly quiet place to live. Situated a few miles inland from the ocean, Fortuna is slightly warmer than towns right on the ocean. Tall redwood trees are scattered throughout its residential districts.

With a population of approximately 10,000, Fortuna is large enough for all services yet basically a small town. The homey business district offers a diverse choice of shopping.

Recreation and Culture

The Fortuna Concert Series offers a wonderfully eclectic selection of programs that include classical, folk, jazz, and ethnic music. Performances are given in a newly restored facility, known for its warmth, intimacy, and acoustics. It has become a favorite of local and regional professional musicians, making for musical events that delight audiences and performers alike. Just 8 miles north of Fortuna is the College of the Redwoods, an outstanding community college.

Real Estate

One of the benefits of living in Fortuna is the wide range of housing. Prices go from $95,000 for a small home to $250,000 for a spacious one with a spectacular view of the Eel River Valley and surrounding mountains. One- and two-bedroom apartments rent from $400 to $650 a month, and homes rent from $600 to $1,000 a month.

Medical Care

The forty-seven-bed Redwood Memorial Hospital serves the southern portion of Humboldt County. The facility has a twenty-four-hour emergency department. St. Luke Manor, a convalescent hospital with eleven beds is located on Newburg Road. Fortuna has thirty physicians, two optometrists, four dentists, three chiropractors, and an ambulance service.

When Grandkids Visit

You must take your grandchildren on a drive through the Avenue of the Giants. Famous for its towering trees, the Avenue of the Giants and the Humboldt Redwoods State Park area is home to the world's largest grove of old-growth redwoods. More than 700,000 people pilgrimage to the Humboldt Redwoods State Park every year to commune among the cathedral-like giants. Several small communities dot the Avenue of the Giants, any one of which would make interesting retirement—in the country but near civilization. The towns include (from the north) Pepperwood, Shively, Redcrest, Dyerville, Weott, Myers Flat, Miranda, and Phillipsville.

Addresses and Connections

Chamber of Commerce: 735 Fourteenth Street, Fortuna, CA 95540
Senior Center: 2130 Smith Lane, Fortuna, CA 95540

Newspaper: Humboldt Beacon, 928 Main Street, Fortuna, CA 95540
Airport: Eureka/Arcata Airport, 30 miles north
Bus/Train: Countywide bus service; Greyhound
Internet: None available.

Fortuna Weather

	JAN.	APR.	JUL.	OCT.	RAIN	SNOW
		In degrees Fahrenheit				
DAILY HIGHS	55	66	86	76	52"	.02"
DAILY LOWS	36	42	53	43		

Ferndale

The Victorian village of Ferndale, settled in 1852, has the distinction of being the westernmost incorporated city in the continental United States. But Ferndale's real claim to fame is that the entire town is a virtual museum of Victorian architecture. Today, with a population of about 1,500, Ferndale is probably the same size as it was in its heyday at the turn of the century. The village is located 5 miles west of Highway 101 across an 86-year-old bridge known as Fernbridge, one of the longest concrete arch spans ever built and one of only two in the world still in use.

Ferndale's first residents were prosperous dairy farmers who established the town in the late 1800s. Then, as now, this was a thriving dairy center. Wealthy dairy farmers spared no expense to build splendidly ornate homes, layered with gingerbread, scallops, gables, and turrets; they were humorously described as "Butterfat Palaces." Ferndale appeared to have a bright future. It was situated on a main north-south road and was the commercial center for the region. But the town's heyday ended in the early 1900s when Ferndale was bypassed by both the railroad and what today is Highway 101. Left as an isolated village, Ferndale began to deteriorate. Empty store windows became ubiquitous, and commerce all but ceased. A destructive flood in 1964 just about finished Ferndale's already moribund business district.

When the waters subsided, it seemed only logical and cost-effective to replace the old Victorian buildings with something more modern.

But a spunky descendant of one of the village's oldest families, Viola Russ McBride, protested. She refused to allow the town to be "improved." A rancher, artist, and tireless activist, Viola single-handedly saved Ferndale from historic desecration. She began buying up abandoned Victorians and championing villagewide restoration efforts. She convinced local artists and crafters of the potential for their endeavors here. She helped them set up studios and galleries in vacant buildings. Eventually the community realized the wisdom in her ways and joined in enthusiastically. Today the beautiful Queen Anne, Carpenter Gothic, and Eastlake Stick–style buildings have been restored to pristine, original condition, complete with "butterfat" trim. Viola McBride died in 1996 at the age of 90, justifiably proud of her accomplishments and delighted to see Ferndale's Main Street district listed on the National Register of Historic Places. The entire village is a state-designated historical landmark.

As a tourist attraction, Ferndale is mostly a "stop-for-lunch, look-around, and get-going-again" sort of place. But retirees find it a great location for a longer stay. They like its small-town atmosphere, artistic ambience, and neighborliness. The village is located in a flat valley bordered by the Eel River on the north, the ocean on the southwest, and mountains in the east. About forty dairy farms are located in the valley, maintaining herds of between 10 and 300 cows. These farmers send their milk to the cooperative Humboldt Creamery in Fernbridge, which produces Challenge Brand milks and butter, as well as ice creams under a variety of brand names.

Recreation and Culture

Some of the village's delights include three art galleries, working artists' studios, and crafts displays. The Ferndale Repertory Theatre, Humboldt County's oldest and largest theater company, offers comedies, mysteries, and dramas year-round. Ferndale Museum, a local history museum, displays a permanent collection of farm equipment and a floating exhibition of Victorian rooms.

Medical Care

The nearest hospitals are Redwood Memorial in Fortuna and St. Joseph and General Hospitals in Eureka. Humboldt Medical Group maintains offices in Ferndale and Fortuna.

Real Estate

An ample supply of homes is available, ranging in price from $100,000 to $175,000. These prices include a good sampling of Victorian-style houses. Older two- and three-bedroom homes near the downtown area sell from $155,000. Homes in private settings sell for up to $400,000.

When Grandkids Visit

Try to have your granchildren's visit coincide with the regionally famous Kinetic Sculpture Race. Wonderfully imaginative, self-propelled vehicles—made of papier mâché, bicycle parts, whatever is handy—run a mock race down Main Street. The true talent of the artists blossoms in these sculptures; the colors and designs are at the same time hilarious and beautiful. A good time is guaranteed to all.

Addresses and Connections

Chamber of Commerce: P.O. Box 325, Ferndale, CA 95536
Senior Center: None available in town.
Newspaper: Eureka Times Standard, 930 Sixth Street, Eureka, CA 95501–1112
Airport: Eureka/Arcata Airport, 32 miles
Bus/Train: Greyhound in Fortuna, 10 miles
Internet: None available.

Ferndale Weather

	JAN.	APR.	JUL.	OCT.	RAIN	SNOW
		In degrees Fahrenheit				
DAILY HIGHS	55	66	86	76	52"	.02"
DAILY LOWS	36	42	53	43		

Eureka

Eureka is yet another town with Gold Rush origins, beginning its picturesque history in 1850. The town's location on Humboldt Bay made it an ideal port to supply the mines in the nearby Trinity Mountains. Eureka flourished overnight as gold seekers poured off the ships, fresh from San Francisco and eager for riches. When the gold fields played out, many prospectors stayed on; they found steady work as fishermen, farmers, and lumberjacks.

The region's stately redwoods became the backbone of the economy in the late 1800s. Victorian homes built of this almost indestructible lumber grace the landscape of Eureka and surrounding communities, as well as the Victorian neighborhoods of San Francisco. Eureka's beautifully constructed homes are showcases for now-forgotten arts of carpentry. Tools and techniques are no longer available to replicate these gems. Since some early settlers were lumber barons, you can imagine the care and attention to detail with which the artisans constructed the homes. For this reason, Eureka has been declared a state historical landmark.

Humboldt Bay fishing highlights Eureka's economy nowadays. More than 300 fishing vessels call this home port and land more rockfish, crab, oysters, and shrimp than any other port in California. Strolling along Eureka's quaint Old Town waterfront is a favorite activity, breathing in the fresh sea air, watching boats returning with catches of salmon and tasty Dungeness crab.

Although its population is less than 30,000, Eureka is the center, culturally and commercially, of another 45,000 residents in the immediate urban area. Approximately 86 percent of Humboldt County's 119,000 population lives within a 20-mile radius of Eureka. The famous Redwood Empire forests begin near the edge of town and climb the mountains beyond and into the Trinity Alps, with backdrops as high as 6,000 feet. This is a place where mountains, forest, and blue Pacific all come together. Although this is primarily a mountainous region encompassing six wild and scenic river systems and stands of majestic redwood groves, Eureka itself is located on a level coastal plain. Eighty percent of the county consists of forested, public lands.

The weather here, typical of beach towns along the Northern California and Oregon coasts, north to Washington, is ideal for retirees who hate the thought of either hot, steamy summers or icy, frigid winters. Except for more rain in the winter months, there's little difference in the weather year-round. A sweater is necessary almost every evening of the year, and noonday weather is seldom, if ever, hot enough to make you sweat. Air-conditioning is something people here only read about. Winters are mild enough that many homes heat with fireplaces or wood stoves. Many older houses have fireplaces in every room. Rainfall here is around 38 inches, a lot for California but much less than most midwestern and eastern cities receive. Snow shovels are as unnecessary as air-conditioning.

Located on Highway 101, a main north-south artery, the Eureka area also has an airport with regional carriers for short flights to San Francisco and other important local cities. The airport is located a few miles north of Arcata, about 15 miles from Eureka, and is served by a bus shuttle.

The Eureka Senior Center, housed in an old grammar school building, is one of the most extensive and comprehensive around. From classes such as arts and crafts to an Alzheimer's day-care center, the services are superb. An excellent volunteer program here counts on more than 700 retirees who contribute their skills and interests in service to the community.

Recreation and Culture

Fishing, of course, is a favorite sport here, with salmon, albacore, and Dungeness crab the catches. Eureka's generally benign weather makes fishing, crabbing, or clamming possible all year. For those who get seasick, the country immediately behind the town, continuing 100 miles or so, is full of great trout streams. Deer, river otters, herons, and other wildlife are plentiful; much of the Coast Range and inland Klamath Mountains are carefully preserved as wildlife areas.

Eureka's College of the Redwoods, a two-year school, and Eureka Adult School, with many community locations, complement the academic atmosphere created by nearby Humboldt State University.

Real Estate

Along this northern coast, all the way to the state of Washington, low wages and living costs are the rule. As a result, housing is quite reasonable—probably as low as you might expect to find anywhere on the West Coast. It's not difficult to find homes selling for $60,000 or less. For $75,000 and up you can buy a new place. We looked at several Victorians—our favorite had high ceilings, a claw-foot bathtub, an antique wood cookstove, and three bedrooms—going for the price of a tract home in some California communities. Away from the city limits and zoning restrictions, a mobile home can be located on a spacious, wooded lot for economical housing.

Medical Care

Three excellent hospitals serve the area, one each for Eureka and the neighboring communities of Arcata and Fortuna. Arcata hospital can boast that its staff makes house calls, since it operates a home-care program for those who need ongoing treatment outside the hospital. The service is carried out by registered nurses, home health aides, and physical therapists under the direction of a physician.

When Grandkids Visit

Take the kids on a fishing excursion in Humboldt Bay. The more than 300 fishing vessels that make Eureka their home berth land more rockfish, Dungeness crab, salmon, shrimp, and oysters than any other region in California. You ought to be able to catch your share. But if you have a tendency to become seasick, you can take the kids for a slow walk along a secluded beach or enjoy a picnic in the shade of a 2,000-year-old redwood tree.

Addresses and Connections

Chamber of Commerce: 2112 Broadway, Eureka, CA 95501
Senior Center: 1910 California Street, Eureka, CA 95501
Newspaper: Times Standard, 930 Sixth Street, Eureka, CA 95501–1112
Airport: Arcata/Eureka Airport, 15 miles
Bus/Train: Greyhound; Mad River Transit System (regional)
Internet: http://www.eurekachamber.com
http://www.tidepool.com/arcatacity/hello.html

Eureka Weather

	JAN.	APR.	JUL.	OCT.	RAIN	SNOW
		In degrees Fahrenheit				
DAILY HIGHS	53	55	61	60	39"	0.2"
DAILY LOWS	42	44	52	48		

Arcata

Established in 1850—the same time as Eureka—the town of Arcata sits on Humboldt Bay about 5 miles north of Eureka. Bret Harte put in a brief stint as editor on the local newspaper here, until some local toughs took exception to his writing. Discretion being the better part of valor, Harte hopped a coastal steamer for San Francisco, where he began publishing his fascinating stories of life in California's mining camps.

Today Arcata is a captivating university town with a complementary blend of traditional and alternative lifestyles. This is the home of Humboldt State University, recognized as one of the top schools in California's educational system. The university is one of the area's economic mainstays and shares frequent cultural and intellectual events with the general public. Arcata's population is 17,000, not counting a student population of several thousand.

Like Eureka, Arcata has been successful in preserving, restoring, and revitalizing the town's many historical structures. A good example of this is Arcata Plaza, centrally located in Arcata's downtown. Surrounded by shops and restaurants located in historic buildings, the plaza is landscaped with flower beds and shrubbery. Park benches invite sitting, people watching, or snacking. Arcata Plaza is also the location of an openair farmers market. On late Tuesday afternoons and Saturday mornings from May to November, the plaza brims over with a full range of fresh fruits and vegetables.

As a tribute to Arcata's early years, when redwood lumber was the backbone of the economy, the city is proud of its Community Forest/Redwood Park. This 575-acre forest of majestic redwood trees is within the city limits, just a two-minute drive from downtown. The park offers nearly 10 miles of trails for hikers, bicyclists, and horseback riders.

Historic Trinidad Beach and Harbor, the location of Humboldt State's renowned marine laboratory, is home to a fleet of commercial fishing boats. The tiny village is situated 15 miles north of Arcata and has a population of 400. The Trinidad State Beach offers miles of undisturbed sand for long walks, as well as numerous, interesting tidepools to explore.

Recreation and Culture

In addition to several art galleries, many restaurants, businesses, and government offices proudly display the work of local artists. Humboldt State presents art exhibits as well and also brings world-class theatrical, musical, and sports events to the community. Arcata is also home to the Humboldt Light Opera Company.

As in other communities in the region, residents here have year-round access to outdoor activities such as fishing, beachcombing, hiking, bicycling, bird-watching, golfing, and tennis. Arcata also has its own semi-pro baseball team, the Humboldt Crabs. Games are played throughout the summer at the Arcata Ballpark.

Real Estate

Arcata's popularity as a place to live has caused demands for housing to exceed supplies in recent years. In spite of more than one hundred new housing units constructed each year, vacancy rates remain low. The median sales price for a home in Arcata in 1997 was $114,900, 4.5 percent higher than the county median of $110,000. Average rent for a two-bedroom apartment is $520.

Medical Care

Arcata's health-care center is the Mad River Community Hospital. A fully accredited facility, it boasts a full range of medical practitioners. Twenty-four-hour emergency care is provided at Mad River Community Hospital.

When Grandkids Visit

Humboldt State University's natural history museum, centrally located near downtown Arcata, provides an extensive fossil collection and exhibits of California fauna and flora that prove interesting for all ages.

Addresses and Connections

Chamber of Commerce: (Arcata) 1062 G Street, Arcata, CA 95521; (Trinidad) P.O. Box 356, Trinidad, CA 95570

Senior Center: 1910 14th Street, Arcata, CA 95521

Newspaper: The Lumberjack (weekly), Humboldt State University, Arcata, CA 95521; *The Union* (weekly), 613 H Street Arcata, CA 95521

Airport: Arcata/Eureka airport, 8 miles north

Bus/Train: Greyhound; Arcata and Mad River Transit System (city); interconnected city and county lines at Arcata's Transit Center

Internet: http://www.arcata.com

Arcata Weather

	JAN.	APR.	JUL.	OCT.	RAIN	SNOW
		In degrees Fahrenheit				
DAILY HIGHS	53	55	61	60	39"	0.2"
DAILY LOWS	42	44	52	48		

Crescent City

This is Redwood Country galore, with a rugged Pacific coastline combining with the world's tallest trees to make this region one of the nation's most enchanting areas. Near the California-Oregon border is Crescent City, California's northernmost coastal town.

Like other north coast locations, Crescent City experiences cool summers and mild winters with almost no freezing weather. There's more rain, however, with precipitation matching the nearby Oregon south coast, and, oddly enough, Crescent City is warmer than nearby coastal towns. The chamber of commerce advertises the region as Oregon's "Banana Belt" because of its warmer temperatures, which are caused by a phenomenon called the Brookings effect. This has to do with a complicated system of wind patterns, air compression, and other factors (none of which sounds at all plausible). Yet there's no question that Crescent City enjoys warmer summers than locations much farther south. Eureka, for example, is six degrees cooler in the summer. If it's warmer weather you want, just go a few miles inland, to places like Willow Creek, and you can find one-hundred-degree days to bask in.

For the most part, Crescent City is a no-frills fishing town. Shopping is adequate and there are some nice restaurants, but it lacks the charm of Arcata and Eureka. A few years ago, a tremendous tidal wave destroyed some of the low-lying neighborhoods.

Recreation and Culture

In addition to unequalled scenery, year-round activities abound. Hiking, beachcombing, camping, and fishing offer rewarding outdoor experiences. You can join in the fun at the winter crab races, a summer seafood festival, and other annual celebrations.

Elk Valley Casino is an Indian gaming establishment with blackjack, poker, and slot machines. The good news is that the casino is open twenty-four hours a day to receive your money. The bad news is they don't serve drinks—no liquor license.

The College of the Redwoods Del Norte has an excellent offering of adult classes that cover subjects such as basic gardening, Italian cuisine, and beginning guitar. An internet class in detective fiction was recently offered. The Del Norte Association for Cultural Awareness brings Crescent City its measure of drama, musicals, and comedy.

Real Estate

Real estate prices are among the lowest in the state. You'll have your choice of a wide range of homes, from places in town starting in the mid-$60,000 range to more expensive lakeside properties in the $180,000 bracket. A few outstanding homes with views and deluxe amenities are available between $300,000 and $350,000.

Medical Care

Sutter Coast Hospital offers inpatient services that include general medicine, surgery, and twenty-four-hour emergency service. With forty-seven beds and state-of-the-art testing and treatment services, Sutter Coast Hospital has become the focus of health care for the region. There are also ten doctors attending to family practice health needs.

When Grandkids Visit

Take your grandchildren elk watching. The redwood region abounds in enormous Roosevelt elks, with bulls weighing as much as 1,200 pounds. Be content to watch them from afar, for the males can become aggressive when guarding the cow elk harems. One of the most popular elk-watching spots is at Prairie Creek Redwoods State Park, along the highway south of Crescent City. As many as thirty cow elk can be seen grazing along here.

Addresses and Connections

Chamber of Commerce: 1001 Front Street, Crescent City, CA 95531
Senior Center: 810 H Street, Crescent City, CA 95531
Newspaper: Triplicate, 312 H Street, Crescent City, CA 95531
Airport: Arcata/Eureka airport, 83 miles south
Bus/Train: Redwood Coast Transit provides local transportation in Crescent and south to Klamath and Klamath Glen. There is also Greyhound service.
Internet: None available.

Crescent City Weather

	JAN.	APR.	JUL.	OCT.	RAIN	SNOW
		In degrees	Fahrenheit			
DAILY HIGHS	52	58	66	64	65"	0.2"
DAILY LOWS	40	43	51	55		

THE NORTHERN
MOUNTAINS

THE NORTHERN MOUNTAINS

One of the nation's most beautiful mountain domains occupies the north and northeastern portions of California. Known as the Shasta Cascade region, it covers more than 30,000 square miles, an area roughly the size of Ohio. Beginning with the foothill city of Redding, north to the Oregon border and east to the Nevada border, the Shasta Cascade region enthralls residents with breathtaking vistas, towering mountains, volcanoes, artesian hot springs, glaciers, waterfalls, white-water rivers, dense forests, and sky-blue lakes. Seven national forests and eight national and state parks make the outdoors very much a public affair here. The major landmarks are the Trinity Alps and the California Cascade Range with two giant glaciated volcanoes: dormant Mount Shasta and the still-active Mount Lassen.

California's northern mountains start at the upper end of the Sacramento Valley, where the scenery changes rather quickly from flat fields of wheat, rice, and grassy pasture to steep mountains. At Redding, the serious foothills begin—rolling at first, then becoming steeper as the Siskiyou Range looms ahead. The ever-present, snow-covered Mount Shasta creates a gorgeous backdrop as you enter the Shasta Cascade Mountains.

Natives here are known to be independent and sometimes chafe at having legislators from Los Angeles and San Francisco making rules for those in the mountain regions. As a way of protest, residents of these towns often talk of seceding from California and forming their own state of Jefferson. They actually did this for a short time—not seriously—just to draw attention to their grievances. The protesters named the town of Yreka as the capital of Jefferson. A local judge was sworn in as governor—in a tongue-in-cheek ceremony—on December 4, 1941. His term of office ended three days later when Pearl Harbor was bombed.

Redding

A city of some 79,000 inhabitants, Redding is the state's largest city north of Sacramento, yet it somehow manages to retain the ambience of a small town. As the shopping and commercial center for a large number of valley and mountain towns, Redding has an unusually large collection of malls, outlets, chain stores, and businesses. Redding has earned a reputation of a safe community with an excellent quality of life. FBI statistics show Redding ranks very favorably in personal safety.

Approximately 222 miles north of San Francisco and 160 miles from Sacramento, Redding sits at the extreme north end of the Sacramento Valley and forms a transition between traditional California and the mountain kingdom of Shasta Cascade. Palm trees grow in Redding—California's northernmost place where palm trees thrive—framed by a background of snow-covered volcano peaks and forested mountain slopes.

People here refer to Redding as the gateway to the northern mountain wonderlands. And it is true: Interstate 5, out of Redding, is the only direct entrance to the Shasta Cascade region, and nearby recreational opportunities are boundless. A short drive takes you to any number of activities that can be enjoyed for the day, and you can return in time for dinner. Within a 70-mile radius of Redding are such natural treasures as Lassen Volcanic National Park, Mount Shasta, Castle Craggs State Park, and Burney Falls. Nearby lakes include Whiskeytown, Shasta, and Trinity.

Most rainfall here, which averages 33 inches annually, occurs in late fall and winter. Temperatures rarely drop below freezing. Snowfall, although abundant in the higher elevations north of the city, is rare in Redding, which has an elevation of only 600 feet.

Recreation and Culture

The Sacramento River winds its way through town, leisurely now, after its frantic dash down mountain canyons on the way to San Francisco. The river offers both fishing and boating fun. Redding's unique Sacramento River Trail is a great place to jog, bike, or take a relaxing river stroll through the heart of Redding's downtown. From house boating to mountain climbing, backpacking to cave exploring, gold panning to skiing, any kind of outdoor sport imaginable can be enjoyed. Did we mention golf, whitewater rafting, and horseback riding?

The Redding Convention Center, which seats more than 2,000, hosts the Community Concert Association, a Broadway series, and concerts by big-name entertainers. Nonprofit organizations such as the Shasta County Arts Council, the Shasta Community Concerts Association, and the Performing Arts Society bring performing artists to Redding throughout the year. Annual events include a jazz festival, rodeo week, air show, and numerous craft fairs. The Shasta Symphony Orchestra, Riverfront Playhouse Theater, and Shasta College Fine Arts also produce shows during the year.

Shasta College is one of the premier institutions in the California community college system. It has as many students as many top-rated universities. The school offers a wide variety of continuing education programs designed for mature and retired students. Shasta College is also one of the largest employers in Redding.

Real Estate

Redding's housing costs, which are among the most reasonable in California, help keep the cost of living down. More than a thousand homes are normally listed for sale, according to the Shasta County Board of Realtors, making Redding a buyer's market. Approximately 40 percent of these are listed at $119,000 or less. The median sales price for a home in Redding is $114,500.

The monthly rental cost for houses ranges from $400 to $1,000; for two-bedroom apartments and duplexes, from $375 to $550. There are also numerous retirement residences and dedicated retirement housing areas.

Medical Care

Redding serves as the health-care center for the region. Three hospitals—Mercy Medical Center, Patients' Hospital of Redding, and Redding Medical Center—have a total of 513 beds. There's also a specialty hospital, one private surgical hospital, and six convalescent hospitals. The city's major hospitals provide state-of-the-art treatment facilities in almost all specialties. Several hospitals have air ambulance service for emergency patients. Redding also has a veterans outpatient clinic and two smaller hospitals. In all, the city is served by 350 physicians (many of whom are specialists), 100 dentists, 36 chiropractors, and 32 optometrists.

When Grandkids Visit

Take a short catamaran ride across to the east shore of the McCloud River arm on Shasta Lake and visit Shasta Caverns, the only privately owned commercial caverns in Northern California. Behind the main falls is a moss-covered wall where countless spouts of sparkling water issue from the rock. Because these limestone and marble tunnels remain a cool fifty-eight degrees, this is an ideal adventure on hot summer days.

Addresses and Connections

Chamber of Commerce: 747 Auditorium Drive, Redding, CA 96001
Senior Services: 2290 Benton Drive, Redding, CA 96003–2152
Newspaper: Record Searchlight, 1101 Twin View Boulevard, Redding, CA 96003–1597
Airport: Redding Municipal Airport
Bus/Train: Local bus service, Greyhound, Amtrak
Internet: http://www.redding-online.com/rec.html

Redding Weather

	JAN.	APR.	JUL.	OCT.	RAIN	SNOW
		In degrees Fahrenheit				
DAILY HIGHS	56	70	99	78	33"	6"
DAILY LOWS	37	48	67	49		

Dunsmuir and Mount Shasta

The Sacramento River, which passes through Redding and Chico on its way to San Francisco Bay, has its origins farther north—past Redding and beautiful Lake Shasta—in the mountains in between the towns of Mount Shasta and Dunsmuir. The drive to and from Redding is one often experienced by residents of these two towns; Redding is the major weekend shopping destination. The highway climbs steeply past gorgeous Lake Shasta and winds through pine-studded mountains with multiple views of the Sacramento River Canyon far below.

Sitting in a steep canyon, **Dunsmuir** is overshadowed by ridges covered with Christmas-tree pines and segmented by streets that climb steeply from river bottom to the interstate highway above town. The town enjoys a spectacular view of snow-covered Mount Shasta in the distance year-round. Its breathtaking beauty dominates the surrounding countryside for miles. Stepping outside first thing in the morning to take in the view is a special delight. Every day the mountain looks just a little different, always spectacular.

Dunsmuir is an old town, with few homes younger than fifty years near the town center. Newer places are tucked away in the woods, on the slopes, or along the river canyon. A sense of history permeates the old-fashioned downtown section, with its one main street. The bus station is still known as the "stage stop" by old-timers, and the Greyhound bus is called the "stage."

Although some mining went on in the area, Dunsmuir originated in 1886 as a roundhouse and repair service for passing trains. Locomotives picked up fuel and water here, and dining cars stocked up on food for the trip north to Portland and Seattle. At one time, if you didn't belong to a railroad family, you were considered an outsider. Even today, 10 percent of the town's 2,300 people work for the railroad.

The town's original name was Pusher because this is where pusher engines were added to the backs of the trains so they could make it up the steep grade toward Mount Shasta. The town acquired the name Dunsmuir when a man of that name, a Canadian coal baron, stepped off the train while it was taking on water and offered to build a fountain at the depot if the town were named after him. He donated the money, climbed back on the train, and never returned to his namesake. The fountain is still there, often with huge trout swimming about.

With the decline of steam engines, the original purpose of the town faded. Some railroaders moved away when they lost their jobs; others retired and stayed there. Thus began a continuing tradition of Dunsmuir as a retirement location. When the railroaders left, the bottom dropped out of the real estate market. (It didn't have far to drop, since property was inexpensive to begin with.) Retirees found this an ideal location—great fishing, economical living, a gorgeous view from the front porch every morning, and unforgettable sunsets.

Lurking trout, sometimes large native ones, tempt the fisherman to the shores of the Sacramento River. Wild blackberry bushes on the banks yield delicious makings for cobblers, should the fish not be biting that day. The river recovered nicely from a horrendous pesticide spill a few years past. Once again the sweet smell of rainbow trout frying for breakfast fills the morning air. Nearby, three of California's finest alpine lakes challenge fishermen: Lake Siskiyou, McCloud Reservoir, and Medicine Lake.

Because Interstate 5 bypasses the town by a quarter mile, the pace along the town's main street is leisurely and unhurried. Dunsmuir's northern location and 2,300-foot elevation ensure at least a couple of good winter snowstorms. Snow here is a special sort—soft, fluffy, and pretty (as long as you don't have to shovel it)—and it piles up quickly. The canyon turns into a billowy white winter fantasyland for a day or two, until a warm rain clears it all away.

People here are proud of their pristine water supply and call Dunsmuir "home of the best water on Earth." The supply comes directly from glaciers on Mount Shasta and is delivered by lava tubes, surfacing in town. It's so pure it needs no treatment.

Farther up the canyon, the interstate climbs steeply, then levels out onto a plateau of gently rolling hills and the town of **Mount Shasta**, Dunsmuir's close cousin. Larger, with a population of 3,700, Mount Shasta sits at an elevation of 3,500 feet, literally at the foot of the majestic peak itself. This ancient volcano, 14,110 feet high, is one of the highest peaks on the continent. Its base-to-summit rise is rivaled only by Mount Kilimanjaro in Africa and Mount Fuji in Japan.

European fur trappers entered the region in the 1820s and encountered several Indian tribes: principally the Shasta, Klamath, and Modoc. In 1851, gold miners poured into the region when large ore deposits were discovered west of Mount Shasta. When gold played out, lumberjacks, ranchers, and farmers staked out their territories. The first settlement was named Strawberry Valley or Berryville, because of the profusion of wild blackberries that still grow there. Then it was named Sisson, after landowner Justin Sisson. Finally residents adopted the name Mount Shasta. For a time Mount Shasta was a bawdy, wide-open town, full of saloons that catered to lumberjacks for wild weekends of carousing. When the logging industry diminished, the local economy turned to tourists and retirees (neither of whom are given to wild weekends or carousing).

Unlike Dunsmuir, the town of Mount Shasta sits on a wide expanse of more-or-less level land instead of a narrow canyon. Room for expansion means you'll find more contemporary housing and upscale residences here than in Dunsmuir. Besides the snow-covered Mount Shasta looming on one side of town, the stark cinder cone of Black Butte presents another ever-present landmark to the north. To get an overview of the town of Mount Shasta, take the local scenic drive about halfway up the slopes of Mount Shasta. Several vista points allow you to check out the magnificent views of the Sacramento River canyon to the southwest, the Eddy Mountains to the west, and glimpses of Mount Lassen to the south. At the Everitt vista turnout, you can enjoy a short hike through pine forests to a lava rock outcrop to view the broad McCloud valley.

The headwaters of the Sacramento River rise from the rocks in Mount Shasta City Park. Icy clear water gushes from a lava tube originating deep within Mount Shasta. The water flows into Cold Creek, which is the northernmost feeder stream of the Sacramento River, and eventually makes its way 270 miles to empty into San Francisco Bay.

Because of the increased altitude, Mount Shasta receives much more snow than Dunsmuir. Ninety-six inches of the stuff falls every winter, compared with Dunsmuir's 38 inches. And it stays on the ground longer here.

Recreation and Culture

Minutes away from Mount Shasta and Dunsmuir are numerous spots for fishing, hiking, rock climbing, downhill and cross-country skiing, river rafting, mountain biking, and boating. Four golf courses are within driving distance, one in Mount Shasta, one in McCloud, and two in Weed. On the southern slope of Mount Shasta, between the town and McCloud, Mount Shasta Ski Park is a full-service winter resort featuring Alpine and Nordic skiing as well as snowboarding in one convenient nearby location. Twenty-one Alpine runs of snowy slopes thrill downhill skiers and snowboarders with 1,100 vertical feet of trails. During the summer the chairlifts take tourists for spectacular alpine scenery. Mount Shasta also has three public tennis courts.

College of the Siskiyous brings performing arts and musical presentations, making Mount Shasta the cultural center of Siskiyou County. Included are drama, music, and art productions staged by the college as well as by internationally renowned performing troupes. The school's learning resources center is geared toward continuing education for older students.

Real Estate

A wide range of housing prices offers newcomers many choices. The average sale price of homes in Mount Shasta is $150,000. Typical rents for two-bedroom homes are $500–$600. Homes in Dunsmuir range from $55,000 to $200,000, with rentals from $375 to $600.

Medical Care

Mercy Medical Center in Mount Shasta is an eighty-bed hospital with nineteen doctors on staff and a twenty-four-hour emergency care center. Hospital services cover a wide range of services in a modern health-care environment assisted by modern technology. The hospital also operates an outpatient clinic in the town of Weed. Dunsmuir has two family doctors and three dentists.

When Grandkids Visit

Take the kids to the volcanic exhibit at the Mount Shasta Ski Park. There they will learn that Mount Shasta is the largest volcano in the United States, and they'll enjoy the free educational exhibit that includes a thrilling videotape of erupting volcanoes, photos, charts, and displays of the West Coast's Ring of Fire. Also at the ski park: You can treat the grandkids to ski lessons in the winter, or take the chairlift up the mountain in the summer. Once at the top, they can rent bikes and ride down one of the several mountain bike trails found here.

Addresses and Connections

Chamber of Commerce: 300 Pine Street, Mount Shasta, CA 96067

Senior Services: 5744 Dunsmuir Avenue, Dunsmuir, CA 96025–2009

Newspaper: Mount Shasta Herald, 924 North Mount Shasta Boulevard, Mount Shasta 96067; *Siskiyou Daily News,* 309 South Broadway, Yreka, CA 96067

Airport: Redding, 70 miles south; Medford (Oregon), 90 miles north

Bus/Train: There is no city bus service in Dunsmuir, but Greyhound and Amtrak stop there. Mount Shasta has local bus service (STAGE).

Internet: (Dunsmuir) http://www.dunsmuir.com/index.html
(Mount Shasta) http://www.mtshasta.com/homepage.html-ssi

Dunsmuir Weather

	JAN.	APR.	JUL.	OCT.	RAIN	SNOW
		In degrees Fahrenheit				
DAILY HIGHS	47	60	88	68	30"	38"
DAILY LOWS	29	37	56	41		

Mount Shasta Weather

	JAN.	APR.	JUL.	OCT.	RAIN	SNOW
		In degrees Fahrenheit				
DAILY HIGHS	42	58	85	65	37"	96"
DAILY LOWS	26	33	51	37		

Weed

The city of Weed is nestled on the western slopes of Mount Shasta at an elevation of 3,467 feet. Weed is located 50 miles south of the Oregon border, at the intersection of Interstate 5 and Highway 97. People here claim this spot marks the beginning of the Alaskan Highway, but just why the Alaskan Highway should begin here isn't clear. Weed sits at a midway point between Redding and Medford, between San Francisco and Portland, and between Los Angeles and Seattle. The town is surrounded by national forests, high desert plains, and interesting volcanic formations. The city derives its name from lumber baron Abner Weed, who started a lumber industry here.

Most people traveling Interstate 5 zip right past Weed, perhaps pausing for gasoline or lunch at the interstate turnoff but seldom driving through the town itself. If they did they would find a delightful little town with all the amenities for a pleasant retirement.

A major attraction for retirees is the recent development of nearby Lake Shastina with homes, condos, and their attendant facilities. A gorgeous view of Mount Shasta serves as a focal point. The lake provides waterskiing, windsurfing, boating, and other water sports. An eighteen-hole Robert Trent Jones professional golf course and a nine-hole executive course are also at Lake Shastina.

Recreation and Culture

Weed has a bowling alley, theater, museum, nine-hole golf course with an unbeatable view, and five golf courses within easy driving distance. The city maintains five parks with room for picnics and play, a swimming pool, and a jogging trail. Within easy reach are a downhill ski area, Nordic ski area, snowmobile park, prime forest for hunting, and lakes for avid anglers.

The College of the Siskiyous has a branch campus here and offers art exhibits, musical and theater performances, and plenty of activities for sports enthusiasts. From Weed there is also easy access to a range of adventures in Siskiyou County. Marked ungroomed trails at Bunny Flat on Mount Shasta's Everitt Memorial Highway are free and open to the public. Mount Shasta Ski Park offers 25 kilometers of power-tilled tracks and skating lanes for beginner, intermediate, and advanced skiers.

Real Estate

Shasta View Golf Village, a planned retirement community for active adults fifty-five and older, is a prime attraction here. Two-bedroom condos start at $149,500. Older homes in the town of Weed are very affordable, with many homes selling in the low $100,000 range, and some even lower.

Medical Care

An outpatient facility of Mount Shasta Mercy Medical Center provides radiological, laboratory, and therapy services. The community also has two physicians, two dentists, and two optometrists.

When Grandkids Visit

You might want to impress your grandchildren with your physical condition and take them on an energetic ascent of 14,162-foot Mount Shasta. The trail is well marked, but this hike takes from six to eight hours, so an overnight trip is recommended. If that sounds too ambitious, you might try the 2.5-mile walk up 6,344-foot Black Butte, a prominent cinder cone that can be seen for miles. On the other hand, your idea of a strenuous day might be to send the kids to the museum in downtown Weed while you wait for them in the saloon. Actually, it's an interesting museum, with a 1923 LaFrance fire truck (in brand-new condition), artifacts from the old lumber company store and company hospital, original tools from a local blacksmith shop, and a homemade still used during Prohibition to make brandy and whiskey.

Addresses and Connections

Chamber of Commerce: P.O. Box 366, Weed, CA 96094
Senior Services: 150 Alamo Avenue, Weed, CA 96094
Newspaper: *Weed Press*, 924 North Mount Shasta Boulevard, Mount

Shasta, CA 96067–9751; *Siskiyou Daily News*, 309 South Broadway Street, Yreka, CA 96097–2905

Airport: Medford; 50 miles north; Redding, 100 miles south

Bus/Train: Local buses (STAGE) serve various towns in the county. Greyhound bus service is available for longer trips.

Internet: http://www.weedchamber.com/

Weed Weather

	JAN.	APR.	JUL.	OCT.	RAIN	SNOW
		In degrees Fahrenheit				
DAILY HIGHS	47	57	85	62	28"	20"
DAILY LOWS	22	31	37	34		

Yreka

Yreka (why-REE-ka) often ranks high in where-to-retire surveys conducted by major U.S. magazines, usually placing in the top fifty small communities in the United States. The name is said to be a Shasta Indian word meaning "north mountain."

Located 22 miles south of the California-Oregon border, Yreka is a quiet little city of 7,150 nestled in the northernmost corner of the majestic Shasta Valley. This is the largest full-service community on Interstate 5 between Ashland, Oregon, and Redding, 120 miles south. The population base provides support for professional services, medical facilities, and a full range of retail businesses, making Yreka the trade center for the county. The town supports several retail shopping areas, many antiques stores, thirty-two restaurants, auto service stores, thirteen motels, two bed-and-breakfasts, and the Yreka Western Railroad/Blue Goose Steam Train.

Downtown Yreka's fascinating historic district reflects its gold mining past. The town's genesis came in 1851, when one of the driver of a mule train from Oregon discovered glittering metal near a ravine called Black Gulch. Within six weeks of the discovery, 2,000 miners had created a Gold Rush boomtown of tents, shanties, and rustic cabins. Before long the substantial brick and gingerbread buildings you see today were under construction. In 1853 Joaquin Miller described Yreka as "a bustling place with a tide of people up and down and across other streets, as strong as if in New York." More than seventy-five homes built in the 1800s have been preserved, as well as many more of those constructed after the turn of the century. The residential district of Third Street is on the National Register of Historic Places.

Although Yreka sits at an altitude of 2,625 feet, it receives much less rain and snow than some of its neighbors. The town catches about 6 inches of snow, compared with 20 inches in Weed (at an altitude of 3,400 feet) and 38 inches in Dunsmuir (at 2,300 feet). Yreka typcially gets no more than one or two snowstorms a year.

Recreation and Culture

Close at hand are recreational opportunities featuring four golf courses within easy driving distance, tennis courts, great fishing, white-water rafting, hiking, backpacking, camping, hunting, waterskiing, bowling, snowmobiling, snow skiing (at two nearby ski parks), racquetball, and bicycling.

The College of the Siskiyous in Yreka sponsors a Senior College to meet the needs of the senior community. A number of classes are tailored to continuing education, such as those in woodcarving, beginning computers, and memoir writing. Some courses are offered during the day, but most are held in the evening. The facility includes a state-of-the-art computer lab and a fitness center. The school recently combined its performing arts series with the Yreka Community Theatre to produce an extensive series of performances. Patrons come from Dunsmuir, Weed, and other communities—even from as far away as Redding—to enjoy opera, jazz, classical music, drama, and ballet.

Real Estate

Prices of existing homes in Yreka range from $55,000 to $250,000, with three suburban residential areas within 8 miles of Yreka offering homes priced from $50,000 to $250,000. Rentals for one- and two-bedroom apartments and duplexes range from $375 to $550 a month. Rentals for two- and three-bedroom houses range from $375 to $750 a month depending on location.

Medical Care

Yreka is the health-care center for the region, boasting two hospitals. The largest is Siskiyou General Hospital, a full-service facility with fifty-seven beds. Fairchild Medical Center is an acute-care hospital with twenty-eight doctors representing a wide spectrum of medical specialties.

When Grandkids Visit

Treat the kids to a ride on the Yreka Western Railroad, a three-hour trip that recaptures the sights and sounds of a working steam locomotive. The Blue Goose, Yreka's historic, shortline railroad, runs from May to September, chugging and puffing through the Shasta Valley, past an old Chinese cemetery and through a working sawmill, across the Shasta River and through cattle ranches that were established in the 1850s. The journey ends at the nostalgic railroad/cattle town of Montague with Mount Shasta looming on the horizon.

Addresses and Connections

Chamber of Commerce: 117 West Miner Street, Yreka, CA 96097
Senior Services: 810 North Oregon Street, Yreka, CA 96097–2452
Newspaper: Siskiyou Daily News, 309 South Broadway Street, Yreka, CA 96097
Airport: Medford, 50 miles; Redding, 100 miles
Bus/Train: Greyhound
Internet: http://www.yrekachamber.com/

Yreka Weather

	JAN.	APR.	JUL.	OCT.	RAIN	SNOW
		In degrees Fahrenheit				
DAILY HIGHS	44	65	92	69	20"	6"
DAILY LOWS	24	44	52	35		

Intermountain Area

One last example of California's northern mountain country: the region around Fall River Mills and Burney, known locally as the intermountain area. The perpetually snow-covered peaks of Mount Shasta (14,162 feet) and Mount Lassen (10,466 feet) tower above the landscape on two sides of Fall River Mills and Burney, while Burney Mountain, Hatchet Mountain, and Big Valley Mountain guard the other directions. Between the mountains the landscape includes flat agricultural and grazing lands, lava beds with gushing springs, and vast areas of forested hills—but the mountains are never out of sight and are only a few miles away in any direction. Three lakes, three rivers, and 80 miles of inland waterways can be found in the approximately one-hundred square miles of the intermountain area.

Because of its isolated position—an hour to an hour-and-a-half drive from Redding, the nearest city—the intermountain area is one of Northern California's best-kept secrets. Nevertheless, hunters, fishermen, and outdoor enthusiasts know about the trophy trout lurking in the streams, the flocks of ducks and geese that frequent the area to raid the wild rice farms, and deer that grow fat on the lush grass in Big Valley. This is where Bing Crosby chose to raise his children, on a large ranch not far from Fall River Mills and Burney. (The ranch is now owned by another well-known Hollywood personality; local residents take pride in respecting the owner's privacy.)

Crosby's favorite sports were golf and fly-fishing. The superb trout streams throughout the intermountain area satisfied his passion for fishing, but he could not survive without golf. This explains the existence of a beautiful eighteen-hole championship course located just west of Fall River Mills on the main highway. Crosby had this course built, and the layout is reputed to rank among the top fifty courses in the United States. The unique arrangement of the course poses a challenge to professionals and amateurs alike. The facility has a restaurant, a clubhouse, and a pro shop, with other facilities planned for the future.

Settled in the shadow of Burney Mountain—one of many dormant volcanoes along the Pacific Rim's ring of fire—**Burney** has a population of approximately 2,300. Timber still plays a role in Burney's economy, although jobs are disappearing as they are in most western lumber operations. But without missing a beat, the town shifted its emphasis toward attracting tourists and retirees while making itself a service center for the region. Here's where you'll find plenty of major supermarkets, retail stores, and specialty businesses.

A recent forest fire devastated large tracts of forest to the west of Burney, but firefighters heroically stopped it before it could damage the town. So tall Douglas pines still shade Burney's quiet streets and lanes. Not far from the main highway is a retirement complex of single-family homes and one-bedroom apartments situated within easy walking distance of shopping and medical facilities. It features a park area, community center, and RV storage, all designed for use by people in the fifty-five or older age group. Free bus transportation for special needs is available to seniors throughout the intermountain area.

About five minutes from Burney's center, the quiet community of Cassels is a particularly popular place for retirement. Housing varies from exceptionally nice to very rustic; the town is overshadowed by large trees and graced by natural landscaping.

Twenty miles away, in a sharply different terrain, is Burney's sister town: **Fall River Mills**. The setting here is a wide, grassy valley circled by tree-clad mountains. A remarkably clear stream (the Fall River) wells up from the depths of a volcanic formation a few miles away and collects the waters of a dozen sparkling trout streams as it meanders through the valley.

Besides cattle ranches, the Fall River Valley is famous for its wild rice fields. This crop is largely responsible for the region's prosperity. Wild rice is not really rice but the seed of the aquatic grass *Zirania aquatica*. This natural "caviar of grains" is the only grain of its type native to North America. Native Americans continue to harvest wild rice by traditional methods, but the majority of today's crop is cultivated by modern farms that produce a reliable harvest of clean, uniform wild rice.

In contrast with Burney's bustling business district, shopping and services in Fall River Mills are scattered over several miles of highway, extending to the even smaller town of McArthur. The nearest city for major shopping is Redding, an hour-and-a-half drive away. Still, the area manages to be self-sufficient with a selection of small shopping centers, banks, and restaurants, as well as an excellent hospital.

The area is known for its lava beds and the springs that seem to well up from nowhere to gush clear, cold water that trout seem to love. A thriving new business in Fall River Mills is a smokehouse (run by two retirees) that prepares tasty morsels of smoked trout for gourmet restaurants in San Francisco.

Not far from Fall River Mills is another quality retirement place for outdoor lovers: the **Hat Creek area**. Hat Creek, a wild trout stream augmented by a large hatchery, yields trophy trout to the dedicated fly fisher. The creek swirls past the many lovely homes that have been built back in the forest. A growing number of bed-and-breakfasts have been popping up here, catering to the avid fishermen from the San Francisco and Los Angeles areas.

Recreation and Culture

The waterways of the intermountain area offer many varieties of fishing. Choose from deep, cold lakes or mountain streams for bass and trout; try the warmer waters for catfish and crappie. Lakes Britton, Eastman, Fall River, Baum Crystal, and Iron Canyon are a lure to all types of fishermen. With a short drive to the northwest, fishermen will find other hot spots on Bear Creek, Medicine Lake, and the McCloud River. (Live bait is prohibited on some streams.)

Thousand Lakes Wilderness Area and Lassen Volcanic National Park are nearby and offer hiking, fishing, bird-watching—and occasional molten lava mud pots in the background. Shasta Ski Park is a little over an hour's drive away, with twenty-one Alpine runs.

Real Estate

Those looking for affordable housing would be hard-pressed to find better bargains than in and around Burney. Older three-bedroom houses can be found for as little as $65,000. Since land is inexpensive, small lots are rare. You can buy a very nice place for $100,000.

Property in Fall River Mills is more costly due to a recent real estate boom, partly caused by an increase in the retiree population. Newcomers have been building expensive homes on the lake and river shores, and many fishing lodges are being built as well. In a small place like this, just a few buyers can push up prices.

Medical Care

Mayers Memorial Hospital, located in Fall River Mills, is a modern, full-service facility. Part of a medical group with its main hospital in Reno, the facility has helicopter service to move serious cases to Reno within a short time.

When Grandkids Visit

Have a picnic at Burney Falls, about 10 miles from Burney, at McArthur-Burney Falls Memorial State Park. "The eighth wonder of the world" is how President Theodore Roosevelt described Burney Falls when he visited here in the early part of the century. Crystal-clear water gushes from openings in the volcanic rock and cascades 129 feet down the vertical rock formation. Water flows over the falls at the same rate all year long—about 100 million gallons every day—unaffected by rainfall variations. At the foot of the falls the air is cool and laced with mist, nourishing ferns, and evergreen plants, creating a miniature rain forest— a wonderful respite from warm summer temperatures. Nearby is a lake with swimming and picnicking facilities.

Address and Connections

Chamber of Commerce: (Burney) P.O. Box 36, Burney, CA 96013; (Fall River Mills) P.O. Box 475, Fall River Mills, CA 96028

Senior Services: 37477 State Highway 299 East, Burney, CA 96013

Newspaper: Intermountain News, 36965 State Highway 299 East, Burney, CA, 96013-4051

Airport: Redding Airport, 50 miles

Bus/Train: No bus or train service

Internet: (Burney) http://www.burneyfalls.com/burney/ (Fall River Mills) http://www.burneyfalls.com/falriver/

Fall River Mills/Burney Weather

	JAN.	APR.	JUL.	OCT.	RAIN	SNOW
		In degrees Fahrenheit				
DAILY HIGHS	40	74	91	69	40"	25"
DAILY LOWS	28	47	68	46		

INDEX

About the Authors

John Howells

John was born in New Orleans and grew up in suburban St. Louis. He is now a resident of California and Costa Rica. John has worked on newspapers from coast to coast—forty in all. He has been a Linotype operator, English teacher, silver miner, and a travel and feature writer. He is the author and co-author of nine travel-retirement books, and serves on the board of directors of the American Association of Retirement Communities.

Don Merwin

Don is a native New Yorker who now lives in the San Francisco Bay Area. He began his career in communications as a writer for Edward R. Murrow in the early 1950s and spent the next three decades as publicist, administrator and planner in health and human service organizations. Don and his wife, Judith, were the founding publishers of Gateway Books.

Joseph Lubow

Formerly a librarian and a fellow of Merrill College at UC Santa Cruz, Joe had a fifteen-year career as a book and magazine editor. He served as senior editor at Strawberry Hill Press in Portland, Oregon, and as managing editor of *Computers, Reading, and Language Arts*. He is currently the assistant to the editor of *Multicultural Education* magazine. Joe lives in California.

Goodbye Tension...Hello Pension

Choose Costa Rica for Retirement • $14.95
Choose Florida for Retirement• $14.95
Choose the Southwest for Retirement• $14.95
Where to Retire • $16.95

Ahhh...Time to Travel!

Driving the Pacific Coast: California • $12.95
Traveler's Companion: California • $22.95
California Lighthouses • $19.95
Recommended Bed & Breakfasts™: California • $16.95
Off the Beaten Path™: Southern California • $12.95

To place an order or request a catalogue:
Call 9-5 EST: 800-243-0495 • Fax: 800-820-2329 • www.globe-pequot.com
The Globe Pequot Press, P.O. Box 833, Old Saybrook, CT 06475

1900526